Re-evaluating the Historicist's
Interpretation of the Revelation

Thy Kingdom Come

Marsue and Jerry Huerta

THY KINGDOM COME
RE-EVALUATING THE HISTORICIST'S
INTERPRETATION OF THE REVELATION

Unless otherwise indicated, all scripture quotations are from the Holy Bible, King James Version (Authorized Version). First published in 1611. Quoted from the KJV Classic Reference Bible.

Scripture quotations marked as ESV are taken from the English Standard Version® (ESV®). Copyright ©2001 by Crossway Bibles, a division of Good News Publishers. Used by permission. All rights reserved.

iUniverse books may be ordered through booksellers or by contacting:

iUniverse
1663 Liberty Drive
Bloomington, IN 47403
www.iuniverse.com
1-800-Authors (1-800-288-4677)

Because of the dynamic nature of the Internet, any web addresses or links contained in this book may have changed since publication and may no longer be valid. The views expressed in this work are solely those of the author and do not necessarily reflect the views of the publisher, and the publisher hereby disclaims any responsibility for them.

Any people depicted in stock imagery provided by Getty Images are models, and such images are being used for illustrative purposes only. Certain stock imagery © Getty Images.

ISBN: 978-1-5320-6271-1 (sc)
ISBN: 978-1-5320-6270-4 (e)

Library of Congress Control Number: 2018914460

Print information available on the last page.

iUniverse rev. date: 01/08/2018

The surreal image on the book-cover is by Eli Huerta and depicts an impressionist perception of the Industrial Revolution. The darkening of the air and the water is reminiscent of the opening of the bottomless pit in Revelation and is the reason such imagery was chosen for the cover of this book, as it fits well with its theme.

And he opened the bottomless pit; and there arose a smoke out of the pit, as the smoke of a great furnace; and the sun and the air were darkened by reason of the smoke of the pit. (Revelation 9:2)

Contents

Introduction

Reevaluating what historicists have written is an ongoing process; it has been going on for centuries, considering what man writes is not sacrosanct. With similar guidelines as historicists, the fourth-century patriarch Jerome interpreted the scarlet colored beast in Revelation 17 as Nero,[1] but in time the Protestant historicists reevaluated this explanation and rejected it. The nineteenth-century historicist E. B. Elliott's interpretation that the first vial of the seven plagues in Revelation 16 was poured out at the French Revolution,[2] was ultimately reevaluated and rejected. In the history of historicism there are numerous examples, too many to mention, of the reevaluation and rejection of their renditions of Daniel and the Revelation that renovated their house, yet left it standing. The foundation of the historicist's house is the Protestant revelation that the papacy fulfills

---

[1] Jerome (A.D. 340- 420): "As for the A ntichrist, there is no question but what he is going to fight against the holy covenant, and that when he first makes war against the king of Egypt, he shall straightway be frightened off by the assistance of the Romans. But these events were typically prefigured under Antiochus Epiphanes, so that this abominable king who persecuted God's people foreshadows the Antichrist, who is to persecute the people of Christ. And so there are many of our viewpoint who think that Domitius Nero was the Antichrist because of his outstanding savagery and depravity." *Commentary on Daniel Translated by Gleason L. Archer St. Jerome* (Wipf & Stock Pub., 2009), 133.

[2] Henry Carre Tucker, "The plague-boil, which broke out over the Papal countries on the pouring out of the first vial, appears to represent that tremendous outbreak of moral and social evil, that mixture of atheism, vice, and democratic fury, which burst forth at the French Revolution." *Brief historical explanation of the Revelation of St. John, According to the 'Horæ Apocalypticæ' of the Rev. E.B. Elliott* (London: James Nisbet & Co., 21 Berners Street, 1863), 103.

the antichrist and that prophetic time, a year-for-a-day, must be considered in determining prophecy; these are the *sine qua non* of historicism.

One of the most significant aspects of the Revelation is that the seven churches were initially perceived as historical, but in modern times they have been reevaluated and acknowledged as prophetic of the seven eras between the intra-advent age as well as having been historic churches. Even futurists recognize their historical aspect as well as their prophetic distinction. Nevertheless, early historicists had difficulty accepting the prophetic interpretation, as expressed by the nineteenth-century historicist Rev. T. Milner.

> Another opinion, equally as unsupported, though not so wild, is, that the description of the Asian churches, prophetically delineates the character of the universal church, divided into seven succeeding periods, extending from the age of the apostles, to the final consummation of all things. This notion, broached by the monkish writers of the middle ages, has been largely asserted and vindicated by Vitringa and many respectable writers of a more recent date, have appeared in its behalf. The interpreter adopting this hypothesis, involves himself in inextricable difficulties.[3]

Milner contested the idea that the churches were prophetic while acknowledging that the monks in the middle ages had broached the notion and that it was being advocated by a contemporary Dutch theologian Campegius Vitringa. Milner's contention lies in his assessment the monks lacked evidence to support the prophetic delineation due to the fact that they lived in the dark ages, which had limited evidence to support the view, and Milner's postmillennial presuppositions, which dominated the time, kept him from seeing

---

[3] Rev. T. Milner, A.M., *History of the Seven Churches in Asia; Their Rise, Progress and Decline* (London: Simpkin, Marshall, and Co.; 1842), 144.

any future harmonizing "with the description given of the ancient Laodiceans."

> for no type appears in any of these communications, of that time of mental darkness, priestcraft, and religious foolery, which preceded the reformation; and it is at once repugnant to all the disclosures of revealed truth, to suppose, that the last period of the church's history will synchronize with the description given of the ancient Laodiceans.[4]

In 1832, the year Milner published his book, the market driven society that we have today was still in its nascent form and being promulgated by the spirit of Protestantism in the first attempt at globalism. Yet, Theologian and author, Udo W. Middelmann, who has written a contemporary book about the consequences of a market driven society in our time, corroborates that we live in the Laodicean era.

> In the course of a very few decades much of the church has embraced the way of mass culture in its drive to reduce everything to play and attractive entertainment. It has bowed to the demands of a consumer society and offers a message that more and often distracts for the moment than comforts for the long run.... Marketing priorities preside.... Instead the church has adapted its soul and life teaching to appeal to modern man, whose whole perception has been altered by a culture that allows him to expect entertainment, fun, and easy success. The believer-to-be expects to be confirmed in views already held, whether they are of his assumed greatness or his experienced inferiority.... To the host of other experiences he now adds also his conversion and

---

[4] Ibid.

> repentance as experiences without much content or
> without much awareness of the consequences.[5]

It repeatedly appears that one must look back to discern the fulfillment of prophecy. This is upheld by a good number of expositors such as Sanford Calvin Yoder, who wrote in his book on prophecy: "In the light of everything that has happened to the interpreters, who so minutely interpret the predictive elements of Scripture, the old adage of the fathers still stands—that prophecies are best interpreted after they are fulfilled."[6]

The traditional historicist's perception that the seven churches were merely historic was ultimately reevaluated and rejected by a progressive revelation, an expression explained shortly. (Hence, the subtitle of the work: Reevaluating the historicist's Interpretation of the Revelation.) Centuries of developing the proper guidelines and the passage of time has led expositors to discern the imagery of the churches in tracing the history of the church. Each church has a pronounced theme, such as the ability to discern apostles in the first church of Ephesus, which is certainly indicative of the early rise of the church. The theme of the second church, Smyrna, is their persecution and martyrdom, which soon followed up to the time of the emperor Constantine, the most severe lasting during the reign of Diocletian. The theme of the following church, Pergamos, is that they dwelt in the seat of Satan and how many were seduced by this fraternization, this being acknowledged also by the preponderance of even secular historians concerning the conversion of the Roman empire to Christianity; the empire continued in many respects with pagan idolatry. The succeeding churches can also be reconciled to history, but none as overtly as the Laodicean church with our modern-day market driven society and its ramifications on the church, which

---

[5] Odo W. Middelmann, The Market Driven Church: The worldly Influence of Modern Culture on the Church in America (Crossway, January 12, 2004), 124-125.

[6] Sanford Calvin Yoder, *He Gave Some Prophets* (Wipf & Stock Pub., October 1, 1998), 73.

past historians, like Max Weber,[7] have inadvertently reconciled to our modern times in which Protestantism, with disestablishment, broke the hold that the church had on commerce and fostered a secular society.

At our present juncture in history, some two centuries after disestablishment by Protestantism, we now have no dearth of church historians, like reformed theologian, Mark A. Noll, who observe that disestablishment freed us to worship according to the dictates of our conscience, but which also wrought ignominious consequences on public morality, especially with its traffic.

> This combination of revivalism and disestablishment had effects whose importance cannot be exaggerated. Analyzed positively, the combination gave the American churches a new dynamism.... Analyzed negatively, the combination of revivalism and disestablishment meant that pragmatic concerns would prevail over principle.[8]

Noll addressed these pragmatic concerns as untrammeled or "liberal economic practices."

---

[7] Wikipedia: "Maximilian Karl Emil, 'Max' Weber ... was a German sociologist, philosopher, jurist, and political economist. His ideas profoundly influenced social theory and social research.... Weber's main intellectual concern was understanding the processes of rationalisation, secularisation, and 'disenchantment' that he associated with the rise of capitalism and modernity. [12] He saw these as the result of a new way of thinking about the world.[13] Weber is best known for his thesis combining economic sociology and the sociology of religion, elaborated in his book *The Protestant Ethic and the Spirit of Capitalism*, in which he proposed that ascetic Protestantism was one of the major 'elective affinities' associated with the rise in the Western world of market-driven capitalism and the rational-legal nation-state." s.v. Max Weber, last modified June 2018, https://en.wikipedia.org/wiki/Max_Weber

[8] Mark A. Noll, *The Scandal of the Evangelical Mind* (Eerdmans, 1995), 66.

By "liberal" in the context of the nineteenth-century, historians mean the tradition of individualism and the market freedom associated with John Locke and especially Adam Smith.... The point again is not whether evangelicals should have embraced liberal economic practice, for a case can be made for the compatibility between evangelical Christianity and moderate forms of market economy. The point is rather *how* evangelicals embraced liberal economic practice. Again this was done without a great deal of thought.... The most important economic questions of the day dealt with the early growth of industrialization. What kinds of obligations did capital and labor owe to each other? How would the growth of large industries, first in textiles and then in railroads, affect community life or provisions for the disabled, aged, and infirm? Each of these questions, and many more like them, posed a potential threat to Christian witness and to public morality. Each of them was also the sort that could be answered only by those who had thought through principles of Scripture, who had struggled to see how the truths of creation, fall, and redemption applied to groups as well as to individuals. Unfortunately, there was very little of such thinking. These problems developed pretty much under their own steam and received little specific attention from Christians wrestling with the foundations of economic thought and practice.[9]

It would hardly behoove a denominational church or church member who has become "rich, and increased with goods, and had need of nothing" to wrestle against an established commerce that had enriched them.

---

[9] Ibid.

Son of man, take up a lamentation upon the king
of Tyrus.... By the multitude of thy merchandise
they have filled the midst of thee with violence....
Thou hast defiled thy sanctuaries by the multitude
of thine iniquities, by the iniquity of thy traffick.
(Ezekiel 28:12, 16, 18 King James Version unless
otherwise stated)

This work is about the detriments to the church and public morality
wrought through the ignominy of untrammeled commerce at
the disestablishment of the church that was fostered by apostate
Protestantism and illustrated at the ordained time of the Laodicean
church in the Revelation given John. Historicism has its own set
of guidelines that this work has observed to advance the tenet that
"prophecies are best interpreted after they were fulfilled," by which
a number of the interpretations of past historicists were corrected.

A forensic analysis has also been observed to vindicate a
restructuring of the historicist's presumptions concerning John's
use of recapitulation in the Revelation, insomuch as it does not
truly conform to the patterns in the Hebraic cultus. By looking
back and grasping the past, a different structuring and portrayal
of the illustrations in Revelation are easily decrypted without the
ad hoc rationalizations and the failures to come to one accord that
have plagued the historicist's paradigm, which has led numerous
commentators, like historical premillennialists George Eldon Ladd
and Leon Morris, to criticize historicists for failing to agree and
suggesting that their guidelines were wanting.[10]

In the course of time the corporate apostasy that the New

---

[10] Historicism has been rejected by contemporary theologians like Leon
Morris and George Eldon Ladd: "Historicist views also labour under the
serious disadvantage of failing to agree. If the main points of the subsequent
history are in fact foreshadowed it should be possible to identify them with
tolerable certainty, otherwise what is the point of it?" Leon Morris, *The Book
of Revelation-An Introduction and Commentary* (Wm. B. Eerdmans Pub. Co.,
1987), 19; "Obviously, such an interpretation could lead to confusion, for there
are no fixed guidelines as to what historical events are meant." George Eldon

Testament prophesied (Matthew 24:12, 7:22–23; 2 Thessalonians 2:2–3; 1 Timothy 4:1–3; 2 Timothy 3:12–13, 4:3–4; 2 Peter 2:1–22, 3:3–4) was accepted as being contemporaneous with the Laodicean church era and upheld by a number of theologians as fulfilled by apostate Protestantism: "prophecies are best interpreted after they are fulfilled." In an internet article, *The Church Today And The Reformation Church: A Comparison* by Prof. David Engelsma of the Reformed Church, this resolution is upheld by looking back upon contemporary history.

> The spiritual condition of the Protestant Church today is wretched. A comparison of it with the Reformation Church shows that the Protestant Church has fallen far from the heights of the Reformation Church. Protestantism now closely resembles the pre-Reformation Church; indeed, in certain respects the Protestant Church today is worse. Its misery is compounded by the fact that, like the Laodicean Church of Revelation 3, it supposes that it is "rich, and increased with goods, and (has) need of nothing." The evil of the Protestant Church today is that it preaches and believes another gospel than did the Reformation Church.[11]

Such work calls for the reevaluation of many of the historicist's interpretations that pale in light of contemporary history. Such a reevaluation is grasped as "progressive revelation."[12] H. Grattan

---

Ladd, *A Commentary on the Revelation of John* (Wm. B. Eerdmans Pub. Co., 1972), 11.

[11] Prof. David Engelsma, "The Church Today And The Reformation Church: A Comparison," *Reformed Spokane.org*, http://www.reformedspokane.org/Doctrine_pages/Reformed/Reformed%20Doctrine%20pages/The%20Reformation%20%26%20the%20PRCA/Today_%26_Ref_Comparison.html

[12] *Theopedia*: "Progressive revelation may be defined as the process of God's own disclosure of Himself and His plan given to man throughout history by means of nature (Rom. 1:18-21; Ps. 19), providential dealings (Rom.

Guinness's 1918 edition of, *The Approaching End of the Age: Viewed in Light of History, Prophecy, and Science*, acknowledges the aforesaid precept that "prophecies are best interpreted after they are fulfilled."

We have Seen that God has been pleased to reveal the future to men only by degrees; that both in the number of subjects on which the light of prophecy has been permitted to fall, and in the clearness and fullness of the light granted on each, there has been constant and steady increase, from the pale arid solitary ray of Eden, to the clear widespread beams of Daniel, and to the rich glow of the Apocalypse. We now proceed to show that human comprehension of Divine prophecy has also been by degrees; and that in certain cases it was evidently intended by God to be so.... It is not too much to assume that the Apocalypse of St John was also designed to be progressively understood; that it forms no exception to the general rule, but was given to reveal the truth by degrees, and only in proportion as the understanding of it might conduce to the accomplishment of God's purposes, and the good of His people. Analogy forbids us to suppose that such a prophecy could be clear all at once, to these to whom it was first given, and it equally forbids the supposition that it was never to be understood or interpreted at all. Can we not perceive reasons why God should in this case act as He had so often acted before, and progressively reveal its meaning? and can we not also perceive means by which such a progressive revelation of the

---

8:28), preservation of the universe (Col. 1:17), miracles (John 2:11), direct communication (Acts 22:17-21), Christ Himself (John 1:14) and through the Bible (1 John 5:39)." s.v. Progressive revelation, accessed October 27, 2018, https://www.theopedia.com/progressive-revelation

meaning of this prophecy, might, as time rolled on, be made?[13]

Historicists are caught in the dilemma of holding to their past interpretations while attempting to concede to the precept of progressive revelation as acknowledged by their most valued proponents. Progressive revelation maintains the phenomena prophesied for the last days in the Revelation or Daniel, especially the Judgment foreshadowed by the festivals in the seventh month, will only be fully grasped upon entering those days, so any past or earlier interpretations concerning this Judgment are salient targets for reevaluation. This work concurs with Guinness on progressive revelation and has tendered another term intended specifically for historicism concerning such sound reevaluation: progressive historicism. This work has applied the term "progressive historicism" wherever the latest advancements, or at least some advancement has occurred correcting the past interpretations of historicists.

One such example of progressive historicism concerns the reevaluation of the throne scene in Revelation 4–5, which the contemporary historicists Frank W. Hardy, Ph.D., creator of Historicism.org, and R. Dean Davis, Professor of Religion at Atlantic Union College in South Lancaster, Massachusetts, have proposed. Historicist's of the past, like H. Grattan Guinness, held that the throne scene depicted in Revelation 4–5 occurred at Christ's ascension in the first-century A.D.

> Lo! The Lamb advances and takes the seven scaled book…. As He opens the seven seals, successive visions appear…. The first seal being opened he saw a white horse and a crowned horseman bearing a bow…. A comparison of this opening vision with that in the nineteenth chapter, of *the rider on the*

---

[13] Henry Grattan Guinness, The Approaching End of the Age Viewed in the Light of History Prophecy and Science (London: Hodder & Stoughton, 1878 ed.), 80.

while horse, whose name was "King of Kings and Lord of Lords," justified in the view of the early Church the application of the first seal. [14]

Davis and Hardy have reevaluated the traditional interpretation with the sound proposal that the throne scene is the same one depicted in Daniel 7 and that it is concurrent with the Laodicean church era.

> The throne scene takes place in the timeframe to which the seven letters have brought us, i.e., the timeframe of the letter to Laodicea, in and after 1844.[15]

> In Rev 5 the portrayal is that of a traditional divine council in session ... an investigative-type judgment.... Contrary to the views of most modern interpreters, there is evidence for interpreting the seven-sealed scroll as the Lamb's book of life. The evidence includes: (1) the occurrences of the phrase (or equivalent) "Lamb's book of life" (13:8; 20:12), (2) the reaction of those who have a definite stake in the contents of the scroll, (3) the corporate solidarity between the Lamb as Redeemer and the righteous saints as the redeemed, and (4) the parallel passage of Daniel7, which describes the same corporate solidarity between the saints of the Most High and one like a son of man who receives the saints of the Most High as his covenant inheritance.[16]

---

[14] Henry Grattan Guinness, *History unveiling prophecy; or, Time as an interpreter* (F.H. Revell, 1905), 14, 15, 29.

[15] Frank W. Hardy, Ph.D., "Historicism and the Judgment A Study of Revelation 4-5 and 19a," *Historicism.org,* (August 8, 2006, Modified April 15, 2010), 1. http://www.historicism.org/Documents/Lecture1Rev4-5.pdf

[16] R. Dean Davis, "The Heavenly Court Scene of Revelation 4-5" (Andrews University Dissertations, Paper 31, 1986), 243-244. https://

Note that the phrase "investigative-type judgment" appears in the quote from Dean so there is no mistake he and Hardy are referring to the same time "the time of the end" which they perceive as the final church era. Their reevaluation of the traditional interpretation of Revelation 4–5 actually furthers a linear progression starting in chapter 1 up until the time of the seventh trumpet in chapter 11, inasmuch as historicism has already reevaluated the seven vials as a break in the pattern of their severe view of recapitulation. This work concerns the in-depth analysis of the symbolism of the seven seals and the seven trumpets as well as the in depth look at the patterns in the Hebraic cultus that warrants a departure from the extreme use of recapitulation for a greater linear narration in the book of Revelation, while still adhering to the historicist's *sine qua non* of a year-for-a-day principle and the recognition of the papacy as the antichrist.

To begin with, prior to any reevaluation of traditional historicism, the issue of errant presuppositions must be broached, which is the subject of our first three chapters. Daniel is held by historicism as relating the ordained and progressive history from the time of Neo Babylon until the second advent, which does not reconcile with the presupposition that God repented on the Old Testament prophecies concerning Israel when the Jews rejected Christ. Upholding the belief that God ordained the progressive history from Neo Babylon until the second advent of Christ is a non sequitur with the presupposition that God repents on his promises and prophecies due to the works of man. In truth, a good many of historicists have followed the traditional interpreters who imbibed the presupposition of Covenant Theology that the biological descendants had a covenant of works as opposed to the gentile's covenant of grace. It has led a good number of historicists to maintain that: "the promises and predictions given through the Old Testament prophets originally applied to biological descendants and were to have been fulfilled to them on

---

digitalcommons.andrews.edu/cgi/viewcontent.cgi?referer=https://www.google.com/&httpsredir=1&article=1030&context=dissertations

the condition that they obey God."[17] To begin to dispel such unsound presuppositions one must one must remind the historicists that the Old Covenant magnified sin and disobedience.

> For when we were in the flesh, the motions of sins, which were by the law, did work in our members to bring forth fruit unto death.... taking occasion by the commandment, wrought in me all manner of concupiscence. For without the law sin *was* dead. For I was alive without the law once: but when the commandment came, sin revived, and I died. And the commandment, which *was ordained* to life, I found *to be* unto death. For sin, taking occasion by the commandment, deceived me, and by it slew *me*. (Romans 7:5, 8–11)

Simply put, the law of the Old Covenant could do nothing to promote obedience but actually magnified sin and disobedience. Paul testified that only Christ breaks the sentence of the curse issued at Adam's fall and frees man from *the law of sin and death*.

> O wretched man that I am! who shall deliver me from the body of this death? I thank God through Jesus Christ our Lord. So then with the mind I myself serve the law of God; but with the flesh the law of sin. (Romans 7:24–25)

> *There is* therefore now no condemnation to them which are in Christ Jesus, who walk not after the flesh, but after the Spirit. For the law of the Spirit of life in Christ Jesus hath made me free from the law of sin and death. (Romans 8:1–2)

---

[17] *The Seventh-day Adventist Bible Commentary*, vol. 4, s.v. "The Role of Israel in Old Testament Prophecy," (Review and Herald Pub. Ass., 1980), 25.

The historicists who assert that the Old Testament prophecies were conditional upon works have overlooked the New Testament affirmation that there was never any such intent by God. In truth, God ordained the Old Covenant to fail and to be replaced by a New Covenant, progressive in grace, which would bring the Old Testament prophecies to fruition.

> For if that first *covenant* had been faultless, then should no place have been sought for the second. For finding fault with them, he saith, Behold, the days come, saith the Lord, when I will make a new covenant with the house of Israel and with the house of Judah: Not according to the covenant that I made with their fathers in the day when I took them by the hand to lead them out of the land of Egypt; because they continued not in my covenant, and I regarded them not, saith the Lord. For this *is* the covenant that I will make with the house of Israel after those days, saith the Lord; I will put my laws into their mind, and write them in their hearts: and I will be to them a God, and they shall be to me a people: And they shall not teach every man his neighbour, and every man his brother, saying, Know the Lord: for all shall know me, from the least to the greatest. (Hebrews 8:7–11)

The same historicists, above, who claim the fulfillment of the prophesies to the biological descendants were works related also maintain that:

> Under the new covenant men's hearts and minds are changed (see on Rom. 12:2; Corinthians 5:17). Men do right, not by their own strength but because

Christ dwells in the heart, living out His life in the believer (see on Gal. 2:20).[18]

The commentary on the New Covenant, above, is to Judah and Israel and conflicts with the presumption that the Old Testament prophecies to the biological descendants were works related.

Election also undermines the covenantalist's perception of the Old Testament prophecies to the biological descendants, insomuch as the Old Covenant builders or tenants of the vineyard of Israel (Matthew 21:33–44), or the house of God, were ordained to reject the stone that becomes the cornerstone (Psalms 118:22–23; Isaiah 8:14–15, 49:7; 1 Peter 2:6–8). Only an ordained remnant of the house of Israel was chosen to avow Christ.

> Peter, an apostle of Jesus Christ, To those who are elect exiles of the dispersion in Pontus, Galatia, Cappadocia, Asia, and Bithynia, according to the foreknowledge of God the Father, in the sanctification of the Spirit, for obedience to Jesus Christ and for sprinkling with his blood: May grace and peace be multiplied to you. (1 Peter 1:1–2 English Standard Version)

The ESV was used due to the poor translation of ἐκλεκτοῖς παρεπιδήμοις Διασπορᾶς in the KJV. The "elect exiles of the dispersion" is a superior translation and historically accurate, as Peter's ministry to the circumscribed (Galatians 2:8) was to the biological descendants, who never returned from the Assyrian exile and who had remained dispersed. Furthermore, they were ordained to avow Christ according to the foreknowledge of God, all of which undermines the presuppositions of the historicists who have imbibed the covenantalist's misapprehension that the Old Testament prophecies to the biological descendants were works related. As stated above, prior to any reevaluation of traditional historicism the

---

[18] Ibid., vol. 7, s.v. "Hebrews 8, Put my laws," 446.

issue of errant presuppositions must be broached, which is the subject of the first three chapters. The New Testament vindicates Samuel's testimony that "the Strength of Israel will not lie nor repent: for he *is* not a man, that he should repent" (1 Samuel 15:29). Everything that was ordained to occur at the first advent happened in accord with the Old Testament prophets. If what is spoken by a prophet does not come to pass then, according to Deuteronomy, the prophet is not of God.

> I will raise them up a Prophet from among their brethren, like unto thee, and will put my words in his mouth; and he shall speak unto them all that I shall command him. And it shall come to pass, *that* whosoever will not hearken unto my words which he shall speak in my name, I will require *it* of him. But the prophet, which shall presume to speak a word in my name, which I have not commanded him to speak, or that shall speak in the name of other gods, even that prophet shall die. And if thou say in thine heart, How shall we know the word which the LORD hath not spoken? When a prophet speaketh in the name of the LORD, if the thing follow not, nor come to pass, that *is* the thing which the LORD hath not spoken, *but* the prophet hath spoken it presumptuously: thou shalt not be afraid of him. (Deuteronomy 18:18–22)

A true reevaluation of the traditional historicist's interpretations must commence with their errant presupposition that all prophecy is conditional. The initial chapters will deal with the doctrine that God spoke to man in either the compound sense or the divided sense.

> In dealing with God's will, we must then ask the question "Does God desire things He does not decree?" First, we must answer this question in

the compound sense.... God, in this sense, never desires anything He does not decree. All things are accomplished in the exact way— the only way— He has ordained from the foundation of the world. His pursuit of His own glory is fulfilled in the execution of His decrees concerning the compound sense, the wide angle lens, of His desire.... However, in the divided sense, in His preceptive will, "Does God desire things He does not Decree?" Do we see things happening in the world around us that seem like God desires them, but has not actually decreed them to come to pass? Absolutely.[19]

As already conveyed, the New Testament revealed that the law could do nothing to promote obedience but actually magnified sin and disobedience, while the New Covenant was ordained to solve the problem of disobedience by having God dwell in his chosen elect. Consequently, it would not have been advantageous to God's plans if the Old Covenant biological descendants had fully grasped this principle. Knowing that the law could not promote obedience would have exacerbated their rebellion and disobedience and so God chose not to convey this revelation until the ratification of the New Covenant. Hence, the difference between the divided and compound senses is revelation: progressive revelation. The divided sense is the nascent, elementary revelations of God, while the compound sense is his consummate or comprehensive revelation. The biological descendants were not ready for the compound sense in revelation, in that the law could not promote obedience; thus, exercising the compound sense would have been counterproductive. Therefore, under the Old Covenant ministration God conveyed security concerning land and life in the divided sense: blessings for obedience and curses for rebellion. Even so, in the compound sense God foreknew that the biological descendants would not keep the

---

[19] C. Matthew McMahon, *The Two Wills of God* (Puritan Publications, 2005), Kindle location 1833-1850.

law until the New Covenant was ratified, which substantiates that conditional prophecy is expressed in the divided sense and further, cannot be used to confirm the argument that man causes God to repent or alter his plans for the unforeseeable. In the Bible, God revealed the fate of humanity in stages because it would not have been advantageous to his plans if that fate of man was known from the beginning. This is what is dealt with in the first three chapters in order to establish the proper presuppositions to expose the errant misapprehensions of the traditional historicists and establish the foundation for progressive historicism.

After dealing with the errant presuppositions that historicists have imbibed, this work moves on to a cursory comparison of the other paradigms of preterism and futurism to expose their most salient defects. This leads to the vindication of the historicist's model and the explanation of the differences between the genres of apocalyptic and classical prophecy. The evidence that Christ held the fulfillment of Daniel's prophecy of the abomination of desolation as yet unfulfilled reveals that the apocalyptic genre is special in prophecy and conforms to the historicist's model of the Revelation; it represents the gradual unfolding of history between the two advents of Christ.

After historicism is vindicated the main thesis is raised, that of reevaluating the historicist's traditional interpretations. In reevaluating traditional historicism, one must commence with the contemporary issue of John's temporal perspective concerning the time that mystery Babylon is judged in chapter 17. The traditional interpretation was that John's perspective was the perspective of the first-century, but in recent times this view was changed to represent a distant future closer to our time in its stead, the phenomenon termed the *Day of the Lord*. The Day of the Lord is an idiom denoting the eschatological Day of the Lord, or the antitype of the Hebraic autumnal festivals of Rosh Hashanah and Yom Kippur. In chapters four and five, historicists as well as futurists are cited to affirm that John was taken in the spirit to a future time closer to our own. The fallacy that mystery Babylon is the papacy and that the sixth king is pagan Rome is exposed by this contemporary reevaluation. The papacy came into existence some four-hundred years after John's time and cannot be viewed as riding on the back of pagan Rome in any logical sense. The fallacy escalates in the evidence that the "fornication" in Revelation 17:2 is in the indicative mood which conveys the act as prior to the indictment of the whore, before she becomes "the habitation of devils, and the hold of every foul spirit, and a cage of every unclean and hateful bird" (Revelation 17:2, 18:2). Without a doubt, one cannot render the sixth king in Revelation 17 as pagan Rome and maintain that the whore is the papacy. Progressive revelation leads to the conclusion that John's temporal perspective was the eschatological Day of the Lord and the sixth king is an entity in our time, which is substantiated by a contemporary historicist in chapter five. The consequence of the progressive revelation is that John was taken by the spirit into the future and shown events in our time, which is also the time of the sixth king. It is also the time of the eighth king that "was" and "is not" and will be again. Maintaining the *sine qua non* of historicism and the true temporal perspective of John, the only entity that fits the king that "was" and "is not" is the papacy, as it was wounded by the Protestant's disestablishment of religion. And since America fostered disestablishment, America is easily reconciled as the sixth king.

The historicists who have acknowledged the progressive revelation that John was taken to the future eschatological Day of the Lord have also opened the door to rendering the seven seals and the seven trumpets in a linear progression, commencing with the final church era, Laodicea. Historicism has acknowledged a linear narration concerning the seven last plagues for some time; the last plagues are a phenomenon concurrent with the seventh and last trumpet. Chapter six continues to follow the progressive revelation by historicists in their acknowledgement of a linear narration between the fifth seal and the sanctuary scene in Revelation 8, which renders the sixth seal as a mere flash-forward, straightening out the past excesses in recapitulation by historicists, while still adhering to the historicist's *sine qua non* of a year-for-a-day principle and the recognition of the papacy as the antichrist. Chapter six also broaches the progressive revelation accomplished on the Hebraic cultus festivals and their antitypes to vindicate the concept that the seven churches are the antitype of the seven months between the spring and autumnal festivals, all of which conforms to the progressive revelation as interpreted by the historicists Davis and Hardy in their rendition of Revelation 4–5 as a phenomenon fulfilled contemporaneously with the last church era, the Laodicean era, our contemporary market driven society. Chapters seven through ten are in support of this inadvertent movement to straighten out the excesses of recapitulation by traditional historicists in favor of the linear narration that was John's intent and its ramifications that the antitypes of the apocalyptic four horsemen are found in our modern-day phenomenon of Protestant missionary imperialism and its consequences of economic global imperialism. Said advances in progressive revelation vindicate that John's use of recapitulation was modest as compared with the traditionalist's view and when this modest application is grasped it resolves the prophecies and illustrations of the seven seals with our modern day market driven society, the prophetic era of the Laodicean church, the seventh month autumnal festivals and the "the time of the end" in Daniel 8:17. The correspondence of the apocalyptic horsemen of the seven seals with the historical accounts of the Protestant's rise to prominence and their termination of the church's influence in our modern-day commerce is incendiary! Moreover, the correspondence with the all the scriptural chronicles pertaining to the autumnal festivals, regarding the final judgment, and the apocalyptic horsemen of the seven seals is no less provocative! As is the case of all such correlations that come to light through progressive revelation they become a blessing for the sons and daughters of God and a reproof for those who walk in darkness (Revelation 1:3).

The Insufficiency of the Presuppositions of Dispensationalism in Rendering John's Apocalypse

Dispensationalists presuppose the transcendence of the historical-grammatical hermeneutic, in many cases to the exclusion of others, depending on the sect. Regarding this issue, dispensationalists R. Bruce Compton confirmed that the prophets were not omniscient and "did not always fully comprehend all of the implications or significance of the text" they wrote,[1] which is an acknowledgment of the weakness in the historical-grammatical hermeneutic by itself. The historical-grammatical view informs us of the author's original intent and meaning but cannot inform us of implications or significance beyond what the prophets were given to know. Such a concession concedes the existence of implications or significance that can be further developed in progressive revelation. True progressive revelation maintains concurrence with the historical-grammatical perception and presupposing the latter's hegemony results in true correspondence between the Old and New Testaments.

Dispensationalism views Israel as a "nation among nations," on a path to salvation different from that of the church, which is "formed

---

[1] R. Bruce Compton, "Dispensationalism, the Church, and the New Covenant," *Detroit Baptist Seminary Journal*, vol. 8 (Fall 2003), 44. http://www.dbts.edu/wp-content/uploads/2016/02/compton_dispensationalism.pdf

from all nations."[2] With this *a priori* Ryrie rendered Matthew 21:43 as the rejection of the Jews, albeit temporarily, and the conception of an *ad hoc* separate institution called the church, bearing the fruit of the vineyard, entered onto the scene. Curiously, Ryrie cross referenced the phenomenon with the nation in 1 Peter 2:9.[3]

> MATTHEW 21:43 taken from you, and given to a nation. I.e., taken from the Jews and given to the church (1 Pet. 2:9).[4]

The Greek term *ethnei*, in Matthew 21:43, does stress singularity, as a nation among nations—but dispensationalism maintains the church is not a nation like Israel; thus, when Ryrie renders the nation that bears the fruit in Matthew 21:43 as the church he violates the rule of non-contradiction. In Ryrie's study bible we are left adrift as to how the nation in 1 Peter 2:9 bears the fruit in Matthew 21:43 and how it pertains to the Jews, especially when Peter was addressing the ten northern bribes of Ephraim. Thomas Ice's rendition of Peter's epistle supposedly has the historical-grammatical interpretation represent a great number of exiled Jews dwelling in the regions conveyed in 1 Peter 1:1.

> Interestingly, most of the post-apostolic early church fathers also agreed that 1 Peter was written

---

[2] One dispensationalist who views Israel as a "nation among nations" is John S. Feinberg: "the place of Israel according to the OT teaching concerning the call and mission of that nation among the nations…. and the church as similarly 'people of God,' but formed from all nations." *In Continuity and Discontinuity: Perspectives on the Relationship Between the Old and New Testaments* (Westchester, Illinois: Crossway Books 1988), 259.

[3] Other dispensationalists such as Scofield interpret the nation bearing the fruit as the Gentiles, but this presents the difficulty that the gentiles represent a "nation", which is untenable in scripture.

[4] .,*The Ryrie Study Bible* by Charles Caldwell Ryrie (Moody Press, 1976), 1378.

to Jewish believers scattered throughout the stated regions of modern-day Turkey.[5]

What is perplexing is that Ice also deviates from the historical-grammatical interpretation; the original intent of the authors that Peter cited was to convey that the promises to the nation of Ephraim, the ten northern tribes, were being fulfilled, as opposed to being fulfilled in Judah (Exodus 19:6; Hosea 1:10, 2:23).

> But ye are a chosen generation, a royal priesthood, an holy nation, a peculiar people; that ye should shew forth the praises of him who hath called you out of darkness into his marvellous light: in time past were not a people, but are now the people of God: which had not obtained mercy, but now have obtained mercy. (1 Peter 2:9–10)

> And I will sow her unto me in the earth; and I will have mercy upon her that had not obtained mercy; and I will say to them which were not my people, Thou art my people; and they shall say, Thou art my God. (Hosea 2:23)

In his railings against replacement theology, Ice produced an essay on 1 Peter 2 that also disavowed the nation as Ephraim by omission, which reveals the omission is pervasive in dispensationalism and this blinds them from the salvific history of the nation of Ephraim as contrasted from Judah. The omission stems from the dispensationalist's presuppositions that renders Matthew 21:43 as referring to the suspension of the calling of Israel at the first advent, and the commencement of the *ad hoc* call concerning the church, which is what Ice conveys in his essay on 1 Peter 2:9–10:

---

[5] Thomas Ice, "The Calvinistic Heritage of Dispensationalism," *pre-trib.org*, http://www.pre-trib.org/data/pdf/Ice-TheCalvinisticHeritag.pdf

While much more could be said about 1 Peter 2, it is abundantly clear that the passage does not support any form of replacement theology. Instead it speaks of a fulfillment of God's Old Testament promises to the Israel of God through Christ.... God will indeed keep all His promises to Israel even though during the Church age He is combining elect Jews and Gentiles into a single co-equal body (Eph. 2:11–22).[6]

As a revised dispensationalist, Ice's perception of the fulfillment of God's Old Testament (OT) promises to Israel is that they are yet future, after the rapture of the church; they were not fulfilled at the first advent in any sense. The restrictive clause "even though during the Church age" juxtaposes the church from Israel in their manipulation of the historical-grammatical sense. In Ice's view, then, God took his kingdom from the Jews when they rejected Christ, which he perceives as meaning that God changed his mind on the offer of the kingdom, and, as an *ad hoc*, fed the church, a contingency summarized as the parenthesis by dispensationalists.[7] Classic and revised dispensationalism's *ad hoc* or contingency forces the open theist's perception; God did not know how the Jews would respond to Christ,[8] which they labeled the parenthesis. Another

---

[6] Thomas Ice, "1 Peter 2 and Replacement Theology-Tom's Perspectives," *pre-trib.org*, http://www.pre-trib.org/articles/view/1-peter-2-and-replacement-theology

[7] Wikipedia: "Dispensationalism is unique in teaching that the Church stands in a dispensation that occurs as a parenthesis in the prophetic Kingdom program, a dispensational 'mystery' or 'grace' period, meaning that it was not directly revealed in prophecy in the Old Testament, and that this 'age of grace' will end with the rapture of the church allowing the prophetic clock for Israel to start up again." s.v. Dispensationalism, last modified June 12, 2018, https://en.wikipedia.org/wiki/Dispensationalism

[8] *Theopedia*: "In libertarianism (not to be confused with the political ideology), free will is affected by human nature but man retains ability to choose contrary to his nature and desires. Man has the moral ability to turn to God in Christ and believe of his own "free will," apart from a divine, irresistible grace.

dispensationalist, Michael J. Vlach, attempts to vindicate the perception of the *ad hoc* or contingency of the church.

> Thus, while the certainty of God's purposes is sure because of God's sovereignty, from the human side of the divine/human curtain the timing of fulfillment of some prophecies can be influenced by human obedience or disobedience. Contingency appears to be explicitly taught in Jeremiah 18:7–10.... Jonah prophesied that Nineveh would be destroyed in forty days, but national repentance delayed God's judgment (Jonah 3).... Thus, contingency in regard to prophecy must be considered.[9]

Vlach proceeds from an open theist's perception of free will, believing man causes God to repent or alter his plans for the unforeseeable. This is incompatible with compatibilism,[10] which is the Calvinist's perception of free will. Yet, Ice has claimed Calvinism as essential to dispensationalism in another essay.

> In concert with the Calvinist impulse to view history theocentricly, I believe that dispensational premillennialism provides the most logical eschatological ending to God's sovereign decrees

---

Indeed, according to Open Theism, God is anxiously waiting to see what each person will do, for he cannot know ahead of time what the choice might be. Or, according to Arminianism, God chooses to save those whom he foresees will believe of their own free will." s.v. Free will, accessed October 27, 2018, http://www.theopedia.com/free-will

[9] Michael J. Vlach, "The Kingdom Program in Matthew's Gospel," *Pre-Trib Research Center*, accessed October 27, 2018, https://www.pre-trib.org/pretribfiles/pdfs/Vlach-TheKingdomProgramInMatthew.pdf

[10] *Theopedia*: "Compatibilism, sometimes called soft determinism, is a theological term that deals with the topics of free will and predestination." s.v. Compatibilism, accessed October 27, 2018, http://www.theopedia.com/compatibilism

for salvation and history. Since dispensational premillennialists view both the promises of God's election of Israel and the church as unconditional and something that God will surely bring to pass, such a belief is consistent with the Bible and logic. A covenant theologian would say that Israel's election was conditional and temporary. Many Calvinists are covenant theologians who think that individual election within the church is unconditional and permanent. They see God's plan with Israel conditioned upon human choice, while God's plan for salvation within the church is ultimately a sovereign act of God. There is no symmetry in such logic.[11]

Vlach supports the open theist claims concerning contingency from texts in Jeremiah and Jonah,[12] which is at variance with Ice's perception of God's sovereignty in Calvinist's terms. Vlach proceeds from the open theist's concept of free will concerning God's foreknowledge as an incompatibilist,[13] while Ice asserts that dispensationalists hold to the Calvinist compatibilist's perception of determinism. It is clear that the parenthesis is incompatible with the Calvinists' view of foreknowledge and even Martin Luther acknowledged this aspect of Calvinism: "God foreknows nothing contingently"[14] In truth, both Ice and Vlach are not compatibilists but labor for the open theist's view of God's foreknowledge as it concerns contingency in regard to prophecy.

---

[11] Ice, "The Calvinistic Heritage of dispensationalism"

[12] Vlach, "The Kingdom Program in Matthew's Gospel"

[13] *Theopedia*: "The incompatibilist says that the free will is 'incompatible' with determinism. The Libertarian is an incompatibilist who consequently rejects any determinism associated with the sovereignty of God." s.v. Compatibilist vs. libertarian views of free will, accessed October 27, 2018, http://www.theopedia.com/libertarian-free-will

[14] Martin Luther, The Bondage of the Will Translated by J. I. Packer and O. R. Johnston (Fleming H. Revell; 1st edition 1990) 13.

Compatibilists claim causal direction concerning human action, which libertarians repudiated at some lengths on the grounds of indifference; freedom and moral accountability must remain indifferent to causation. Modern libertarians have abandoned indifference and conceded to endorse the causal direction, but claim such must be under man's sole direction in order to maintain their perception of free will. When the libertarian concept of free will is repudiated open theism must fall, insomuch as it is built upon libertarianism. And then contingency in regard to prophecy must logically fall. In truth, the libertarian perception of free will was repudiated by Paul in his epistle to the Romans in the texts below.

> For that which I do I allow not: for what I would, that do I not; but what I hate, that do I. If then I do that which I would not, I consent unto the law that it is good. Now then it is no more I that do it, but sin that dwelleth in me. For I know that in me (that is, in my flesh,) dwelleth no good thing: for to will is present with me; but how to perform that which is good I find not. For the good that I would I do not: but the evil which I would not, that I do. Now if I do that I would not, it is no more I that do it, but sin that dwelleth in me. I find then a law, that, when I would do good, evil is present with me. For I delight in the law of God after the inward man: But I see another law in my members, warring against the law of my mind, and bringing me into captivity to the law of sin which is in my members. (Romans 7:15–23)

Paul affirms that ultimately man has no power over his carnal nature (CN); it causes sin even when the will resists. Concerning man, dispensationalist John Nelson Darby stated: "when he wills good, sin is too strong for him."[15] The CN efficaciously circumvents the will to consummate sin; this repudiates libertarianism. First, man's will is not in complete control of his actions; the CN also directs man and resists his will. Secondly, man is conscious of his sins; it troubles his conscience as Hebrews 10:2 states, which establishes accountability. Paul clearly affirms that the mind is aware when it wrongs. The incompatibilist's arguments pertaining to accountability and causal determination are overcome by Paul's testimony. Furthermore, Old and New Testament revelation affirms that we do not die for Adam's sin, but for our own; death follows sin.

> Therefore to him that knoweth to do good, and doeth it not, to him it is sin. (James 4:17)

> The soul that sinneth, it shall die. The son shall not bear the iniquity of the father, neither shall the father bear the iniquity of the son: the righteousness of the righteous shall be upon him, and the wickedness of the wicked shall be upon him. (Ezekiel 18:20)

This also concurs with the Calvinist perception that the elect are called by God and not vice versa, as no man is able to free himself from the CN.

> Behold, I stand at the door, and knock: if any man hear my voice, and open the door, I will come in to him, and will sup with him, and he with me. (Revelation 3:20)

Arminianists and open theists think they stand on God's door and knock and he answers to their beckoning. But only the causal direction of "the law of the Spirit of life in Christ" (Romans 8:2) emancipates man from the CN and allows him to answer God's call.

---

[15] *John Darby's Synopsis*, s.v. Romans 7, *Christianity. Com*, accessed October 27, 2018, https://www.christianity.com/bible/commentary.php?com=drby

For the law of the Spirit of life in Christ Jesus hath made me free from the law of sin and death. For what the law could not do, in that it was weak through the flesh, God sending his own Son in the likeness of sinful flesh, and for sin, condemned sin in the flesh: That the righteousness of the law might be fulfilled in us, who walk not after the flesh, but after the Spirit. (Romans 8:2–4)

The Calvinist's perceptions of God's foreknowledge in texts such as Romans 8:29–30, indicate that God was familiar with the elect before creation (Jeremiah 1:5; Ephesians 1:4), which also concurs with his foreknowledge of how they respond, in what appears to man as contingency (conveyed appropriately as anthropomorphic shepherding). In summary, scripture affirms that sin is caused by an organic influence capable of overpowering the will, while maintaining accountability, which repudiates the perception of free will by libertarianism and contingency in regards to prophecy.

What is also garnered from the circumstance of the CN is that the power of the flesh was sanctioned until an appointed time, when manumission would be made possible for the elect by the propitiation of Christ, at the inauguration of the Israel's New Covenant (NC). Both Scofield and Ryrie indirectly affirm this appointed time in their commentary on Daniel, below; yet, both fail to grasp the ramifications of accurately calculating this appointed time from the Babylonian captivity as vindicating the concept that man does not cause God to repent nor alter his plans for the unforeseeable.

The seventy weeks are divided into seven = 49 years; sixty-two = 434 years; one = 7 years (Daniel 9:25–27). In the seven weeks = 49 years, Jerusalem was to be rebuilt in "troublous times." This was fulfilled, as Ezra and Nehemiah record. Sixty-two weeks =

434 years, thereafter Messiah was to come (Daniel 9:25).[16]

> Certain important events were to happen after the 62 weeks (plus the 7 weeks, or a total of 69 weeks): the crucifixion of Messiah, and the destruction of Jerusalem in A.D. 70 by the Romans who are the people of the prince that shall come.[17]

The appointed time for the propitiation of sin was determined from the seventy weeks in Daniel 9, which was due to Judah's rejection of God's call to repent in Jeremiah 18:7–10. Said dependency vindicates that God had foreknowledge that Judah would not repent; consequently, Jeremiah 18 cannot be used to show that man causes God to repent nor alter his plans for the unforeseeable. Such foreknowledge finds confirmation in the NT evidence that man was in subjugation to the CN and could not keep the law until this manumission, at the appointed time, which was God's will.

What is indicated in Jeremiah 18:7–10 and the book of Jonah from the evidence presented is the appearance of contingency, from whence Vlach drew his conclusions concerning contingency in regard to prophecy. God ordained that Israel would ultimately fail to comply with the law under the Sinai Covenant (SC), with the consideration that ultimate obedience was ordained with the NC. God either moves[18] against the CN or allows it to run its course and it is the former case which we see in the example of the book of Jonah. In Jonah, God moved the Ninevites and the prophet to act contrary to their CN, which demonstrates compatibilism, as opposed to open theism. It is man's perception of contingency that leads to the misapprehension of open theism. Covenantalist C. Matthew

---

[16] *Scofield's Reference Notes*, s.v. Daniel 9, Verse 24, *Study Light.org*, accessed October 27, 2018, https://www.studylight.org/commentaries/srn.html

[17] The Ryrie Study Bible, 1238.

[18] Moves: meaning God's ability to overpower the CN by his causal direction as a display of his power, stated in Romans 9:21-24 and Revelation 17:17

McMahon properly analyzed the narrative in Jonah as giving "us a glimpse of God's true intention for the Ninevites through Jonah's actions (the compound sense), while the stated text exhibits His coming wrath against the city in forty days (the divided sense)."[19] McMahon developed the seventeenth-century Calvinist's work of Francis Turretin, using his hermeneutics tool of the compound and divided sense, which agrees with what has been presented thus far. In Jonah, the compound sense perceives God moving against the CN of Jonah and the Ninevites to perform his will; the divided sense perceives a contingency. The account in the book of Jonah conveys the same sovereignty as the prophecy in Revelation 17:17, where God puts his will into the hearts of the ten kings to "give their kingdom unto the beast, until the words of God shall be fulfilled."

The concept of election also undermines the perception that the OT prophecies to the biological descendants were conditional, insomuch as the Old Covenant builders or tenants of the vineyard of Israel (Matthew 21:33–44), or the house of God, were ordained to reject the stone that becomes the corner (Psalms 118:22–23; Isaiah 8:14–15, 49:7; 1 Peter 2:6–8). Only an ordained remnant of the house of Israel was chosen to avow Christ.

> Peter, an apostle of Jesus Christ, To those who are elect exiles of the dispersion in Pontus, Galatia, Cappadocia, Asia, and Bithynia, according to the foreknowledge of God the Father, in the sanctification of the Spirit, for obedience to Jesus Christ and for sprinkling with his blood: May grace and peace be multiplied to you. (1 Peter 1:1–2 English Standard Version)

The ESV was used due to its poor translation of ἐκλεκτοῖς παρεπιδήμοις Διασπορᾶς in the KJV. The "elect exiles of the dispersion" is a superior translation and historically accurate, as Peter, the apostle to the circumscribed (Galatians 2:8), ministered to

---

[19] McMahon, *The Two Wills of God*, Kindle location 5224.

the biological descendants who never returned from the Babylonian exile and remained dispersed. Furthermore, they were ordained to avow Christ according to the foreknowledge of God, all of which undermines the misapprehension that the OT prophecies to the biological descendants were conditional. The New Testament (NT) vindicates Samuel's testimony that "the Strength of Israel will not lie nor repent: for he *is* not a man, that he should repent" (1 Samuel 15:29). Everything that was ordained to occur at the first advent happened according to the testimony of the OT prophets. If what is spoken by a prophet does not come to pass then, according to Deuteronomy, the prophet is not of God.

> I will raise them up a Prophet from among their brethren, like unto thee, and will put my words in his mouth; and he shall speak unto them all that I shall command him. And it shall come to pass, *that* whosoever will not hearken unto my words which he shall speak in my name, I will require *it* of him. But the prophet, which shall presume to speak a word in my name, which I have not commanded him to speak, or that shall speak in the name of other gods, even that prophet shall die. And if thou say in thine heart, How shall we know the word which the LORD hath not spoken? When a prophet speaketh in the name of the LORD, if the thing follow not, nor come to pass, that *is* the thing which the LORD hath not spoken, *but* the prophet hath spoken it presumptuously: thou shalt not be afraid of him. (Deuteronomy 18:18–22)

As already conveyed, the NT revealed that the law could do nothing to promote obedience but actually magnified sin and disobedience, while the New Covenant would solve the problem of disobedience by having God dwell in his chosen elect. Consequently, it would have inhibited God's plans if the Old Covenant biological descendants had fully grasped this principle. Knowing that the law could not promote obedience would have exacerbated their rebellion and disobedience and so God chose not to convey said revelation until the ratification of the New Covenant. Hence, the difference between the divided and compound senses is revelation: progressive revelation. The divided sense is the nascent, elementary revelations of God, while the compound sense incorporates his consummate or comprehensive revelations. The biological descendants were not ready for the compound sense in revelation, knowing that the law could not promote obedience; giving them such understanding would have been counterproductive to their walk with him. Therefore, under the Old Covenant ministration God conveyed security in land and life in the divided sense: blessings for obedience and curses for rebellion. Even so, in the compound sense God foreknew the biological descendants ultimately could not keep the law until the New Covenant was ratified, which substantiates that conditional prophecy is expressed in the divided sense and as such it cannot be used to confirm the premise that man causes God to repent nor does he alter his plans for the unforeseeable.

Returning to Ice's essay on 1 Peter 2 and replacement theology, his interpretation supports the concept that conditional prophecy is a fallacy by his affirmation that there were unsaved reprobates mixed with the elect of Israel.

> Since Hosea is a type of God in that book, the Lord is saying that not all of the children of Israel are His offspring. (I take it this is the Lord's way of saying many within national Israel were unbelievers in relation to their individual salvation while still a part of national Israel.)[20]

Ice acknowledges that the promises to Israel were only to the elect and not to the reprobate that mixed with them.

---

[20] Ice, "1 Peter 2 and Replacement Theology"

However, since Peter is writing to "the Israel of God" or Jewish believers, he is listing these Old Testament descriptions of Israel to let them know that everything promised them in the Old Testament is being fulfilled through their faith in Jesus as their Messiah. This is juxtaposed by a comparison with unbelieving Jews who have not trusted Jesus as the Messiah of Israel in verses 7–8. Peter speaks of "the stone which the builders rejected" (2:7) as a likely reference to Jewish leadership that lead the nation to reject Jesus as the Messiah. Peter further describes Jewish unbelievers as ones that view Jesus as "a stone of stumbling and a rock of offense" (2:8a). He notes that these Jewish unbelievers "stumble because they are disobedient to the word, and to this doom they were also appointed" (2:8b).[21]

Yet, the elect of Israel did avow Christ and since the kingdom did not appear there can be no other sound conclusion than that it simply was not the appointed time and that it was not offered by any means. God is not a God of *ad hoc* contingencies. Ice faltered, above, where he states Peter's epistle informed the Jewish believers that "everything promised them in the OT is being fulfilled through their faith in Jesus as their Messiah." This substantiates that the OT prophesies concerning Ephraim were being fulfilled at the first advent and there was no intent to establish the kingdom. It upholds the church as the vehicle to "raise up the tribes of Jacob, and to restore the preserved of Israel," as well as being a "light to the Gentiles" (Isaiah 49:6). Ice's interpretation of Peter's citation from Hosea 2:23 vindicates that the prophecy was being fulfilled literally at that time, an expression Ice used in still another of his essays: *Dispensational Hermeneutics.*[22]

The omissions of the historical-grammatical interpretation of the

---

[21] Ibid.

[22] Ice cites Arnold Fruchtenbaum in his thesis: "When a literal prophecy is fulfilled in the New Testament, it is quoted as a literal fulfillment." Thomas

OT citations in 1 Peter 2:9–10 are a failure to account for the salvific history of the nation of Ephraim as contrasted from Judah in Hosea, Jeremiah, Isaiah, Zechariah and especially in the anthropomorphic motif of the unfaithful, divorced wife returned to her husband, as idiomatic of the obstacle of Deuteronomy 24:4. More than one prophet idiomatically presented the obstacle of Deuteronomy 24:4 with the return of the divorced woman of Hosea.

> Her former husband, which sent her away, may not take her again to be his wife, after that she is defiled; for that is abomination before the LORD: and thou shalt not cause the land to sin, which the LORD thy God giveth thee for an inheritance. (Deuteronomy 24:4)

> They say, If a man put away his wife, and she go from him, and become another man's, shall he return unto her again? shall not that land be greatly polluted? but thou hast played the harlot with many lovers; yet return again to me, saith the Lord. (Jeremiah 3:1)

> Thus saith the Lord, Where [is] the bill of your mother's divorcement, whom I have put away? or which of my creditors [is it] to whom I have sold you? Behold, for your iniquities have ye sold yourselves, and for your transgressions is your mother put away. (Isaiah 50:1)

Omitting the historical-grammatical perspective of Ephraim taints any rendition of an OT citation in the NT. Ice concedes that at the first advent many exiled Jews dwelt in what is now southern Turkey,[23]

Ice, "Dispensational Hermeneutics" (2009), Article Archives Paper 115, http://digitalcommons.liberty.edu/pretrib_arch/115
[23] Ice, "The Calvinistic Heritage of Dispensationalism"

but as mentioned above, he neglects the historical-grammatical hermeneutic by omitting Ephraim from the context of 1 Peter 2:10. Instead, he calls the descendants of Israel abiding in the provinces of 1 Peter 1:1 Jews, as if all Israelites were Jews. Even so, Peter's citations from Hosea pertained to the reinstatement of the elect descendants of Ephraim, as an unfaithful, divorced wife returned to her husband.

Deuteronomy 24:4 pertains to the idiom of the unfaithful, divorced wife returned to her husband in an eschatological context, which is precisely what Paul relates in his Romans epistle concerning the release from the condemnation of the law.

> Know ye not, brethren, (for I speak to them that know the law,) how that the law hath dominion over a man as long as he liveth? For the woman which hath an husband is bound by the law to her husband so long as he liveth; but if the husband be dead, she is loosed from the law of her husband. So then if, while her husband liveth, she be married to another man, she shall be called an adulteress: but if her husband be dead, she is free from that law; so that she is no adulteress, though she be married to another man. Wherefore, my brethren, ye also are become dead to the law by the body of Christ; that ye should be married to another, even to him who is raised from the dead, that we should bring forth fruit unto God. (Romans 7:1–4)

Dispensationalists like Scofield and Ryrie were silent upon Paul's allusion to Deuteronomy 24:1–4. Ryrie certainly does not even attempt to explain how in Romans 7 the gentiles were "in bondage to the law," as he put it.[24] Furthermore, his assertion that the law was "not the Mosaic law here" cannot be sustained by the context.[25] The

---

[24] *The Ryrie Study Bible*, s.v. Rom 7:4, 1604.
[25] Ibid.

contemporary dispensationalist Ernest L. Martin acknowledged that the law in Romans 7:1–4 hindered Ephraim's remarriage, but held that the remarriage "will take place, contrary to the law of God in Deuteronomy 24."[26] Dispensationalists like Martin fail to grasp that Paul's allusion to Deuteronomy 24 in Romans 7:1–4 affirms that the SC ended with the cross, and the betrothal of Hosea 2:23 began. According to Paul, Israel's marriage to the covenant maker (Jeremiah 3:14; Isaiah 54:5–6; Hosea 2:7) ended when Christ died on the cross, freeing them from the SC and leaving them free to remarry the risen Christ in the NC. Further, Martin is in conflict with one of the founders of dispensationalism, Charles Stanley of Rotherham (1821–1890), who grasped that the association of the marriage to the husband conveyed in Romans 7:2–4 pertained strictly to Israel's marriage in the OT, as opposed to any association with the gentiles.

> Here, then, we have the two husbands. The old husband the Jews had had; that is, the law … so is it shown that the believer cannot be married to both Christ and the law…. if we carefully examine the holy oracles of God, we shall find that the Jews had been under law, or married to the first husband, 1,500 years…. But of the Jews the apostle says, "Wherefore, my brethren, ye also are become dead to the law by the body of Christ, that ye should be married to another, even to him who is raised from the dead, that we should bring forth fruit unto God." (Rom. 7:4) Hence, do not you see, my reader, the passages that follow, instead of being the proper experience of the Christian, really are the strongest possible contrast.[27]

---

[26] Ernest L. Martin, "The Book of Hosea" *Associates for Scriptural Knowledge (ASK)*, (Number 10/12, October 2012), accessed October 27, 2018, http://www.askelm.com/prophecy/p121001.PDF

[27] Charles Stanley, "The Two Husbands of Romans 7," *Bible Truth Publishers.com*, accessed October 27, 2018, https://bibletruthpublishers.com/

Stanley was correct in one sense only: excluding gentiles, only Israelites were married to the husband in the anthropomorphic depiction of the covenant relationship in the OT, but Stanley failed to ascribe concurrence with the husband in Jeremiah 3:14, Isaiah 54:5–6 and Hosea 2:7; concurrence must affirm a divine being as the husband in the illustration, not the law. Another contemporary dispensationalist, Arnold Fruchtenbaum, concurs that the husband is a divine being and correctly rendered the SC, the law, as the marriage contract in the anthropomorphic equivalence.

> The entire format of the Book of Deuteronomy is that of both an ancient treaty and an ancient marriage contract. In this book, Moses took all the various facets of the three earlier books and presented them in the form of an ancient marriage contract. In this book we find the marriage contract signed between Israel and God whereby Israel becomes the Wife of Jehovah.... The relationship of Israel as the Wife of Jehovah is viewed throughout the Scriptures in various ways and facets.... if one makes the Wife of Jehovah (Israel) and the Bride of the Messiah (the Church) one and the same thing, he is faced with numerous contradictions because of the different descriptions given.[28]

The problem Fruchtenbaum faces is, how does Jehovah himself release Israel from the SC by his death? Yahweh cannot die. The prophets reckoned Deuteronomy 24:1–4, the law, as an impediment to Ephraim's restoration and Paul revealed the impediment was surmounted by the death and resurrection of Christ in Romans 7:1–4. This is a revelation; it was pre-incarnate Christ who was

---

the-two-husbands-of-romans-7/charles-stanley/pamphlets/c-stanley/la61593
[28] Arnold Fruchtenbaum, "The Wife of Jehovah and the Bride of Messiah," *Bible Prophecy Blog.com*, accessed October 27, 2018, http://www.bibleprophecyblog.com/2009/07/wife-of-jehovah-and-bride-of-messiah.html

the husband that divorced Ephraim. This is also affirmed in the revelation of Christ, who, as the angel of the Lord, declared "I will never break my covenant" (Judges 2:1). The comprehension that Christ was the angel who gave Israel its covenant flourished in the eighteenth- and nineteenth-century Evangelical movement, which is written by Louis Goldberg in *Baker's Evangelical Dictionary.*

> The connection between the angel of the Lord and the preincarnate appearance of the Messiah cannot be denied. Manoah meets the angel of the Lord, and declares that he has seen God. The angel accepts worship from Manoah and his wife as no mere angel, and refers to himself as "Wonderful," the same term applied to the coming deliverer in Isaiah 9:6 (Jud 13:9–22). The functions of the angel of the Lord in the Old Testament prefigure the reconciling ministry of Jesus. In the New Testament, there is no mention of the angel of the Lord; the Messiah himself is this person.[29]

Ryrie in truth concedes that Christ was the husband in the OT and in Romans 7:2–4 when he interpreted that Christ was the "spiritual rock" that "actually followed the Israelites" in 1 Corinthians 10:4.[30] Even so, Ryrie completely missed the allusion to the SC in Romans 7:1–4, specifically the law of Deuteronomy 24:1–4. Fruchtenbaum's perception of the husband in the OT presents the fallacy of the death of an immortal being necessary to release Israel from the SC.

---

[29] *Baker's Evangelical Dictionary of Biblical Theology,* s.v. Angel of the Lord, *Bible Study Tools.com,* accessed October 27, 2018, https://www.biblestudytools.com/dictionaries/bakers-evangelical-dictionary/angel-of-the-lord.html

[30] The rock in 1 Corinthians 10:4 is affirmed as Christ by C. C. Ryrie: "that spiritual Rock which provided water (Ex. 17:1-9; Num. 20:1-13). Since the rock is mentioned twice, and is in different settings, a rabbinic legend held that a material rock actually followed the Israelites. Paul, however, says that it was Christ who was the with Israel all the way." *The Ryrie Study Bible,* s.v. the spiritual Rock, 1632.

Stanley misrepresented the law as the husband. Martin missed the phenomenon altogether, that Christ's death released both houses of Israel from the SC. The failure of these dispensationalists to grasp the significance of Deuteronomy 24:1–4 as it pertains to Romans 7:1–4 stems from their omissions of Ephraim from the historical-grammatical perspective, when rendering NT texts such as 1 Peter 2:9–10. They fail to account for the salvific history of the nation of Ephraim as contrasted from Judah in Hosea, Jeremiah, Isaiah, Zechariah and especially in the anthropomorphic motif of the unfaithful, divorced wife returned to her husband, as idiomatic of the obstacle of Deuteronomy 24:1–4.

Vlach, like any dispensationalist, sees two distinct anthropological groups at the first advent.

> Revised dispensationalists did not emphasize the eternal dualism and separation of heavenly and earthly peoples like classical dispensationalists did. Yet they did emphasize that there were two distinct anthropological groups— Israel and the church which are always kept distinct. These two groups are structured differently with different dispensational roles and responsibilities, but the salvation they each receive is the same.... The distinction between Israel and the church, as different groups, will continue throughout eternity even though both groups inherit the millennial kingdom and the eternal state.[31]

As revealed above, Ice's essay on 1 Peter 2 also conveys two anthropological groups—but from God's perspective:

> Peter is writing to "the Israel of God" or Jewish believers, he is listing these Old Testament

---

[31] Michael J. Vlach, *Dispensationalism: Essential Beliefs and Common Myth* (Theological Studies Press December 28, 2010), Kindle Locations 171-179.

descriptions of Israel to let them know that everything promised them in the Old Testament is being fulfilled. This is juxtaposed by a comparison with unbelieving Jews who have not trusted Jesus as the Messiah of Israel in verses 7–8.... He notes that these Jewish unbelievers "stumble because they are disobedient to the word, and to this doom they were also appointed" (2:8b).[32]

Ice clearly affirms two bodies within the biological descendants of Jacob, an anthropological division, where only the elect biological descendants of Jacob are "the Israel of God." The biological descendants are anthropologically divided as either the seed of the woman or the seed of the serpent (Genesis 3:15). Many are called, but few are chosen (Matthew 20:16). Moreover, Ephraim and Judah are two nations with differing salvific histories in the scriptures, which is an anthropological division in itself and this is what dispensationalism omits. This is the dualism Vlach conveys but he fails to perceive that it pertains more accurately to the distinction of the salvific destiny of Ephraim as contrasted with Judah. Dispensationalists' omissions have blinded them to the evidence that the church is the vehicle to "raise up the tribes of Jacob, and to restore the preserved of Israel" as well as being a "light to the Gentiles" (Isaiah 49:6).

Ephraim's unique salvific histories commenced with Solomon. Ice unwittingly acknowledged that the Ephraimites were dwelling in exile when he stated Jews had "been there since their dispersion by the Assyrians and Babylonians."

It is clear, Peter, an apostle who was specifically called to minister to the Jews, is writing a letter to encourage Jewish believers who are in the diaspora. It makes no sense to speak of Gentile Christians as aliens living in Gentile nations. It makes good

---

[32] Ice, "1 Peter 2 and Replacement Theology"

sense to speak of Jewish believers as aliens living in Gentile lands who had likely been there since their dispersion by the Assyrians and Babylonians.[33]

Ice makes a good point that Peter and other epistles pertained primarily to the biological descendants; yet, Ice misrepresented them as Jews, as not all Israelites are Jews. Ice's citation of the Assyrian dispersion concedes that the descendants of Ephraim as well as those of Judah were dwelling in the dominions where Peter directed his epistles. Dispensationalist William D. Barrick indirectly affirms this in his essay on the promises that are yet to be fulfilled to Israel.

> Note that several of these characteristics were undeveloped or unfulfilled during the return of Israel to the land following the Babylonian Exile (viz., altered topography, climate changes, and extension of boundaries). This would seem to contradict those theologians who insist that the promises to Israel for restoration were all fulfilled when Zerubbabel, Ezra, and Nehemiah led their various groups of Israelite exiles back into the land from Babylon. If these promises were fulfilled by the return of the Jews from the Babylonian exile, "How then shall we explain the prophecy in Zechariah 10:8–12 that announces in 518 B.C. a still future return, which would not only emanate from Babylon, but from around the world?"[34]

Here we have evidence from a dispensationalist that Zechariah 10 pertains to a subsequent return from a dispersion that occurs in this age, an age that commenced at Christ's first advent. Judah is clearly dispersed again in this age after the temple was destroyed in 70

---

[33] Ibid.

[34] William D. Barrick, Th.D., "The Kingdom of God in the Old Testament," *Master's Seminary Journal*, 23/2 (Fall 2012) 173–192, https://www.tms.edu/m/msj23j.pdf

A.D. This by itself substantiates that Christ's first advent was not to offer the kingdom but to disperse the Jews again. Nevertheless, Barrick omits the prophecy that Ephraim is saved in a protracted, multi-generational dispersion, which only proves the omission of Ephraim in the grammatical-historical hermeneutics is pervasive in dispensationalism.

> And they of Ephraim shall be like a mighty man, and their heart shall rejoice as through wine: yea, their children shall see it, and be glad; their heart shall rejoice in the Lord. I will hiss for them, and gather them; for I have redeemed them: and they shall increase as they have increased. And I will sow them among the people: and they shall remember me in far countries; and they shall live with their children, and turn again. (Zechariah 10:7–9)

Zechariah 10 is the inspiration for the parables of the marriage of the king's son and that of the wheat and the tares and its examination is so appropriate here. As Barrack affirms, Zechariah 10:8–12 prophesied of another diaspora after the return from Babylon, specifically concerning Ephraim. Scofield cited 1 Peter 2:8 to interpret the "corner" in Zechariah 10:4 as Christ,[35] which is tantamount to conceding that it was Christ's whose anger was kindled against the shepherds and the goats (v 3). Clearly, the text pertains to the diaspora resulting from the kingdom being taken from the shepherds (Matthew 21:43), which is the subject the following chapter, Zechariah 11. In abstracts, the initial verses relate that Christ strengthens the remnant of Judah and saves Ephraim by gathering them in Christ, according to the NT (Matthew 13:24–30, 36–43; Romans 12:5; 1 Corinthians 15:22; 1 Peter 5:14).

---

[35] Scofield's Reference Notes, s.v. Zech 10:4

> I will hiss for them, and gather them; for I have
> redeemed them: and they shall increase as they have
> increased. (Zechariah 10:8)

Through the gospel the elect of Ephraim are called and gathered in Christ, while the promise of fecundity is fulfilled. Then, God sows them in the world according to the parable of the wheat and the tares.

> And I will sow them among the people: and they shall
> remember me in far countries; and they shall live with
> their children, and turn again. (Zechariah 10:9)

The neglectful shepherds correspond to those sitting on Moses's seat who refused to come to the marriage; consequently, God destroys the city and also scatters the reprobate who are no longer the husbandmen of the vineyard of Israel. Ephraim becomes a great multitude in fulfillment of the promise of fecundity passed down to Ephraim and Manasseh, the sons of Joseph (Genesis 48:17, 49:22). Zechariah 10:7–9 affirms, Ephraim is redeemed and then sown in distant countries and this runs concurrent with the betrothal of Ephraim "in righteousness, and in judgment, and in lovingkindness, and in "mercies" and "in faithfulness" before they are sown in the earth (Hosea 2:19–23). The death of Christ releases Ephraim from the marriage contract, the SC, and frees them to marry Christ under the NC. Ephraim is the nation that bears the fruit of the vineyard in Matthew 21:43. This is not the history of the Jews (Romans 9–11; Galatians 4:25). The prophets agree, many of the elect which are the biological descendants of Abraham propagated with gentiles in a protracted exile (Jeremiah 31:27; Hosea 2:23, 7:8, 8:8–9; Amos 9:9; Micah 5:7; Zechariah 10:7–9). They also agree, these descendants populated the world due to Ephraim's fecundity (Genesis 12:3, 17:5–6, 35:11, 41:52, 48:16, 19; Hosea 1:10; Zechariah 10:7–9). They agree further that the Ephraimites are redeemed or saved, their sins blotted out, while in exile, and are dispersed throughout the world (Isaiah

43:1, 5, 25, 44:22, 24, 51:5, 11; Hosea 2:23; Jeremiah 31:1–2, 5–6; Zechariah 10:6).

It is hard to conjecture as to exactly what Ice meant when he interpreted Peter's citations of Hosea to the Jewish believers as imparting "everything promised them in the Old Testament is being fulfilled" when regarding the dispensationalist belief that God interrupted his plans for Israel when they rejected their Messiah. What is revealed in the NT is that Christ released Israel from their marriage under the SC and his resurrection made them eligible to be espoused to him (Romans 7:1–4) under the NC, particularly Ephraim, the unfaithful, divorced wife who now returns to her husband. Ephraim's fecundity is consummated as she returns to her husband. Ice's interpretation of 1 Peter 2 does substantiate that the eschatological promises to Israel are protracted over time and not merely at a precipitous event at the return of Christ.

In Christ, elect Jews and Ephraimites are no longer held to the Old Covenant laws prohibiting intermarriage (Deuteronomy 7:3–5; Galatians 3:28; Romans 7:1–4; Ephesians 2:13); even so, in another sense they still remain the biological descendants, and it can be maintained that God's elections are irrevocable—as they are the Israel of God's irrevocable choice, by whom the Gentiles are blessed (Genesis 12:3, 18:18, 26:4). In Christ, the Jew, Ephraimite and Gentile become corporately perceived as one, but in the biological sense as women remain women, Ephraimites remain biological heirs of Abraham no matter how diminished that biological sense becomes due to the end of the prohibitions against intermarriage and the concern for genealogies is quashed (1 Timothy 1:3; Titus 3:9). Moreover, dispensationalists omit the birthright of fecundity passed down from Jacob to the descendants of the northern tribes of Zechariah above (Genesis 48:3–4, 16–20), which renders them a copious people in providence, much greater than the hardened Jews who dispensationalists perceive as the only Israel. First Samuel 15:29 affirms that God "is not a man, that he should repent." God did not repent concerning the biological descendant's commission to bless the nations at the first advent even as their biological identity diminished; in a sense, the obfuscation of their lineage became the means to bless the nations. Any principle in determining how one discerns the term Israel in an eschatological context must avoid tension between OT and NT revelation, which dispensationalism has not evaded.

The dispensationalist's argument against any protracted and gradual development of Israel's NC is that the OT affirms the NC is fulfilled in the precipitous event of the second-advent. In reference to the promises of the NC and citing Compton, again, he asserts that the "promises without exception occur in the OT in eschatological contexts.... in connection with the Lord's coming to gather the Jews from the lands in which they have been dispersed, reconstituting them as a nation, and restoring them to their geographical homeland."[36] Again, the fallacy in Compton's assertion is that he is not applying his own supposition that the prophets did not fully grasp all the implications of the words they were superintended to write,[37] and nowhere is this more striking than in the prophecy of the two advents of the Messiah—the greatest of mysteries! One of the most noted dispensationalists, Cyrus Ingerson Scofield affirmed that "Malachi, in common with other O.T. prophets, saw both advents of Messiah blended in one horizon, but did not see the separating interval described in Matthew 13."[38] But only NT revelation provides the hermeneutics to discern this distinction in the OT; Scofield must rely on NT revelation to make such a statement. Scofield essentially supports the idea that the prophets were not given to know of two advents but this does not affirm that two advents were not planned. NT revelation affirms two advents; in the first Christ would be wounded for our transgressions (Isaiah 53:5) and after a mysterious interval, he would return as king. Scofield's concession verifies Israel's promises of the redemption from sin and regeneration in the NC, anticipated in Jeremiah 31:31–33, were not committed to the second advent, as Compton perceives, but to the first advent.

---

[36] Compton, "Dispensationalism, the Church, and the New Covenant"
[37] Ibid.
[38] Scofield's Reference Notes, s.v. Malachi 3:1

From Peter's perspective, the present salvation of the descendants of the ten tribes, still in exile, to whom he addressed his epistles, was seen by the prophets in the sufferings of Christ (1 Peter 1:10–12). Moreover, their existing "trials" correspond to the chastisements also anticipated by Isaiah 27:8–9 and Zechariah 13:8–9, which will be examined presently, along with the provisions of the NC from which the salvation of the descendants of Israel originates.

After his resurrection Christ unveiled to his disciples the record from the prophets where he was to die and be raised to his Father's right hand (Luke 24:25–27). With this inspiration Peter's monologue in Acts affirms that David had prophesied Christ's suffering and death in Psalms 16:8–11 and how it was being fulfilled at the first advent, but his return or second advent was held in abeyance until his enemies are made his footstool, fulfilling Psalms 110:1 (Acts 2:25–36). Peter's renditions of Psalms 16 and 110 provide the hermeneutic by which dispensationalists like Ryrie render Zechariah 9:9 as "fulfilled completely at the first advent of Jesus Christ" and then interpret the consummation of the subsequent verses is held in abeyance until "the second advent of Christ."[39] In like manner, Ryrie and the preponderance of dispensationalists, such as J. Dwight Pentecost, render the birth of Israel's ruler in Micah 5:2, along with the consequence in verse 3, as being fulfilled by Christ at the first advent, and verses 4–15 of the same context are held in abeyance until the second advent.[40] The point being is that dispensationalists must concede, the NT reveals the Savior in a greater capacity than the OT. Discernment between first and second advents in the OT is only possible from an NT revelation. Scofield was right, the OT prophets knew nothing of "the separating interval described in Matthew 13," but their lack of knowledge does not preclude a protracted eschatology. The protracted eschatology revealed in Matthew 13 actually explains OT texts such as Hosea 2:19–23 and Zechariah 10:7–9. The dispensationalist's acknowledgement that

---

[39] *The Ryrie Study Bible*, s.v. Zech 9:9-10, 1319.
[40] Ibid., 1288; J. Dwight Pentecost, *Things to Come: A Study in Biblical Eschatology* (Grand Rapids: Zondervan, 1958), p.289.

the two advents in the OT were often in the same context destroys Compton's issue concerning context and the NC. The fact that both advents were often spoken of in the same context substantiates that Compton's issue is impractical. Finding both advents prophesied in the same context rather substantiates that the NC is fulfilled in a protracted manner in which some parts are immediately fulfilled while others are held in abeyance until the second-advent.

The NT substantiates that the judgment on the reprobate shepherds prophesied in Zechariah 11 and Ezekiel 34 was fulfilled at the first advent. Christ took the kingdom from the reprobate shepherds and then pardoned and prospered a remnant who would sojourn in the nations to be sifted (Amos 9:8–9; Mark 10:30). Intercession for the remnant is evidence that God continued to feed and work with Israel in this age. The parables in Matthew 13 illustrate that the remnant of Israel, especially the nation Ephraim, would be sown throughout the world to fulfill the promise that Abraham would be the "father of many nations (Genesis 17:4–5). In contradiction, Scofield's notes on Micah 5 assert that "The meaning of Micah 5:3 is that, from the rejection of Christ at His first coming Jehovah will give Israel up till the believing remnant appears; then He stands and feeds in His proper strength as Jehovah (Micah 5:4)."[41] Scofield's presuppositions have him see Israel's remnant only at the second advent, at the last scene of the present age, dismissing the evidence that the copious remnant of exiled Ephraimites actually avowed Christ, migrated and intermarry with the gentiles and are still being fed by God in this age. As already established, God appointed certain reprobates to wrath and to reject Christ (Romans 9:21), which renders it a fallacy to interpret that he offered the kingdom to those who were never ordained to inherit it. Darby, the author of classic dispensationalism, also held the literalist view believing the remnant of Israel will be fed at the second advent.

Another very important element of this last scene of the present age is pointed out in this verse.

---

[41] Scofield's Reference Notes, s.v. Mic 5

Israel is given up to judgment, forsaken of God, in a certain sense, for having rejected the Christ, the Lord. But now she who travaileth has brought forth. Afterwards (and this is the element I refer to) the remnant of the brethren of this first-born Son, instead of being added to the church (Acts 2), return unto the children of Israel. The Christ is not ashamed to call them His brethren; but at this period they no longer become members of His body. Their relation is with Israel.[42]

Notwithstanding, their supposition concerning "context" and the quelling of the evidence that the remnant of Israel was fed at the first advent is thwarted by their concession that there is a transition from one advent to the other without chronological notation in the OT which can only be resolved by NT revelation. Such a concession substantiates that the feeding of the biological descendants of Israel was not held in abeyance at the first advent (John 21:17; Acts 20:28; 1 Peter 5:2). Dispensationalists force Micah 5:4, Ezekiel 34 and sometimes even Zechariah 11 to pertain to the second advent by circumventing the fact that the remnant of Israel was fed by God at the first advent. Acknowledging that these texts pertain to the first advent substantiates the gradual development of eschatological provisions of the NC in Hebrews. Major provisions were fulfilled at the first advent and others await the second, a premise clearly sustained in the epistle to the Hebrews.

Darby stressed the discontinuity between the OT and NT relationship with God while underestimating the continuity, which led to his failure to properly render the sense in which the woman is given up in Micah 5:3. Notwithstanding, the judgment at the first advent did not depart from the precedent established when Israel was sent into Babylonian captivity; God interceded for the faithful remnant that submitted to his judgment, while the reprobate

---

[42] John Darby's Synopsis, s.v. Mic 5

were hardened and endured the wrath of God, thus, the continuity between Israel and the church and the glory of God is maintained.

Build ye houses, and dwell in them; and plant gardens, and eat the fruit of them; Take ye wives, and beget sons and daughters; and take wives for your sons, and give your daughters to husbands, that they may bear sons and daughters; that ye may be increased there, and not diminished. And seek the peace of the city whither I have caused you to be carried away captives, and pray unto the LORD for it: for in the peace thereof shall ye have peace... Then shall ye call upon me, and ye shall go and pray unto me, and I will hearken unto you. (Jeremiah 29:5–7)

And the LORD said unto me, A conspiracy is found among the men of Judah, and among the inhabitants of Jerusalem. They are turned back to the iniquities of their forefathers, which refused to hear my words; and they went after other gods to serve them: the house of Israel and the house of Judah have broken my covenant which I made with their fathers. Therefore thus saith the LORD, Behold, I will bring evil upon them, which they shall not be able to escape; and though they shall cry unto me, I will not hearken unto them. Then shall the cities of Judah and inhabitants of Jerusalem go, and cry unto the gods unto whom they offer incense: but they shall not save them at all in the time of their trouble. For according to the number of thy cities were thy gods, O Judah; and according to the number of the streets of Jerusalem have ye set up altars to that shameful thing, even altars to burn incense unto Baal. Therefore pray not thou for this

people, neither lift up a cry or prayer for them: for
I will not hear them in the time that they cry unto
me for their trouble. (Jeremiah 11:9–14)

Writing from a revised dispensationalist supposition Gary E. Yates
confirms the two responses and the ramifications:

> While steadfastly refusing to extend "peace" (מֹלְשׁ)
> to Jerusalem, the prophet Jeremiah then encourages
> the Judean exiles in Babylon to pray for the "peace"
> (מֹלְשׁ) of Babylon (29:7). Jeremiah opposes the
> prophets who proclaim an unconditional "peace"
> (מֹלְשׁ) for Jerusalem (cf. 4:9–10, 6:14, 8:11) and
> asserts instead that Babylon has replaced Jerusalem
> as the place of blessing and security for the people of
> Israel … this same prophet … exhorts the exiles to
> seek the "welfare" (מֹלְשׁ) of Babylon (29:7a) because
> in its "welfare is your welfare" (בִשְׁלוֹמָה לָכֶם יִהְיֶה שָׁלוֹם)
> (29:7b). Following the subjugation of Judah to
> Babylon in 597 B.C., the prophet Jeremiah asserts
> that the exiles in Babylon actually enjoy a position
> superior to the citizens and king who remain in
> Jerusalem. The promise for a new Israel is connected
> to the return of the Babylonian exiles after seventy
> years (29:10–14). In contrast, the inhabitants of
> Jerusalem remain the object and target of Yahweh's
> decree of judgment (29:16–18).[43]

The Hebrew word *palal* translated pray, literally imparts: intervene
or interpose. Jeremiah substantiates that God continued to intercede
for the remnant of Israel during the Babylonian captivity, which the

---

[43] Gary E. Yates, "The People Have Not Obeyed: A Literary and Rhetorical
Study of Jeremiah 26-45" (Published dissertation presented to the Dallas
Theological Seminary, 1998), 173-174. http://digitalcommons.liberty.edu/cgi/
viewcontent.cgi?article=1025&context=fac_dis

book of Esther also corroborates. The dichotomy between the two responses to Christ at the first advent was explained by Paul as the distinction between the children of the promise and the children of the flesh (Romans 9:6–8). The same distinction conveys the response to Jeremiah's prophecy to Jerusalem. At the first advent the majority of Judah represented the children of the flesh destined to be cast off, which brought about the circumstances where God interceded for the remnant, the children of the promise, and they became a blessing upon the nations (Genesis 12:3; Romans 11:11–29). In like manner, the remnant that went peaceably to Babylon become the means by which those cities prospered as in the case of Daniel, Hananiah, Mishael, and Azariah (Daniel 1–6). Christ, as the supreme prophet Moses anticipated (Deuteronomy 18:15–19; Acts 3:22–23), represented the anti-type of Jeremiah who rebuked the false prophets that claimed God would save Jerusalem (Jeremiah 29:8–9; John 11:45–53) and who also interceded for the children of the promise—those who submitted to him and ultimately went peaceably into the world and propagated the gospel, in fulfillment of the parables of Matthew 13 and the prophesies of Hosea 2:19–23 and Zechariah 10:7–9.

In their zeal to stress the discontinuity, while underestimating the continuity between the OT and the NT relationship with God, dispensationalists force Zechariah 13, just as they do Micah 5:4, into pertaining to the second advent. However, Christ cited Zechariah 13:7 in Matthew as being fulfilled at his death and the scattering of the sheep is confirmed by history.

> Then saith Jesus unto them, All ye shall be offended because of me this night: for it is written, I will smite the shepherd, and the sheep of the flock shall be scattered abroad. (Matthew 26:31)

Furthermore, the refinement of the remnant of Israel, the third part brought through the fire,[44] is substantiated as commencing at the first advent through the vehicle of the church that runs concurrent with this age, according to Peter's epistles addressed to the elect exiles of the dispersion (1 Pet. 1:1), which even Ice held as pertaining to Israel and not the gentiles.[45]

> That the trial of your faith, being much more precious than of gold that perisheth, though it be tried with fire, might be found unto praise and honour and glory at the appearing of Jesus Christ. (1 Peter 1:7)

> Every man's work shall be made manifest: for the day shall declare it, because it shall be revealed by fire; and the fire shall try every man's work of what sort it is. If any man's work abide which he hath built thereupon, he shall receive a reward. If any man's work shall be burned, he shall suffer loss: but he himself shall be saved; yet so as by fire. (1 Corinthians 3:13–15)

Scofield asserts Zechariah's use of recapitulation when he stated that "Zechariah 13 now returns to the subject of Zechariah 12:10,"[46] but while Zechariah uses recapitulation it is not to be applied between these two chapters. As stated, the smiting of the shepherd is clearly a first advent phenomenon. Christ was prophesied to be stricken and afflicted at his first advent in correspondence with Isaiah 53:4 and Micah 5:1 and other texts. Premillennialism renders the second advent of Christ as his return in power to smite the nations (Isaiah

---

[44] The proportions need not be rendered as precise, but merely a majority as opposed to a remnant, as there is a remnant at any time that God chooses from those who are called.
[45] Ice, "1 Peter 2 and Replacement Theology"
[46] Scofield's Reference Notes, s.v. Zech 13:8

11:4; Revelation 19:15) as opposed to the first advent when he was afflicted. Furthermore, it was at the first advent when Christ fulfilled the scripture of a fountain being "opened to the house of David and to the inhabitants of Jerusalem for sin and for uncleanness" (Zechariah 13:1). Hebrews 9:28 confirms that Christ died once for sin at the first advent and when he returns it is not to remit sin again but to save his people and end the persecution at the hands of their enemies. It was Christ's first advent that caused "the names of the idols" to be cut "out of the land" and caused the false "prophets and the unclean spirit to pass out of the land" (Zechariah 13:2). The propagation of the gospel overpowered paganism wherever the gospel and Christ were avowed, which maintains Zechariah 13 as pertaining to the first advent. It is in this age that the promise that Jacob would become a nation and a company of nations is fulfilled (Gen. 35:11).

In Mark, Christ proclaimed the continued intercession for the Jews who avowed him at the call of the gospel, post diaspora, expressed in the same language in Jeremiah 29:7.

> And Jesus answered and said, Verily I say unto you, There is no man that hath left house, or brethren, or sisters, or father, or mother, or wife, or children, or lands, for my sake, and the gospel's, But he shall receive an hundredfold now in this time, houses, and brethren, and sisters, and mothers, and children, and lands, with persecutions; and in the world to come eternal life. But many that are first shall be last; and the last first. (Mark 10:29–31)

Hebrews 4 corroborates that the Jews who entered into the rest for the people of God at the first advent obtained mercy and grace through the intercession of Christ as high priest, who ministers the NC anticipated in Jeremiah 31 (Hebrews 10:9–10, 12:22–24). First Peter 2:8 affirms many were appointed to disobedience and would inherit wrath. Again, the judgment at the first advent did not deviate from the precedent established prior whereby God sent Israel into the Babylonian captivity and interceded for the faithful remnant who submitted to the judgment, while those who resisted were hardened and endured the wrath of God. And lastly, here, the intercession for the remnant substantiates that Micah 5:4 pertains to the first advent. The woman in Micah 5:3–4 represents the "remnant" in Romans 9:27–28 that is fed by God, while his wrath fell on the children of the flesh that were cast off. The sense in which the remnant woman in Micah 5:3 was given up at the first advent, then, was to persecutions and trials in correspondence with Mark 10:30 and 1 Peter 1:7; yet, at the same time she entered into God's rest by receiving Christ's intercession to find "grace to help in time of need" (Hebrews 4). But as for those who disavowed Christ "because of unbelief" they were not able to enter into his rest as God had so sworn.

In their continued zeal to stress the discontinuity, while underestimating the continuity between the OT and the NT relationship, dispensationalists claim gentiles have no standing as parties to the NC, that the covenant was strictly promised to Judah and Israel. Standing is accentuated in support of their doctrine that God set aside Israel at the first advent and will not feed them again until Christ's return, in fulfillment of Micah 5:4. The evidence presented here that God interceded for the scattered remnant of Israel at the first advent and continued to feed them substantiates that the church was foreseen in the OT as the remnant women in Micah 5, albeit veiled until God's appointed time. In one of the controversies concerning this issue an essay by Elliott Johnson in The Master's Seminary Journal stresses the dispensationalist's view.

> Discontinuity exists also in the application of the New Covenant benefits. The discontinuity is present because the party to the New Covenant is specified as the house of Israel and the house of Judah (8:8 and 10:16). And Judaism had not accepted a partnership in the New Covenant since they continued to practice their worship under the

terms set by the first covenant. Hebrews views the recipients (3:1 and 9:15) as merely beneficiaries. Benefits promised in the New Covenant have now been applied to called ones because of the death and ministry of Jesus Christ.... And Hebrews' quotation of the passage from Jeremiah (8:8:12 and 10:16–17) leaves open the expectation, as the quotations claim, that the houses of Israel and Judah will be called in the future. That would then involve a fulfillment of Jeremiah's prophecy of the covenant at some future time, in the same terms as prophesied[47]

Concerning Hebrews 9:16–17, Johnson argued that the author's intent was that of an application of a Hellenistic or Roman civil bequeathal, instead of interpreting the scripture more appropriately in accord with the Hebraic cultic mea*ning of* diathēkē.

> The transition from 9:15 to 9:16–17 introduces a strange anomaly in the use of *diathēkē* ... it has the sense of last "will" or "testament" according to the majority of translations and interpreters.... the "death of the one who made it" most naturally requires a sense of "last will" or "testament," since covenants did not involve the death of their makers before being inaugurated. Likewise, in 9:17 the statement that a *diathēkē*, takes effect at death and is not in force while the maker is alive applies only to a testament. In 9:18, however, the topic returns again to the first *diathēkē*, that is, the Sinai arrangement, which is clearly regarded as a covenant. Accepting such a change in translation suggests profound implications in the hermeneutics of Hebrews. It is not a change in arrangement but a change in

---

[47] Elliott Johnson, "Does Hebrews Have a Covenant Theology?" (*Masters Seminary Journal*, 21/1 Spring 2010), 31-54.

perspective in looking at the same arrangement.... That does not mean that the second party is unnecessary, or subject to change.[48]

The second party is Judah and Israel. Faithful to dispensationalism's presuppositions Johnson chose to stress the discontinuity of a secular concept or a Hellenistic or Roman legal practice in place of appropriately interpreting the Septuagint's meaning of *diathēkē* in Hebrews 9:16–17. He and the many others that hold this view stress that "covenants did not involve the death of their makers," in order to enforce its provisions. Even so, Scott W. Hahn points out that the Greco-Roman arrangement departs from the theme in Hebrews.

> This runs counter to a testamentary model, in which only God (the Father, 1:5) could function as the testator, since he dispenses the inheritance. Ironically, it is not God, the "testator," but Christ, the heir, who must die to receive the heavenly inheritance. In the understanding of inheritance in Hebrews, God gives a heavenly inheritance to Christ, "the heir of all things," after the death, resurrection, and exaltation of Christ the heir, whereas in a Hellenistic testament, a testator gives an earthly inheritance to his heir(s) near the end of his (the testator's) life—in the case of *donatio inter vivos*—or at this death. The most striking difference between the model of inheritance in Hebrews and a testament is that, consistently in Hebrews, it is the heir rather than the testator who must die before the inheritance is bestowed.[49]

---

[48] Ibid., 46-47.

[49] Scott W. Hahn, "A Broken Covenant and the curse of Death: A Study of Hebrews 9:15-22," *Catholic Biblical Quarterly* (Jul 2004, vol. 66 Issue 3), 421-22.

Hahn stresses the point that in the Hebrew concept of *diathēkē* God fulfills the part of the testator and it is Christ who dies and is "heir of all things" (Hebrews 1:2). Christ, then shares his gift with the elect who are called. The Greco-Roman arrangement has the heir live and the testator ultimately die. Moreover, the Greco-Roman arrangement was not made valid by the death of the testator but when it was written, witnessed and notarized, and it was often distributed prior to the death of the testator. Hahn's essay analyses syntax, secular issues, grammar and the liturgical cultist issues that become an insurmountable argument against the perception of a Greco-Roman arrangement in the meaning of *diathēkē*. Furthermore, Hahn drew on the Septuagint to substantiate that in the arrangement of the SC the sacrifice of animals ratified the covenant and symbolized the death of the covenant violator. The death of the animal ratified the covenant and preceded its enforcement: "vv. 18–22 points out that, in fact, the first covenant was established in just this way, with the blood of the representative animals being sprinkled over the people and over all the physical implements of the covenant cult."[50]

Johnson's endeavor is one of the copious attempts in dispensationalism to play down the relationship of the NC with the church. Ryrie revealed that dispensational premillennialism has taught that "the church has no relation to the new covenant," or that there were "two new covenants, one with Israel and another with the church," or that the church merely "receives some of the blessings."[51] Dispensationalists simply cannot concede that the church is party to the covenant as it would substantiate that Israel and the church are not a separate people. Johnson attempts to substantiate the same by asserting that God departed from a covenantal arrangement with the church and based his relationship with them upon a secular civil arrangement. Hahn's work dispels any notion that the author of Hebrews departed from the Septuagint's concept, which corroborates that the church is party to the NC and eschatological prophecy was

---

[50] Ibid., 430.
[51] Charles C. Ryrie, *Dispensationalism* (Moody Publishers; Revised, Expanded edition, February 1, 2007), 137, 172.

intended as a gradual development in fulfillment of major provisions of the NC at the first advent, while holding others in abeyance until the consummation at the second.

Johnson's sentiments found their way into another dispensationalist's composition by Stephen R. Lewis in the Chafer Theological Seminary Journal entitled: *The New Covenant: Enacted or Ratified?* Lewis attempts to assert the same doctrinal views as Johnson, drawn from the same presuppositions and making the same assertions.

> Those who assert the enactment of the New Covenant for the Church must ponder the following questions: Which part of the Church is the house of Judah and which, the house of Israel? Did God lead our fathers out of Egypt and make a covenant with them? The Holy Spirit's choice of words proves that the Church (predominantly Gentile in composition) is not the entity with whom the Lord Jesus Christ enters into the New Covenant.[52]

Lewis, like Johnson, forces the anachronism of a greater constituency of the gentiles as members of the church in their exegesis of Romans 11, while underestimating the circumstances that the Jews were the overwhelming majority at the inception of the church and the constituency that founded it. The latter view must be accentuated in any presupposition concerning Romans 11 and the grafting in of the gentiles. Accurate analysis renders that Israel did not fail; in the compound sense God interceded for the preordained remnant to remain on the olive tree in the imagery of Romans 11. This intercession corresponds with the precedent in Jeremiah where the prayers of the remnant promoted the welfare of the nations where they sojourned (Jeremiah 29:5–7). Therefore, by design the fall of those whom God hardened had the effect of "Salvation is come

---

[52] Stephen R. Lewis, "The New Covenant: Enacted or Ratified?" *Chafer Theological Seminary Journal*, (vol. 8, October–December 2002), 55.

unto the Gentiles" as affirmed in Romans 11:11. Furthermore, Paul was cognizant of the fact that Peter, James and the other disciples had carried the gospel to northern-eastern Asia Minor where the descendants of Ephraim, the ten tribes, had favorably received the good news in great numbers which corresponds with the parable of the marriage of the king's son (Matthew 22:1–14). This occurrence as evidenced in the epistles of James and Peter is supported by the first-century Jewish historian Flavius Josephus, who observed that the ten tribes "beyond Euphrates till now" were as "an immense multitude, and not to be estimated by numbers."[53] Peter's epistles to the elect exiles of the dispersion in the dominions of Pontus, Galatia, Cappadocia, Asia, and Bithynia (1 Peter 1) are supported by Josephus's observation, as the dominions that were beyond and westwards of the Euphrates. Christ prophesied Jerusalem would be laid waste and would cease to be the center of worship as the gospel was commissioned to the world (Matthew 24, 28:19–20; John 4:21–24), which was integral to Paul's testimony that Israel's fall was the catalyst to present salvation to the gentiles as well as to the elect exiles of the dispersion; worship becoming centrifugal in its form. Such analysis renders the queries of Lewis shortsighted; the remnant of Judah and Israel and the elect gentiles are redeemed by the invitation to the marriage which is proclaimed through the gospel to the highways, again, in complete harmony with the parable of the marriage of the king's son.

Lewis also makes the highly untenable claim that "Nowhere does the Scripture say the NC has already come into existence"[54] in order to sustain the church as a separate people from Israel.

> the author of Hebrews says to second or third generation Hebrew Christian believers in the Church Age that the enactment of the New Covenant will be in the future (cf. Hebrews 8:6–13). He states: *Now what is becoming obsolete and growing old is ready*

---

[53] Josephus, Antiquities of the Jews, 11.133.
[54] Lewis, "The New Covenant: Enacted or Ratified," 59.

to vanish away (8:13b)—literally, "Now that which is growing old and aging is near disappearing." The old has not yet disappeared because the new has not come.[55]

Not only did Lewis fail to grasp the significance of Romans 7:1–4 but he failed to grasp that the author of Hebrews is relaying that the offering of Christ for sin ended the lawful standing of the SC when he established the NC.

> But into the second went the high priest alone once every year, not without blood, which he offered for himself, and for the errors of the people: The Holy Ghost this signifying, that the way into the holiest of all was not yet made manifest, while as the first tabernacle was yet standing. (Hebrews 9:7–8)

Hebrews 9:8 avows that so as long as the first tabernacle remained standing the way into the holiest was yet to be manifest. The revelation that the way into the holiest occurred at Christ's ascension in Hebrews 10:19 confirms that the term "standing" or *stasis* in Hebrews 9:8 cannot be rendered literally, as pertaining to the destruction of the temple at Jerusalem. Such examination substantiates *stasis*, rendered standing, should be comprehended abstractly as the authority from God to enforce the Aaronic priesthood and minister his covenants. Hebrews 10:19 verifies that the authority of the SC was taken away, also indicated by the veil being rent (Matthew 27:51). Only this abstract rendering of *stasis* corresponds with the need of changing the law at the change of the priesthood (Hebrews 7:12), which disannuls the commandment that only the descendants of Aaron could mediate as high priests (Hebrews 7:18) and substantiates the "first" and "second" in Hebrews 10:9 as pertaining to the old and new covenants, which dispensationalist Rodney J. Decker substantiated.

---

[55] Ibid.

If this is a valid assessment of the text (and I think it is), then in light of the larger argument of chapters 7–10, it appears quite certain that we are talking about the first and second covenant, whether we explain it more generally or more specifically.... The negative term, ἀναιρέω, means "to take away, abolish, set aside".... The positive, ἵστημι, is "to put into force, establish," often with legal or covenantal overtones.[109] The first covenant comes to an end; the second take its place.[56]

Decker concludes that the NC came into force at the first advent, and that it is not "possible to divorce Christians from *some* relationship to the new covenant" falling short of confirming that the church is the party to the covenant.[57]

The propitiation for sin was at an appointed time, according to Daniel 9:25. The NT reveals the ratification and ramifications of this appointed time (Hebrews 9:15, 24–28, 10:10, 14; Romans 8:29–30; Acts 13:48; Ephesians 1:4–5, 11). Lewis concedes this appointed time where he stated, "When Christ returns to the nation of Israel and appears the second time, He will appear without need to deal with man's sin problem (Hebrews 9:28)."[58] Yet, he attempts to hold, in the same composition, the fallacy that Israel's sins had not been forgiven.

God did not forgive Israel at Christ's first coming. In fact, just the opposite took place—the sins from Abel to Zecharias God required of that generation (Matthew 23:34–36).[59]

---

[56] Rodney J. Decker Th.D., "The Law, the New Covenant, and the Christian; Studies in Hebrews 7–10," *NT Resources.com*, (September 2009), 23. http://ntresources.com/blog/wp-content/uploads/2009/09/New CovenantHebrews7-10_CDH_09x.pdf

[57] Ibid., 28, 29.

[58] Lewis, "The New Covenant: Enacted or Ratified," 61.

[59] Ibid. 60.

Lewis attempts to hold conflicting views because of dispensationalism's misapprehension of Romans 11:27, which they misinterpret as proof that the NC is not in effect.

> And so all Israel shall be saved: as it is written, There shall come out of Sion the Deliverer, and shall turn away ungodliness from Jacob: For this is my covenant unto them, when I shall take away their sins. (Romans 11:26–27)

Paul conflated Isaiah 59:20–21 and 27:9. This does not mean that Christ returns to ratify the NC of Jeremiah 31:31–34 again, as most dispensationalists believe (Hebrews 9:28). Isaiah 27:9 pertains to correction or purification before the consummation of the kingdom, while the reference to Isaiah 59 pertains to God's spirit abiding in those who are the chosen of Jacob.

> And the Redeemer shall come to Zion, and unto them that turn from transgression in Jacob, saith the LORD. As for me, this is my covenant with them, saith the LORD; My spirit that is upon thee, and my words which I have put in thy mouth, shall not depart out of thy mouth, nor out of the mouth of thy seed, nor out of the mouth of thy seed's seed, saith the LORD, from henceforth and for ever. (Isaiah 59:20–21)

Romans 11:27 cannot be perceived as pertaining to the second advent. Jeremiah 59:21 occurred at the first advent. The Spirit of God fell upon the biological descendants at the first advent according to the NT, fulfilling Isaiah 59:21.

> And they were all filled with the Holy Ghost, and began to speak with other tongues, as the Spirit gave them utterance. (Acts 2:4)

Nevertheless, the continuance of the chastening of the elect proves that the kingdom is not yet consummated. John Owen, a theologian from the seventeenth-century, wrote a voluminous commentary on Hebrews in which he stated the purpose of chastisement.

> It is required in chastisement, that the person be in a state wherein there is sin, or that he be a sinner; so that sin should have an immediate influence to the chastisement, as the meritorious cause of it: for the end of it is, "to take away sin," to subdue it, to mortify it, to increase holiness.[60]

Owen was not speaking of taking away sin in the sense that Christ did at the first advent, which justified man before God, but in the sense of sanctification, conforming the life to live victoriously over sin. He prefaced this statement with his comments upon Hebrews 10:4.

> The cessation of offerings follows directly on the remission of sin, which is the effect of expiation and atonement; and not of the turning away of men from sin for the future. It is, therefore, our justification, and not even sanctification, that the apostle discourseth of.[61]

Owen's conclusion in the matter of Isaiah 27:8–9 affixes God's acts as chastisement and not as the propitiation for sin.

> In the balance against this matter of sorrow in divine chastisements, the apostle lays down the advantage and benefit of it. "It yieldeth the peaceable fruit of righteousness." It yieldeth fruit; not it will do so,

---

[60] John Owen, D.D., *An Exposition of the Epistle to the Hebrews; With the Preliminary Exercitations*, vol. 4 (Boston: Printed and Sold by Samuel T. Armstrong; No. 50, Cornhill 1812.), 315.
[61] Ibid., 18.

but it doth so. It is not a dead useless thing. When God purgeth his vine, it is that it may "bear more fruit," John xv, 2. Where he dresseth the ground, it shall "bring forth herbs meet for himself," Heb. vi, 8. By this therefore, shall the iniquity of Jacob be purged, and this is all the fruit, "to take away his sin," Isa. xxvii, 9.[62]

The most essential matter exposing dispensationalism's fallacy concerning Romans 11:27 is that the provisions of the NC for the forgiveness of sin and regeneration were fulfilled for the remnants of Judah and Israel, and as well as the gentiles, who are called from the highways (representing the world) to the marriage. The church is the vehicle by which the house of God is built (Ephesians 2:11–22) as they answer the call to come to the marriage. Such evidence corresponds with the law and the prophets, which vindicates the inclusion of the gentiles as partners to Israel's covenant that, dispensationalist turned Epangelicalist, Walter C. Kaiser, Jr. develops in his essay published in the *Journal of the Evangelical Theological Society*.

> Consequently, we conclude that the extent of that kingdom had already in its earliest design embraced the steady absorption of Gentiles as well as Jews. Furthermore, there were numerous illustrations of this historical inclusion of the Gentiles. Witness the presence of Melchizedek, Jethro, Zipporah, Balaam, Rahab, Ruth and possibly the Gib-eonites, the Rechabites, the Ninevites and the entire books (e.g., Obadiah, Jonah, Nahum), or sections of books (e.g., prophecies to the nations in Isa 13–23, Jeremiah 45–51, Ezek 25–32, Amos 1–2), addressed to Gentiles.[63]

---

[62] Ibid., 327.

[63] Walter C. Kaiser, Jr., "The Davidic Promise and the Inclusion of the Gentiles," *Journal of the Evangelical Theological Society*, vol. 20:2 (June,

The law and the prophets, such as Isaiah and Ezekiel, witnessed the inclusion of the gentiles in God's covenants concerning the consummation of the kingdom.

> The Lord GOD which gathereth the outcasts of Israel saith, Yet will I gather others to him, beside those that are gathered unto him. (Isaiah 56:8)

> For the LORD will have mercy on Jacob, and will yet choose Israel, and set them in their own land: and the strangers shall be joined with them, and they shall cleave to the house of Jacob. (Isaiah 14:1)

> So shall ye divide this land unto you according to the tribes of Israel. And it shall come to pass, that ye shall divide it by lot for an inheritance unto you, and to the strangers that sojourn among you, which shall beget children among you: and they shall be unto you as born in the country among the children of Israel; they shall have inheritance with you among the tribes of Israel. And it shall come to pass, that in what tribe the stranger sojourneth, there shall ye give him his inheritance, saith the Lord GOD. (Ezekiel 47:21–23)

In relation to Zechariah 10:7–9 and Hosea 2:19–23, the gospels confirm that Christ came initially for Israel, to repair the tabernacle of David that had fallen and to gather from the nations the gentiles that are called by God's name.

> In that day will I raise up the tabernacle of David that is fallen, and close up the breaches thereof; and I will raise up his ruins, and I will build it as in the days of old: That they may possess the remnant of

1977), 99.

Edom, and of all the heathen, which are called by my name, saith the LORD that doeth this. (Amos 9:11–12)

Again, Kaiser stresses that the texts from Amos 9, cited by James in Acts 15:16–17, substantiated that the rebuilding of David's tabernacle is a protracted phenomenon between the two advents.

> The "things" James wanted to highlight were the predicted judgments that Amos had said were to fall on Israel, causing the outward and material collapse of the "house of David".... However, the political and national aspects of that same promise could not be deleted from Amos" truth-intention. As the suffixes in Amos 9:11 indicate, the northern and southern kingdom, the Davidic person, the people of Israel and the remnant of humanity at large were all encompassed in that rebuilding of the "tent of David," even though its outward fortunes would appear to sag in the immediate events of the eighth century.[64]

Kaiser reveals dispensationalists contradict the historical-grammatical hermeneutic in an "interpolation" of Acts 15:14–16. Kaiser's exegesis renders James's intent of the prepositional phrase "after this" in Acts 15:16 as the "day" Amos conveyed to be the *sifting* of Israel (Amos 9:9–11).

> Now "after these things"—the destruction of the temple, the fact of the diaspora, and the end of Samaria—warned James, with an eye to the Amos

---

[64] Ibid., 105-106.

context, God "would turn again" (anastrepsō) to re-establish the house of David.[65]

The interpolation of the dispensationalists has the conversion of the gentiles as heralding the rebuilding of David's tabernacle; Kaiser corrects the misrepresentation to affirm that it is the diaspora and sifting that herald the rebuilding of David's tabernacle, which is followed by the conversion of the gentiles. It is a subtle but significant difference.

Dispensationalist, Les Feldick, a TV evangelist, teaches that the sifting of Israel is concurrent with the end of this age and that "not a kernel … will be lost."[66] This is restated in another lecture where he maintains that the prepositional phrase "after this" in Acts 15:16 pertains to the Christ's "Second Coming," or "after the Rapture and the Body of Christ is removed from the earth to Heaven."[67] Kaiser maintains James's intent was that the tabernacle be restored inchoately by the sifting in this age, which commenced with the destruction of the second temple and the precipitous dispersion of the Jews. The presuppositions of dispensationalists prevent their objectivity concerning the scriptural and enduring research in archeology and etymology that confirm that the descendants of Israel became the church to which the gentiles were joined. The illustrations in Ephesians 2:19–22 and 1 Peter 2:4–5 attest that God is building a supernatural house by redeeming the members who are predestined and fits them upon his building, which, when one acquires the proper hermeneutical presuppositions, is comprehended as the repairing of David's tabernacle.

Without doubt, there is a sense of redemption as well as chastisement implicit in the sifting that compels dispensationalists

---

[65] "Now 'after these things'—the destruction of the temple, the fact of the diaspora, and the end of Samaria—warned James, with an eye to the Amos context, God 'would turn again' (anastrepsō) to re-establish the house of David." Ibid., 106.

[66] Les Feldick, "Through the Bible with Les Feldick," (Les Feldick Ministries on Smashwords, 2015, Book 16), Kindle location 1032.

[67] Ibid., (Book 76), Kindle location 167.

like Feldick to exclaim, "not a kernel … will be lost," regarding the ordained of Israel. Dispensationalist W. Edward Glenny concedes the sifting has a sense of redemption in his affirmation that Amos 9:9, in the LXX, is not a message of judgment as in the MT (where Israel will be "sifted" and none will escape). Instead, the last clause of Amos 9:9 conveys salvation.[68] Feldick's description of the sifting as being ordained is tantamount to acknowledging predestination, which contradicts his view that "God expected Israel to receive her King, get the Kingdom set up, and the Jew to go out and evangelize the world."[69] One must concede the presupposition that God ordains the future and with that standard, one is able to perceive the fallacy of believing that God did not know how Israel would respond to Christ. This is what Ice alludes to in his assertion, "I believe that dispensational premillennialism provides the most logical eschatological ending to God's sovereign decrees for salvation and history."[70] Even so, according to the prophets, not all of Israel are prophesied to avow Christ their king; this is the prophecy of the stone rejected—and is exactly what happened. Calvinism, specifically the compatibilists, wrongly perceives that the reprobate who rejected Christ and were appointed to wrath (Romans 9:21) were offered the kingdom, a kingdom they were never destined to inherit. The sifting is redemptive, corrective, centrifugal and precedes the Messianic Kingdom. God knew the cornerstone, his Son, would be rejected by many of his own; it was his plan. But in mercy God would intercede for an avowed remnant to include the gentiles, who would become the body of Christ, the church, by which God brings Jacob again to himself (Isaiah 49:5), the tribes of Ephraim playing the dominate role as his first-born (Jeremiah 31:9), as the prodigal son who returns in the parable and the nation bringing forth the fruit of the vineyard

---

[68] W. Edward Glenny, "The Septuagint and Apostolic Hermeneutics: Amos 9 in Acts 15," *Bulletin for Biblical Research* 22 1 (2012), 1-26. http://www.nakedbiblepodcast.com/wp-content/uploads/2015/05/Glenny-The-Septuagint-and-apostolic-hermeneutics-Amos-9-in-Acts-15.pdf
[69] Feldick, "Through the Bible with Les Feldick" (Book 5), Kindle location 999
[70] Ice, "The Calvinistic Heritage of dispensationalism"

(Matthew 21:43). With the proper presuppositions one can see that the prophecies of God are proceeding according to plan and in their appointed times, including those both in Daniel and the apocalypse of John. But those proper presuppositions are not to be found in dispensationalism or covenantalism.

The Insufficiency of the Presuppositions of Covenantalism in Rendering John's Apocalypse

Paul's testimony concerning God's foreknowledge and other NT evidence pertaining to God's attributes provide the premise by which covenantalists deduce their doctrines and concepts on predestination.[1] Reformed theology maintains that a fixed number of predestined heirs are chosen "before the foundation of the world" (Ephesians 1:4).[2] Predestination is an expression of God's foreknowledge about all his *chosen* or elected-as grasped in covenantalism's reading of Paul, specifically Romans 8:29·30, which they call the *Golden Chain*: foreknowledge, predestination, effectual calling, justification, and glorification.

> For whom he did foreknow, he also did predestinate *to be* conformed to the image of his Son, that he might be the firstborn among many brethren. Moreover, whom he did predestinate, them he also called: and whom he called, them he also justified:

---

[1] Arminianism and Calvinism acknowledged God's foreknowledge but parts ways on the issue of free will.

[2] John Calvin held double predestination, that man was "predestinated either to life or to death." *Institutes*, (Book Ill, Ch. XXI, Sec. 5)

and whom he justified, them he also glorified. (Romans 8:29–30)

Covenantalists hold a predestined salvation position concerning individuals but until recent times have had little regard for *predestined corporate salvation* to continue their traditional perception that God repented on Israel's future destiny. Covenantalism still maintains that God repented on the destiny of the elect biological descendants of Abraham as the means by which the conversion of the gentiles was to ensue. In truth, this is an acknowledgement that corporate Israel had been *destined* to convert the gentiles, contrary to what covenantalist Russel Moore asserts.[3] The eighteenth- and nineteenth-century commentators John Gill and Adams Clarke express covenantalism's traditional perception of Israel's future in their comments concerning *the Parable of the Tenants* in Matthew 21:33·44.

> *and given to a nation bringing forth the fruits thereof....* Though God may take away the Gospel from a people, as he did from the Jews; yet he does not, nor will he, as yet, take it out of the world: he gives it to another "nation"; to the Gentiles, to all the nations of the world, whither he sent his apostles to preach and where it must be preached before the end of the world comes, in order to gather his elect out of them: for not one particular nation is meant, unless the nation of God's elect, among all nations, can be thought to be designed.[4]

---

[3] Avowed covenantalist and president of *Ethics and Religious Liberties Commission of the Southern Baptist Convention* (ERLC), Russell Moore, states: "Covenant theologians argue that the future restoration of Israel will be fulfilled-but fulfilled in the church, a largely Gentile body that has 'replaced' the Jewish theocracy since the nation rejected her Messiah at Jesus' first advent." Russell Moore, "Is There a Future for Israel?" *Russel Moore.com*, https://www.russellmoore.com/2009/01/09/is-there-a-future-for-israel/

[4] *John Gill's Exposition on the Whole Bible*, s.v. Matthew 21:43, *Study Light.org*, https://www.studylight.org/commentaries/geb.html

Therefore, say I - Thus showing them, that to them alone the parable belonged. The kingdom of God shall be taken from you—the Gospel shall be taken from you, and given to the Gentiles, who will receive it, and bring forth fruit to the glory of God. *Bringing forth the fruits*—As in Matthew 21:34; an allusion is made to paying the landlord in kind, so here the Gentiles are represented as paying God thus. The returns which He expects for his grace are the fruits of grace; nothing can ever be acceptable in the sight of God that does not spring from himself.[5]

Their commentary supports the idea that God had elected the *nation of Israel* to inherit the promises to Abraham—founded on his "oath which he had sworn" to the patriarch—as opposed to merit of any construct (Deuteronomy 7:6–8; Isaiah 41:8–9, 43:10, 20, 44:1–2). As such, the OT substantiates that the nation's salvific destiny is about the same efficacy as individual election—the destiny of the nation corresponds to the election of its chosen citizens. Covenantalism has failed to perceive that the corporate election of the body of Israel was correlative with the election of its individual citizens, which fostered the fallacy that the former election upon the biological descendants was grounded on merit and was forfeited at the first advent.

Foundational to the issue of corporate predestination is the nature of the body elected in texts such as Deuteronomy 7:6–8.

For thou *art* an holy people unto the LORD thy God: the LORD thy God hath chosen thee to be a special people unto himself, above all people that *are* upon the face of the earth. The LORD did not set his love upon you, nor choose you, because ye were more in number than any people; for ye *were* the fewest of all people: But because the LORD loved

---

[5] *Adam Clarke Commentary*, s.v. Matthew 21:43, *Study Light.org*, https://www.studylight.org/commentaries/acc.html

you, and because he would keep the oath which he had sworn unto your fathers, hath the LORD brought you out with a mighty hand, and redeemed you out of the house of bondmen, from the hand of Pharaoh king of Egypt. (Deuteronomy 7:6–8)

Adjective clauses in the context such as "thou art an holy people" and "them that love him and keep his commandments" introduce a distinction that omits the reprobate in the election of the corporate body of Israel. (The ordination by grace substantiates that *keeping the commandments* is also by grace as expressed in Ephesians 2:10.) Paul maintains this same distinction concerning corporate Israel in Romans 9–11 when addressing the remnant, Israel, that had not been cast off, in contrast to those who were cast off and hardened. The nineteenth-century covenantalist David Brown affirmed this distinction when he commented on Romans 9:6, concerning *the Israel of God's irrevocable choice.*

> *for they are not all Israel which are of Israel*—better, "for not all they which are of Israel are Israel." *Here the apostle enters upon the profound subject of* ELECTION, the treatment of which extends to the end of the eleventh chapter – "Think not that I mourn over the total loss of Israel; for that would involve the failure of God's word to Abraham; but not all that belong to the natural seed, and go under the name of "Israel," are *the* Israel of God's irrevocable choice" … the argument of this verse is, that "all Israel *is not* rejected, but only a portion of it, the remainder being *the* "Israel" whom God has chosen in the exercise of His sovereign right." And that this is a choice not to mere external privileges,

but to eternal salvation, will abundantly appear from what follows.[6]

Brown substantiates the correspondence between individual and corporate salvation, which substantiates the distinction expressed in Deuteronomy 7:6–8. Covenantalist Thomas R. Schreiner also addresses the distinction and notes that the elect are correspondingly regarded as the "church."

> All God's choice of a corporate group means is that God chose that all who put their faith in Christ would be saved. Those who put their faith in Christ would be designated the Church. Those who defend corporate election are conscious of the fact that it is hard to separate corporate from individual election, for logic would seem to require that the individuals that make up a group cannot be separated from the group itself.[7]

In Schreiner's zeal to renounce Arminianism, which is the object of his essay, he substantiates the correspondence between corporate and individual election but fails to comprehend that his acknowledgement is at variance with covenantalism's claims that God *repented* on the corporate election of the biological descendants of Israel and replaced them with the gentiles. Schreiner's, or covenantalism's continuity between Israel and the church is contradictory to their assertion that God repented on the corporate election of ethnic Israel; it would be more precise to say that God merely changed the management and gave it to the other house of Israel, Ephraim, which is the subject of the next chapter.

---

[6] Jamieson, Fausset, and Brown's Commentary on the Whole Bible, s.v. Rom 9:6, Study Light.org, https://www.studylight.org/commentaries/jfb.html

[7] Thomas R. Schreiner, "Does Romans 9 Teach Individual Election Unto Salvation? Some Exegetical and Theological Reflections," *JETS* 36/1 (March 1993), 38

Concerning the dispensationalist's failure to affirm the continuity between the Church and Israel, covenantalist Russell Moore posits that their view stems from their misapprehension that the promises were to the "regenerate and unregenerate members," but in contradiction, the "future restoration of Israel has *never* been promised to the unfaithful, unregenerate members of the nation."[8] Moore inadvertently corrects the traditional covenantalist view and affirms the concept that the promises to the body of the church and Israel were to the elect individuals as distinct from the reprobates who mixed with them, which corroborates the distinction in Deuteronomy 7:6–8 as well as corporate and individual correspondence in salvation. This distinction is not new and has long been perceived as the *visible* and *invisible* church,[9] the latter being comprised of only the elect, but covenantalists resist the notion that this applies to *corporate* Israel also. As stated, Moore unintentionally avows this by acknowledging that the promises to Israel were strictly to the elect. Moore's analysis "The future restoration of Israel has *never* been promised to the unfaithful, unregenerate members of the nation" is synonymous with David Brown's commentary on Romans 9:6 and his perception of *the Israel of God's irrevocable choice*. Their analyses call for the recognition of the distinction in Deuteronomy 7:6–8 mentioned above, which conveys *salvific corporate predestination*.

Covenantalist C. Matthew McMahon has also deviated from replacement theology by acknowledging *corporate predestination* in his analyzation of the Hebrew term *bachar*, translated as *chosen* in Deuteronomy 7:6. After producing the few extraneous uses of the word he analyzes where,

---

[8] Moore, "Is There a Future for Israel?"

[9] *Wikipedia*: "The invisible church or church invisible is a theological concept of an 'invisible' body of the elect who are known only to God, in contrast to the 'visible church'—that is, the institutional body on earth which preaches the gospel and administers the sacraments." s.v. Church invisible, last modified July 2017, https://en.wikipedia.org/w/index.php?title=Church_invisible&action=history

it is used of God to choose the ultimate destinies and eternal salvation of particular people or of the nation Israel.... It is a specific choosing of a people who will be holy before Yahweh to do His will. This choosing or election is not based on their own merit but on God's good pleasure and for His glory as seen in (Deuteronomy 7:7.)[10]

In McMahon's book, *The Two Wills of God*, he perceives a hermeneutic that God expressed his will in more than one *sense*. Unless we accurately perceive these *senses* tension results in revelation and the truth does not prevail. As mentioned previously, McMahon develops another theologian's work, Francis Turretin's, as the hermeneutics of the compound and divided *senses*. McMahon clearly asserts that God chose the corporate body of Israel to do his will and decreed a salvific destiny in the *compound sense*, which also agrees with Brown's commentary on Romans 9:6 and his perception of *the Israel of God's irrevocable choice*.

It is apparent that both McMahon and Moore agree with Brown's perception that the election of the body of Israel pertained to *the Israel of God's irrevocable choice*, as distinguished from the reprobate mixed with them, which epitomizes both individual and corporate salvific correspondence. They perceive that God cannot change his mind regarding the salvific calling in Deuteronomy 7:6–8 because it did not apply to the reprobate, which conflicts with their notion that Israel forfeited its destiny to the gentiles at the first advent. Furthermore, it is inaccurate to view the diaspora of the elect biological descendants simply as punishment when Christ declared,

> And Jesus answered and said, Verily I say unto you,
> There is no man that hath left house, or brethren,
> or sisters, or father, or mother, or wife, or children,
> or lands, for my sake, and the gospel's, But he shall
> receive an hundredfold now in this time, houses, and

---

[10] McMahon, *The Two Wills of God*, Kindle location 5856.

> brethren, and sisters, and mothers, and children,
> and lands, with persecutions; and in the world to
> come eternal life. (Mark 10:29–30)

Promised prosperity cannot be reconciled with the loss of inheritance and exile but rather substantiates that the gifts and calling of Israel as irrevocable, which is precisely what Peter, below,[11] and Paul (Romans 11:29) affirmed.

> Peter, an apostle of Jesus Christ, to the
> strangers scattered throughout Pontus, Galatia,
> Cappadocia, Asia, and Bithynia, Elect according
> to the foreknowledge of God the Father, through
> sanctification of the Spirit, unto obedience and
> sprinkling of the blood of Jesus Christ: Grace unto
> you, and peace, be multiplied. (1 Peter 1:1–2)

The unbiased evidence shows that Peter addressed members of the ten still-scattered northern tribes who, to some degree, were still aware of their heritage, and his epistles truly overcome any objections to the contrary. Further evidence is provided by the first-century Jewish historian, Flavius Josephus, who wrote, "the ten tribes are beyond Euphrates till now, and are an immense multitude, and not to be estimated by numbers."[12] This also confirms the fulfillment of Israel's birthright of fecundity, particularly Joseph's branch (Genesis 48:16, 49:22). But as previously mentioned, these circumstances were prophesied by Ezekiel and Zechariah concerning the house of Ephraim, also known as Joseph, Israel, and Samaria—as contrasted from Judah. As revealed, some covenantalists like McMahon and Moore have made advances in viewing "the gifts and calling" of the descendants of Abraham "are without repentance" (Romans 11:29) but have failed to grasp that this understanding undermines

---

[11] As stated previously, the superior translation of ἐκλεκτοῖς παρεπιδήμοις Διασπορᾶς is "elect exiles of the dispersion."

[12] Josephus, Antiquities of the Jews

their perception that Israel forfeited its destiny at the first advent, specifically the destiny to convert the gentiles.

Calvinists McMahon and Moore believe they have something more exact than earlier covenantalists had to relate concerning *sense* in scripture, although Moore does not use the same terminology. Coming from a determined compatibilist[13] *sense* they rightly perceive that God does not change his mind,[14] which is why it is contradictory for them to also assert any form of change in destiny for the biological descendants of Abraham at the first advent. Further analysis of McMahon's book, *The Two Wills of God*, reveals a fallacy, concerning 1 Peter 2:8. He proposes that the reprobates were ordained to reject Christ and at the same time he asserts they had a choice.

> But Peter does not simply leave us to our imagination to decide what it means for those who reject Christ to "stumble." He says that they were appointed to stumble. God appoints men to stumble at Christ. The word "appoints" is τίθημι (*tithemi*) which means "to set, put, place," or "to establish, and ordain." God appoints men to eternal damnation according to His good pleasure, just as He elects men to salvation accordingly as well.[15]

He continues to affirm predestination further into his book.

> Peter says, "They [those whom God passes by] stumble because they disobey the message—which is also what they were destined for" (1 Peter 2:8).[16]

---

[13] *Theopedia*: "Compatibilism . . . teaches that people are free, but defines freedom differently." s.v. Basic beliefs, accessed October 27, 2018, https://www.theopedia.com/compatibilism

[14] God never changes his mind according to C. Matthew McMahon: "God never repents, never gets angry, never is jealous, etc. He is without passions and emotions in the compound sense." *The Two Wills of God*, Kindle location 370.

[15] Ibid., Kindle location 3034.

[16] Ibid., Kindle location 6249.

In finishing his analysis, he writes,

> God had told Abraham that he would be a blessing to many nations, and that the whole world would be blessed by him. The Pharisees, Scribes and rulers of Jerusalem should have taken up that commission to bless the nations with the Word of God, but they did not … they turned in on themselves, reveling in ethnic privilege rather than in converting the nations … Jesus gives His reaction to this when he says that their house has become "desolate" as a result of this hardness towards Him.[17]

McMahon has failed to grasp that he has violated the rule of non-contradiction.[18] He asserts the fallacy that those who were destined to be lost "should have taken up that commission to bless the nations." The commission to bless the nations was to the elect, not to the reprobate. McMahon shifts from a compatibilist to an Arminian or open theist *sense* here. In the *corporate sense* the *nation* was irrevocably chosen as a people with an ultimate destiny and salvation, which McMahon acknowledged concerning the use of *bachar*, above.[19] The only relief from such a fallacy is to concede that the reprobates did exactly what they were ordained to do as it was not their destiny to convert the gentiles; rather, it was the destiny of the biological elect remnant of Israel to convert the gentiles, *the Israel of God's irrevocable choice*, which is precisely what happened. McMahon succumbs to Arminianism and even open theism in his assertion that the Jewish ruler's choice determined their destiny when in truth, God preordained their destiny apart from the elect (1 Peter 2:7–8). Thus, McMahon is a typical covenantalist attempting

---

[17] Ibid., Kindle location 6825.
[18] "What does the law of non-contradiction teach? The *law of non-contradiction* states the following: 'A' cannot be both 'A' and non-A at the same time and in the same relationship." Ibid., Kindle location 445.
[19] Ibid., Kindle location 5856.

to maintain the contradiction that God does not change his mind—and at the same time, says that those who were appointed to disavow Christ "should have taken up that commission to bless the nations." It was those who were appointed to avow Christ that were destined to convert the gentiles, not those who disavowed him. The only view that satisfies the compatibilist perception is the Two House theological model.[20] The Two House model is the object of this discourse and it will be substantiated as the only model consistently holding to the compatibilist perception proving to be sufficient in properly rendering the NT and John's apocalypse.

As stated, McMahon contradicts himself when proposing that the reprobate Jews at the first advent were ordained to reject Christ and then argues they should have avowed him. With inconsistency he acknowledges that the prophecy of Psalms 118:22–23 prophesied Christ, as the cornerstone, who was ordained to be rejected by the builders.[21] This is also prophesied in Isaiah 8:14–15 where Christ is prophesied as "a rock of offence to both the houses of Israel." The Arminian perception of prevenient grace is incompatible with the requisite that God appointed the time of Christ's rejection by the reprobate who mixed with Israel; the Arminian concept of free will would have the disposition of men determine the appointed time—not God. When those who hold the Arminian perception concede that God influences man's will, it destroys their conceptualization of freewill. Matthew 10 speaks directly to the reaction of the biological descendants of Israel to Christ in verse 23: "Ye shall not have gone over the cities of Israel, till the Son of man be come." This text conveys how long Israel would continue to stumble on the cornerstone.

> These twelve Jesus sent forth, and commanded them, saying, Go not into the way of the Gentiles,

---

[20] *Theopedia*: "God is said to influence our desires, and thus is able to have exhaustive control of all that goes on." s.v. compatibilism, God's involvement, accessed October 27, 2018, http://www.theopedia.com/compatibilism
[21] McMahon, *The Two Wills of God*, Kindle location 3031.

and into *any* city of the Samaritans enter ye not: But go rather to the lost sheep of the house of Israel. And as ye go, preach, saying, The kingdom of heaven is at hand.... verily I say unto you, Ye shall not have gone over the cities of Israel, till the Son of man be come.... Whosoever therefore shall confess me before men, him will I confess also before my Father which is in heaven. But whosoever shall deny me before men, him will I also deny before my Father which is in heaven. (Matthew 10:5–7, 23, 32–33)

The pronouncement in Matthew 10:23 that preaching the Gospel would continue "till the Son of man be come" affirms that the first advent was not the appointed time of the Davidic kingdom foreseen in 1 Samuel 7:10–11 but was rather the appointed time of Jeremiah 31:2, when the elect descendants of both houses of Israel would find "grace in the wilderness," as they were dispersed throughout the nations. It was from this circumstance that they were to play the major role in converting the gentiles. The phrase "till the Son of man be come" pertains to the second-advent, not to the first. Jeremiah 31:2 as well as Ezekiel 34:17–31, Hosea 2:14–23, Amos 9:9–10 and Zechariah 10:7–9 are but a few OT texts that prophecy Israel, specifically the biological descendants of the northern tribes, finds *grace in the wilderness*, in exile, but we see that they are not directly restored to the promised land when all the relevant texts are properly examined. In anthropomorphic illustrations, the remnant of Israel is redeemed and then sown throughout the world, like the good seed in Christ's parables of the sower and of the tares; the correspondence between the aforementioned OT texts and Christ's parables is an integral object of this work and substantiates the Two House model.

In returning to the reaction of the biological descendants to Christ, McMahon conveys they "should have taken up that commission to bless the nations ... but they did not."[22] McMahon exhibits the

---

[22] Ibid.

continuing influence of past covenantalists who mistakenly viewed the end of the biological descendant's administration of the kingdom of God in their interpretation of Matthew 21:43 and 23:38, as if the elect biological descendants merely ceased to exist and who are given no consideration as being the singular, the fruit bearing *nation* of Matthew 21:43. As stated, this conflicts with Moore and McMahon's *sense* that God's elections are inviolable. It also conflicts with the NT testimony relating the accepted knowledge that there were great numbers of the descendants of the northern tribes dwelling as exiles in communities scattered throughout the known world at the time (John 7:35, 11:51–52; James 1:1; 1 Peter 1:1). The nineteenth-century covenantalist Adam Clarke's writing is of some use here in that he conceded that the phrase *"the children of God that were scattered abroad"* in John 11:52 pertained to the *Jews* and not the gentiles, differing from the view held by many of his fellow covenantalists.

> John 11:52 … *Children of God that were scattered abroad* - Probably John only meant the Jews who were dispersed among all nations since the conquest of Judea by the Romans; and these are called the dispersed, John 7:35, and James 1:1; and it is because he refers to these only, that he terms them here, the children of God, which was an ancient character of the Jewish people: see Deuteronomy 32:5; Isaiah 43:6; Isaiah 45:11; Jeremiah 32:1. Taking his words in this sense, then his meaning is this: that Christ was to die, not only for the then inhabitants of Judea, but for all the Jewish race wheresoever scattered; and that the consequence would be, that they should be all collected from their various dispersions, and made one body. This comports with the predictions of St. Paul: Romans 11:1–32.[23]

---

[23] Adam Clarke Commentary, s.v. John 11:52

It speaks well of Clarke that he did not make the same mistake that many of his contemporaries make who interpret the phrase as referring to the elect gentiles;[24] nevertheless, the epistles of James and Peter carry significant bearing on the issue and correctly render the phrase pertaining to the twelve tribes, properly addressed as Israel, as opposed to *Jews*, as not all Israelites are Jews. Failure to recognize John 7:35, 11:52, James 1:1 and 1 Peter 1:1 as pertaining to the hitherto exiled northern tribes at the first advent is an anachronism that subordinates the accuracy of covenantalism in interpreting the scriptures, specifically the NT; they apply contemporary perceptions to terminologies that must be rendered *first* from the historical-grammatical point of view.[25] Their contemporary views of the Jews as the nation of Israel cannot be reconciled to the texts, which affirms that the other house of Israel, Ephraim, must be considered in eschatological phenomena. Caiaphas spoke in terms of the tribes of Israel that had not dwelt as one sovereign nation in the promised land since the time of David and Solomon but who as such were still aware to some degree of their origins (John 11:51–52). Samaria has never been re-occupied by the ten tribes, which substantiates that Ephraim did not return with the Jews from the Babylonian captivity; the dominion of Samaria had been settled by foreigners who still dwelt in the land at the first advent. It strays from reason that Caiaphas's, a Pharisee, intent in John 11:51–52 pertained to gentiles. McMahon's comment, above, that the Jews "should have taken up that commission to bless the nations ... but they did not" violates the rule of non-contradiction when one considers that the other house of Israel had taken up the commission in fulfillment

---

[24] John 11:52 is interpreted as the gentiles by John Gill: "*the children of God that were scattered abroad*; by which may be meant . . . the Jews, who were scattered amidst the nations of the world . . . but rather the elect of God among the Gentiles, called "the children of God", in opposition to a notion of the Jews." *John Gill's Exposition on the Entire Bible*, s.v. John 11:52.

[25] Wikipedia: "The historical-grammatical method is a Christian hermeneutical method that strives to discover the Biblical author's original intended *meaning* in the text." s.v. Historical-grammatical method, last modified May 2018, https://en.wikipedia.org/wiki/Historical-grammatical_method

of Hosea 2:23 and Zechariah 10:7–9. Peter and James testify that Ephraim took the commission; the other house of Israel did not just cease to exist and has relevance as the singular, a fruit bearing *nation* of Matthew 21:43.

Matthew 10 and other NT evidence substantiate that the Messianic kingdom was not offered at the first advent as it was predetermined to be consummated only upon the return of the Son of man at the second advent. Matthew and Mark agree, Christ came *not to be ministered unto, but to minister, and to give his life a ransom for many*—which affirms that Christ's first advent presented us with a suffering redeemer and *Ishi's* (husband) in Hosea 2—who returns as king, depicted in Revelation 19. The evidence that Christ came not to be ministered unto undoubtedly defeats the presumption of a *conditional offer* of the kingdom that the Jews expected. The prophets grasped the phenomenon as the sole will of God at his appointed time; God must first *circumcise their hearts* before the consummation of the kingdom (Deuteronomy 30:6). Evidence that the kingdom was not offered at that time is witnessed subsequently to the commission portrayed in Matthew 10, where Christ dismissed the impression that "the kingdom of God should immediately appear" (Luke 19:11–27). "Ye shall not have gone over the cities of Israel till the Son of man be come" (Matthew 10:23) can only be interpreted as being protracted phenomenon as conveyed in Luke 19:11–27. From this evidence, the phrase "the cities of Israel," verse 23, achieves a greater *sen*se than merely the cities of Judah, but develops to include wherever the descendants of Israel abide in the illustrate*d sow*ing in Hosea 2:23 and Zechariah 10:9. The OT affirms that the children of God were to be scattered throughout the world in this age, which renders Christ's testimony "Ye shall not have gone over the cities of Israel, till the Son of man be come" as a greatly protracted phenomenon over the expanse of the world. Christ's parables affirm that this is the *world* in which the good seed, the remnant of Israel, is planted.

Moore also exhibits the continuing influence of past covenantalists who ignore the biological *sense*, lineage and heritage in the preordained administration of the kingdom of God in their misinterpretation of Matthew 21:43 and 23:38. In Moore's essay, *Is There a Future for Israel*, he wrote:

> Covenant theologians argue that the future restoration of Israel will be fulfilled-but fulfilled in the church, a largely Gentile body that has "replaced" the Jewish theocracy since the nation rejected her Messiah at Jesus' first advent.... The future of Israel then does belong to Gentile believers but only because they are in union with a Jewish Messiah.... The church, as Israel was promised, does now "bear fruit"—the fruits of the Spirit (Galatians 5)—but it does so only because Jesus is the vine of Israel.[26]

In the same essay he writes:

> The future restoration of Israel has *never* been promised to the unfaithful, unregenerate members of the nation (John 3:3–10; Romans 2:25–29)—only to the faithful remnant.[27]

In the latter quote Moore clearly concedes Israel's irrevocable corporate election in his affirmation that the reprobate who were mixed with them were not regarded in the election. This is simply another way of affirming, God's appointment of the corporate body of the biological descendants of Jacob was predetermined as *the Israel of God's irrevocable choice*, apart from the reprobate who were mixed with them.

One can concede that the NT Gentile converts are perceived as joining *the Israel of God's irrevocable choice*, but in what *sense* are they *restored* according to Moore—or in what *sense* does Moore interpret the verb *restore* in texts such as Acts 1:6. The *sense* he eschews is the

---

[26] Moore, "Is There a Future for Israel?"
[27] Ibid.

principal biological *sense*; only the biological descendants can suffer loss, be *given up* for a time in Micah 5 and ultimately be *restored.*

> Therefore, will he give them up, until the time
> *that* she which travaileth hath brought forth: then
> the remnant of his brethren shall return unto the
> children of Israel. (Micah 5:3)

Only the biological descendants of Ephraim can be *restored* in the historical-grammatical sense in Hosea.

> And I will sow her unto me in the earth; and I will
> have mercy upon her that had not obtained mercy;
> and I will say to them which were not my people,
> Thou art my people; and they shall say, Thou art
> my God. (Hosea 2:23)

In the *principal sense,* only the elect biological descendants, the northern *nation* can represent the woman in Hosea and Micah, above, that is *restored* at an appointed time. In this work, the phrase, *principal sense,* pertains to the *first-thought meaning* as defined by covenantalist and amillennialist Vern S. Poythress in his book: *Understanding Dispensationalists.*

> This example shows that for most words there is
> something like a first-thought meaning, a meaning
> that one would naturally give when asked, "What
> does this word mean?" Not everyone might say
> exactly the same thing, but one sort of answer would
> usually dominate.[28]

Sound reasoning maintains that the historical-grammatical interpretation corresponds with the *first-thought meaning* or *principal*

---

[28] Vern S. Poythress, *Understanding Dispensationalists* (Presbyterian and Reformed Pub. Co., 1994), 79.

sense and in this sense the woman in Micah 5:3 and Hosea 2:23 must be rendered as the elect biological descendants of Jacob, specifically the elect of the northern nation of Ephraim. Poythress is not examining the term *Israel*, above, but the word "battle" to argue that context can alter the meaning of words into other less used *senses* or can become idiomatic of another word or phrase altogether.

> When, however, once we are given even a little bit of
> context, our guesses about the meaning may change
> radically.[29]

Poythress is setting up the covenantalist's argument which radically alters the term *Israel* with the reasoning that the distant and earthshaking eschatological context warrants the drastic shift from the historical-grammatical, *principal sense.*

> The important question at this point is not about a
> specific passage but about principle, a principle of
> prophetic interpretation. I claim that there is sound,
> solid, grammatical-historical ground for interpreting
> eschatological fulfillments of prophecy on a different
> basis than preeschatological fulfillments. The
> Israelites of Jeremiah's day should have absorbed
> (albeit often unconsciously) the earthshaking,
> transformational character of the eschatological
> coming of God. It is therefore a move away from
> grammatical-historical interpretation to insist that
> (say) the "house of Israel" and the "house of Judah"
> of Jeremiah 31:31 must with dogmatic certainty be
> interpreted in the most prosaic biological sense, a
> sense that an Israelite might be likely to apply as a
> rule of thumb in short-term prediction.[30]

---

[29] Ibid.
[30] Ibid., 107.

Poythress violates the rule of non-contradiction when later he states this shift "should not undermine or contradict grammatical-historical interpretation" even as it "goes beyond its bounds."

> In other words, one must compare later Scripture to earlier Scripture to understand everything. Such comparison, though it should not undermine or contradict grammatical-historical interpretation, goes beyond its bounds. It takes account of information not available in the original historical and cultural context.... True, grammatical-historical interpretation exercises a vital role in bringing controls and refinements to our understanding of particular texts. But we must also undertake to relate those texts forward to further revelation that they anticipate and prepare for.[31]

One must agree with Poythress that the distance and earthshaking event of the eschatological context and NT revelation does diminish "the most prosaic biological sense" in the way the term Israel must be interpreted, but it would be wrong to maintain that the context *ends* the *principal sense* altogether, which unequivocally "undermines or contradicts the grammatical-historical interpretation," and this is precisely what covenantalists attempt concerning eschatological prophecy. Herein lies Poythress's violation. In returning to Moore's use of the term *restoration* concerning Israel, the biological *sense* simply cannot be omitted without "undermining or contradicting the grammatical-historical interpretation" which Poythress affirmed must be avoided, as perplexing as his statement is, in light of the fact that covenantalists undermine the hermeneutic persistently. Furthermore, it must be considered that the gentiles "were without Christ ... aliens from the commonwealth of Israel, and strangers from the covenants of promise, having no hope, and without God

---

[31] Ibid., 116.

in the world" (Ephesians 2:12) and as such they cannot be *restored* in the *principal sense* as the biological descendants.

As stated above, one can concede Poythress's assertion that "the earthshaking, transformational character of the eschatological coming of God" has its effects on how Israel is perceived, but only in the *sense* that "in Christ" elect Jews and Ephraimites are no longer held to the Old Covenant (OC) laws prohibiting intermarriage or that genealogies are germane (Deuteronomy 7:3–5; Galatians 3:28; Ephesians 2:13). Even so, in another *sense* they still remain the distant biological descendants which maintains that God's appointments are irrevocable, as they are *the Israel of God's irrevocable choice*, by whom the gentiles are blessed (Genesis 12:3, 18:18, 26:4). Certainly, this is one of "the earthshaking, transformational" changes "of the eschatological coming of God," using Poythress's words above. In Christ, the Jew, Ephraimite and Gentile become corporately perceived as one, but in the biological *sense*, women remain women, as Ephraimites remain biological heirs of Abraham no matter how diminished that biological *sense* becomes due to the end of the prohibitions against intermarriage and when the concern for genealogies is quashed (1 Timothy 1:3; Titus 3:9). Moreover, the covenantalist's perception omits the birthright of fecundity passed down from Jacob to the descendants of the northern tribes (Genesis 48:3–4, 16–20) which renders them a copious people in Providence, much greater and more numerous than the hardened Jews who covenantalists perceive as the only Israelites. First Samuel 15:29 affirms that God "is not a man, that he should repent." Poythress, McMahon and Moore fail to maintain this principle in comprehending the term *Israel* in scripture, specifically in eschatological prophecy. God did not repent concerning the biological descendant's commission to bless the nations at the first advent, even as their biological identity diminished; in a *sense*, it became the means to bless the nations. It is precisely this perception that accounts for "information not available in the original historical and cultural context" of the prophets, as Poythress expressed it above, as this understanding neither harms, nor *undermines or contradicts* the historical-grammatical interpretation of Judah and Ephraim. Any principle in determining how one discerns the term *Israel* in an eschatological context must avoid tension between OT and NT revelation, a tension which Poythress disavows, perplexing as that may be.

Poythress's work is described as perplexing because in truth, covenantalism does not maintain the "principle of accounting for information not available in the original historical and cultural context" while preserving correspondence between the Old and NT revelation. As previously mentioned, it violates the rule of non-contradiction to maintain that the gentiles are *restored* in the same *sense* as the biological descendants of Ephraim, or that the free will of the reprobate shepherds of Judah determined the destiny of the elect biological descendants of Israel. The covenantalist's perception of the title *Israel* in eschatological prophecy also violates the rule of non-contradiction concerning the omniscience and omnipotence of God when covenantalists acknowledge these attributes but maintain prophecy as conditional. The perception of *conditional prophecy* violates the OT revelation that when a prophet spoke for God it must come to pass, which is deduced from Deuteronomy below.

> When a prophet speaketh in the name of the LORD, if the thing follow not, nor come to pass, that is the thing which the LORD hath not spoken, but the prophet hath spoken it presumptuously: thou shalt not be afraid of him. (Deuteronomy 18:22)

Eschatological prophecy was essentially linked to the immediate predictions of the prophets, Jeremiah being a salient example. The seventy years of exile determined upon Judah were promptly fulfilled, relatively, while the promise or prophecy of the institution of the NC was eschatological in relation, dealing with the distant future as affirmed by NT revelation (Jeremiah 29:10, 31:31–43; Hebrews 12:24). Texts such as Jeremiah 7:1–7, 18:7–10 as well as the book of Jonah are cited by covenantalists, not unlike the use of dispensationalists, to assert that all promises and prophecies concerning Israel were conditional or contingent, and that God is restrained by man's will, in contradiction to the reality of God's omniscience and omnipotence. As stated, concerning the dispensationalists, the perception of contingency in prophecy stems from a libertarian and the open theist view of free will, [32] which is incompatible with the compatibilist's view. [33] While one expects this from dispensationalists because of their notion of the parenthesis, covenantalists are Calvinist and should know better. In the previous chapter, we established that progressive revelation vindicates the fact that the law was not intended to promote obedience according to Romans 7:5 and 8–11. It was the NC that was intended to put God's laws into the mind and write them in the hearts of the chosen or elect (Hebrews 8:7–11). Furthermore, this work conveyed that the libertarian or open theists's perception of free will cannot endure against Paul's testimony in Romans 7 that man's will is subject to his CN and causes him to sin against his will however, without nullifying his accountability. Paul concludes that only those "in Christ" are manumitted from the CN and are released to obey God's law and will receive justification for their sins (Romans 8:1–4). The Calvinist's perceptions of God's foreknowledge in texts such as Romans 8:29–30 indicate that God was familiar with the elect before creation (Jeremiah 1:5; Ephesians 1:4), which also concurs with his foreknowledge of how a man responds to what appears as contingencies (conveyed appropriately as anthropomorphic shepherding). Scripture affirms that sin is caused by an organic influence capable of overpowering the will and reminds us that man is accountable, which repudiates contingency in regards to prophecy and the perception of free will by Libertarianism. What we can also garnered from the examination of the CN, is that the power of the

---

[32] *Theopedia,* "In libertarianism (not to be confused with the political ideology), free will is affected by human nature but man retains ability to choose contrary to his nature and desires." s.v Free will, Libertarian freedom, accessed October 27, 2018, http://www.theopedia.com/free-will

[33] *Theopedia,* "Libertarian free will maintains that for any choice made, one could always equally have chosen otherwise, or not chosen at all." *Compatibilism,* s.v. Basic beliefs, http://www.theopedia.com/compatibilism

flesh was sanctioned until an appointed time, when manumission would be made possible for the elect by the remarkable sacrifice of Christ, and the glorious inauguration of the Israel's NC.

Like dispensationalists, Calvin affirmed that God had an appointed time when Christ would come as determined from the Persian decree to restore Judah's nationhood and the Hebraic cultus in the prophecies of Daniel 9.

> We shall now treat the sense in which the going forth of the edict ought to be received. In the meantime, it cannot be denied that the angel pronounces this concerning the edict which had been promulgated about the bringing back of the people, and the restoration of the city. It would, therefore, be foolish to apply it to a period at which the city was not restored, and no such decree had either been uttered or made public. But, first of all, we must treat what the angel says, *until the Christ, the Messiah*. Some desire to take this singular noun in a plural sense, as if it were the Christ of the Lord, meaning his priests; while some refer it to Zerubbabel, and others to Joshua. But clearly enough the angel speaks of Christ, of whom both kings and priests under the law were a type and figure.[34]

As stated previously, the incompatibilist's arguments pertaining to accountability and against causal determination are overcome by Paul's testimony concerning the subjection of the will to the CN. Again, Paul revealed that it was Christ's propitiation that released man from the CN (Romans 8:1–4), which confirms that Calvin actually refutes the covenantalist's understanding of conditional prophecy. Just like the dispensationalists, Calvin's commentary on Daniel 9:25, concerning the appointed time of "Messiah the Prince," actually

---

[34] *Calvin's Commentary on the Bible*, s.v. Daniel 9:25, *Study Light.org*, accessed October 27, 2018, https://www.studylight.org/commentaries/cal.html

advocates that the time for the propitiation of sin was determined from the seventy weeks in Daniel 9, which was determined from Judah's rejection of God's call to repent in Jeremiah 18:7–10. This important correlation substantiates that God indeed, had foreknowledge that Judah would not repent and this is a representative application of the divided sense in prophecy; consequently, Jeremiah 18 cannot be used to prove that man causes God to repent or alter his plans for the unforeseeable. Such foreknowledge confirms, with NT evidence, that man was in subjugation to the CN and could not keep the law until the manumission mentioned above, being God's will, at God's appointed time. What appears as contingencies to man is rudimentary revelation, perceived as contingencies, where God merely abstains from moving against the CN in order to carry out his Divine Providence. The appearance of contingency in Jeremiah 18:7–10 and the book of Jonah, from whence covenantalists draw their conclusions concerning contingency in regards to prophecy, are only contingencies as they appear to man, but God's plans are ordained. The lesson to be learned in this case is that man is incapable of complying with God's law without his causal direction (Psalms 37:23; Proverbs 3:6; Jeremiah 31:9, 28; 2 Thessalonians 3:3; 2 Peter 2:9). Could Yahweh be Elohim without divine providence?

> Lord, thou hast heard the desire of the humble: thou wilt prepare their heart, thou wilt cause thine ear to hear. (Psalms 10:17)

> A man's heart deviseth his way: but the LORD directeth his steps. (Proverbs 16:9)

Without God's direction, the will of man is enslaved to the CN. Texts such as Jeremiah 7:1–7 and 18:7–10 are conveyed in the divided sense, the appearance of contingency, as only God can cause men to amend their ways and their doings. The assertion of contingency in prophecy stems from the fallacy that the declarative law could be complied with without the need of the NC but Paul makes it very plain that the SC was never intended as such but was a schoolmaster to bring us to Christ and justification (Galatians 3:24). The doctrine of contingency in prophecy is a fallacy. Prophecy is preordained, it is the foreknowledge of God, his compound will and the decretive sense (Isaiah 41:21–23, 42:9, 44:7, 45:11, 46:10, 48:3,5,6; Jeremiah 1:5; Act 15:8; Romans 8:29).

God knows how man will respond beforehand, which may seem to man as contingency but is just mere appearance. All the prophets anticipated that Israel would fail to comply with the SC. God well knew it and planned to intervene at an appointed time and establish the NC which would impart the ability to comply with his law—so necessary for the consummation of the kingdom (Jeremiah 31:31–34; Ezekiel 11:14–21). Romans 9–11 affirms that in God's judgments upon Israel he hardens more than a few and intervenes for an elect remnant.

> Except the LORD of hosts had left unto us a very small remnant, we should have been as Sodom, and we should have been like unto Gomorrah. (Isaiah 1:9)

> What if God, willing to shew his wrath, and to make his power known, endured with much longsuffering the vessels of wrath fitted to destruction: And that he might make known the riches of his glory on the vessels of mercy, which he had afore prepared unto glory, Even us, whom he hath called, not of the Jews only, but also of the Gentiles? (Romans 9:22–24)

At the first advent the vessels of wrath were ordained to reject Christ (Psalms 118:22–23; 1 Peter 2:7–8), while those who avowed him were chosen "before the foundation of the world" (Romans 8:29–30; Ephesians 1:4). This affirms that God did not offer the kingdom of heaven at the first advent. It is this perspective that informs us that *God foreknows nothing contingently*.[35] Covenantalists maintain the fallacy that the reprobate Jews who were appointed to wrath (Romans 9:21) were offered the kingdom which they were never destined to inherit, wrongfully surmising the notion of contingency in prophecy.

The epistles of Peter are fundamental in determining the *sense* in which the title *Israel* is comprehended in eschatological fulfillment, specifically 1 Peter 2:10. The covenantalist's presuppositions in interpreting Israel in Peter's epistles fail to maintain the historical-grammatical hermeneutic and Calvin's own misinterpretations are a salient example of the same. Calvin acknowledged the biological *sense* in Hosea's phrase "in time past were not a people" when he stated that "Hosea, after having in God's name declared that the Jews were repudiated, gives them a hope of a future restoration."[36] The historical-grammatical principle maintains the texts from Hosea pertain to Ephraim, not Judah. Calvin went on to describe the first-century Jewish condition as "they seemed to be no longer God's people, no worship remained among them, they were become entangled in the corruptions of the heathens,"[37] which can hardly be applied to the Jews of the time still scattered in the nations, as substantiated in Acts 2:5. The citation from Hosea pertains to the northern kingdom, the ten tribes of Israel, also called Ephraim, who were cast off and scattered by God because of their idolatry and because they entered into alliances with the Syria and Egypt, which was clearly anthropomorphically depicted by Hosea. No doubt, Calvin misconstrued a number of texts in Peter's epistles on the basis of his defective hermeneutics. These same texts in recent times have been used by Covenantalists to assert that Peter addressed his epistles to the gentiles, and such positing moves them even farther away from correspondence between the Old and NT revelation. The mention of past *idolatries* in 1 Peter 4:3 has been used in their contemporary assertions to endorse the claim that

---

[35] Luther, The Bondage of The Will
[36] Calvin's Commentary on the Bible, s.v. 1 Peter 2:10
[37] Ibid.

Peter addressed his epistles to the gentiles, making his citation from Hosea 1:10 and 2:23 allegorical as opposed to actual execution. Such perceptions are wanting in the *principal sense* in that the *idolatries* mentioned in Hosea pertained to the ten northern tribes taken captive by the Assyrians, clearly conveyed to Hosea. Peter's epistle was addressed to the elect descendants of these ten tribes that were still dwelling in great numbers in the provinces he mentioned, thus the Covenantalist's perception is found wanting.

Concerning Hosea 2, the historical-grammatical rule conveys a distinction between the biological descendants of the northern and southern nations, descended from Jacob. The anthropomorphic betrothal pertains specifically to the descendants of Ephraim, the northern nation, which we dealt with in the previous chapter. The most relevant *information not available in the original historical and cultural context* in the NT is Romans 7:1–4, which alludes to Deuteronomy 24:1–4 and reveals that Ephraim's release from the marriage contract (Jeremiah 2:3, 3:14, 31:32; Ezekiel 16:32) was required before they could become eligible to return to their husband again, anthropomorphically depicted in Hosea. While God had not divorced Judah, they also needed to be released from the covenant to be betrothed to Christ. It is perceivable that in the *original historical and cultural context* Israelites were not allowed to see the particulars concerning their release from the SC; nevertheless, they were aware of the prophecies of Hosea and aware of the impediment of Deuteronomy 24:4 conveyed in Isaiah 50:1 and Jeremiah 3:1, 8.

Romans 7:1–4 provides the particulars in resolving the impediment—it was the death of Christ and his resurrection by which the elect biological descendants were released from the OC to be betrothed to Christ in the NC. This confirms that the husband in Hosea who divorced Ephraim was Christ, before his incarnation. By deduction, Christ is revealed as the entity that Israel married at Sinai, as it was he that had to die to release them. It is not acceptable to say that it is the gentiles who fulfill the prophecy in Hosea as they were not joined to Christ by the OC as was Israel.

> Wherefore remember, that ye being in time past Gentiles in the flesh, who are called Uncircumcision ... being aliens from the commonwealth of Israel, and strangers from the covenants of promise, having no hope, and without God in the world. (Ephesians 2:11–12)

Only Ephraim fulfills the type to be the woman in Hosea 2 as it was only Ephraim that was divorced in Hosea's narrative, as well as Jeremiah and Isaiah's. Isaiah 50 pertains specifically to Christ and God's call to Israel to obey his servant Christ.

> The Lord GOD hath opened mine ear, and I was not rebellious, neither turned away back. I gave my back to the smiters, and my cheeks to them that plucked off the hair: I hid not my face from shame and spitting.... Who is among you that feareth the LORD, that obeyeth the voice of his servant, that walketh in darkness, and hath no light? let him trust in the name of the LORD, and stay upon his God. (Isaiah 50:5–6, 10)

Calvin failed to accurately account for the historical-grammatical interpretation, the *principal sense*, pertaining to the query, "Where is the bill of your mother's divorcement?" in Isaiah 50:1.

> In order to have a general understanding of it, we must observe that union by which the Lord everywhere testifies that his people are bound to him; that is, that he occupies the place of a husband, and that we occupy the place of a wife. It is a spiritual marriage, which has been consecrated by his eternal doctrine and sealed by the blood of Christ.[38]

---

[38] Ibid., s.v. Isaiah 50:1

In Calvin's assertion that this marriage is sealed *by the blood of Christ* Calvin clearly interprets the marriage as the one under the NC (Hebrews 10:12–13); the OC was sealed by the blood of animals (Exodus 24). Calvin is guilty of omitting the *principal sense* that the divorced women represents Ephraim and the divorce was under the OC. Calvin reveals the "servant" as Christ, who gives his "back to the smiters" and his "cheeks to them that plucked off the hair."[39] Again, Calvin misses the historical-grammatical sense of interpreting Isaiah 50 as pertaining to the Jews and disregarding Ephraim altogether.

> Thus, when the Jews were oppressed by calamities
> so many and so great, that it was easy to conclude
> that God had rejected and divorced them, the cause
> of the divorce came to be the subject of inquiry.[40]

Nevertheless, Calvin renders Isaiah 50:10 as still pertaining to a remnant, which Calvin labels *believers*, who answer the voice of the servant, and these *believers* can be none other than the elect, which by necessity must be acknowledged as predestined and foreseen by God.

> Yet he addresses them separately, that they may
> detach themselves from the mixed crowd, and not
> take part in counsels which are wicked, and which
> God has condemned … there are some left who
> shall profit by his doctrine.[41]

Calvin wisely used the NT to interpret the identity of the servant in Isaiah 50 as Christ, but in obscurity he omitted the historical-grammatical *principal sense*, which blinded him from seeing the people in Isaiah as the very people in the narratives of the gospels and epistles: "God hath not cast away his people which he foreknew …

---

[39] Ibid., s.v. Isaiah 50:4
[40] Ibid.
[41] Ibid., s.v. Isaiah 50:10

Even so then at this present time also there is a remnant according to the election of grace" (Romans 11:2, 5). The promise and prophecies concerning the remnant, elect, are determined by God's decrees, for appointed times; they are not to be perceived in the divided *sense*. The first advent was the determined time for the divorced woman in Hosea, Jeremiah and Isaiah to be betrothed to her husband once again. It is then this *nation* that bears the fruit in Matthew 21:43, a premise which is maintained in the Two House model.

Paul's analysis of the circumstances of the first advent corresponds with the precedent in Jeremiah 29:4–7, which the book of Esther also confirms. In times of judgement and reform God intercedes for the elect remnant in exile and the gentiles are blessed because of them.

> Thus saith the LORD of hosts, the God of Israel, unto all that are carried away captives, whom I have caused to be carried away from Jerusalem unto Babylon; Build ye houses, and dwell in them; and plant gardens, and eat the fruit of them; ye wives, and beget sons and daughters; and take wives for your sons, and give your daughters to husbands, that they may bear sons and daughters; that ye may be increased there, and not diminished. And seek the peace of the city whither I have caused you to be carried away captives, and pray unto the LORD for it: for in the peace thereof shall ye have peace. (Jeremiah 29:4–7)

The dichotomy between the two responses to Christ at the first advent was explained by Paul as the distinction between the children of the promise and the children of the flesh. The same distinction conveys the response to Jeremiah's prophecy in the Babylonian exile. At the first advent the majority of Judah represented the children of the flesh and caused the nation to be cast off, which brought about the circumstances whereby God interceded for the remnant, the children of the promise, and they became a blessing upon the nations in fulfillment of Genesis 12:2–3. In like manner, the remnant that went peaceably to Babylon became the means by which the heathen cities prospered as in the cases of Daniel, Hananiah, Mishael, and Azariah (Daniel 1–6). Christ, as the supreme prophet Moses anticipated (Deuteronomy 18:15–19; Acts 3:22–23), represents the anti-type of Jeremiah, who rebuked the false prophets that claimed God would save Jerusalem (Jeremiah 29:8–9; John 11:45–53). As the anti-type, Christ interceded for the children of the promise who submitted to him and ultimately went peaceably into the world to propagate the gospel, in fulfillment of the parables of Matthew 13, and the prophecies of Hosea 2:19–23 and Zechariah 10:7–9, as related in the first chapter.

The covenantalist's presuppositions of God's omniscience, omnipotence, immutability and etcetera, are touted as forming the basis of their perceptions on predestination and God's foreknowledge but are not taken to their logical conclusions when they continue to foster fallacies in contradiction to the aforementioned. They continue to violate the rule of non-contradiction when they maintain that gentiles are *restored* in the same *sense* as the biological descendants of Ephraim, or that the free will of the reprobate shepherds of Judah determined the destiny of the elect biological descendants of Israel. They violate the rule of non-contradiction when they maintain the fallacy that the Jews could comply with the declarative law without the establishment of the NC or that they could avow Christ without the aid of the Holy Spirit moving on the human will, which under their doctrine only applies to the predetermined elect. One cannot hold that God does not repent like a man and render the NT as anything other than the fulfillment of God's declarative will, which is proceeding precisely according to how the prophets anticipated. The NT merely compliments the historical-grammatical *principal sense*; it clearly does not end or abolish the *first-thought meaning* of the title of Israel.[42] Because of their fallacies they are simply unqualified to properly render John's apocalypse or prophecy in general. They hold the presupposition that God does not change his mind, but as

---

[42] Poythress, Understanding Dispensationalists, 79.

to the identity of Israel in Revelation 7 they fallaciously maintain God does exactly that, he changed his mind.

> Keep not thou silence, O God: hold not thy peace, and be not still, O God. For, lo, thine enemies make a tumult: and they that hate thee have lifted up the head. They have taken crafty counsel against thy people, and consulted against thy hidden ones. They have said, Come, and let us cut them off from being a nation; that the name of Israel may be no more in remembrance. (Psalms 83:1–4)

Only the Two House model adheres to the presuppositions of predestination and compatibilism and reconciles the Old and New Testaments.

CHAPTER

THREE

Israel and the Church

As mentioned in chapter one, God is not a man that repents or changes his mind (1 Samuel 15:29). Conflict arises with the text from Samuel when one views scripture through an open theist[1] lens to perceive that God offered the Messianic kingdom (MK) at the first advent and did not know how the Jews would respond and then reacted to their response precipitously. In other words, God changed his mind. And a libertarian lens does not lessen conflict either, as it still has God repent in his offer of the kingdom. Even so, according to Peter the "elect according to the foreknowledge of God the Father" avowed Christ—and those who disavowed him were ordained to do so.

> Behold, I lay in Sion a chief corner stone…. Unto you therefore which believe *he is* precious: but unto them which be disobedient, the stone which the builders disallowed, the same is made the head of the corner, And a stone of stumbling, and a rock of offence, *even to them* which stumble at the

---

[1] *Theopedia*: "Open theism, also called *free will theism* and *openness theology*, is the belief that God does not exercise meticulous control of the universe but leaves it 'open' for humans to make significant choices (free will) that impact their relationships with God and others." s.v. Open theism, https://www. theopedia.com/open-theism

word, being disobedient: whereunto also they were
appointed. (1 Peter 2:6–8)

Peter presents problems to libertarians or open theists. And for the
same reason Paul confuses them also.

Hath not the potter power over the clay, of the same
lump to make one vessel unto honour, and another
unto dishonour? (Romans 9:21)

Libertarians and open theists attempt to assert that Paul conveyed
only a corporate sense in Romans 9 to avoid compatibilism but,[2] as
affirmed in chapter two, in election the corporate and individual
senses are synonymous; they cannot be separated. The elect body of
Israel is made of its elect individuals as contrasted from their doomed
brethren, concerning the promises, prophecies and restoration: "As
it is written, Jacob have I loved, but Esau have I hated" (Romans
9:13). Dispensationalist Thomas Ice acknowledged this distinction
in his essay of 1 Peter 2, which is tantamount to conceding the
correspondence between individual and corporate election.

since Peter is writing to "the Israel of God" or
Jewish believers, he is listing these Old Testament
descriptions of Israel to let them know that
everything promised them in the Old Testament is
being fulfilled through their faith in Jesus as their
Messiah. This is juxtaposed by a comparison with
unbelieving Jews who have not trusted Jesus as the
Messiah of Israel in verses 7–8. Peter speaks of "the
stone which the builders rejected" (2:7) as a likely
reference to Jewish leadership that lead the nation to

---

[2] In his essay, *Does Romans 9 Teach Individual Election Unto Salvation? Some
Exegetical and Theological Reflections*, Thomas R. Schreiner conveys that
the Arminian view of Rom 9-11 is a "corporate view," as opposition to an
"individual" interpretation, *JETS* 36/1 (March 1993), 38.

reject Jesus as the Messiah. Peter further describes Jewish unbelievers as ones that view Jesus as "a stone of stumbling and a rock of offense" (2:8a). He notes that these Jewish unbelievers "stumble because they are disobedient to the word, and to this doom they were also appointed" (2:8b).[3]

Ice goes on to vindicate the tie between corporate and individual election.

> Since Hosea is a type of God in that book, the Lord is saying that not all of the children of Israel are His offspring. (I take it this is the Lord's way of saying many within national Israel were unbelievers in relation to their individual salvation while still a part of national Israel.)[4]

Covenantalists such as Thomas R. Schreiner and Russell Moore also have inadvertently agreed to the concurrence between corporate and individual election in their statements below.

> All God's choice of a corporate group means is that God chose that all who put their faith in Christ would be saved. Those who put their faith in Christ would be designated the Church. Those who defend corporate election are conscious of the fact that it is hard to separate corporate from individual election, for logic would seem to require that the individuals that make up a group cannot be separated from the group itself.[5]

---

[3] Ice, "1 Peter 2 and Replacement Theology"
[4] Ibid.
[5] Schreiner, "Does Romans 9 Teach Individual Election Unto Salvation? Some Exegetical and Theological Reflections," 38.

Both covenant theology and dispensationalism, however, often discuss Israel and the church without taking into account the Christocentric nature of biblical eschatology. The future restoration of Israel has *never* been promised to the unfaithful, unregenerate members of the nation (John 3:3–10; Rom 2:25–29)—only to the faithful remnant. The church is not Israel, at least not in a direct, unmediated sense. The remnant of Israel—a biological descendant of Abraham, a circumcised Jewish firstborn son who is approved of by God for his obedience to the covenant—receives all of the promises due to him.[6]

Covenantalist C. Matthew McMahon also deviated from replacement theology by acknowledging the correspondence between corporate and individual predestination in his analyzation of the Hebrew term *bachar*, translated as *chosen* in Deuteronomy 7:6. After producing the few extraneous uses of the word he analyzed where,

it is used of God to choose the ultimate destinies and eternal salvation of particular people or of the nation Israel.... It is a specific choosing of a people who will be holy before Yahweh to do His will. This choosing or election is not based on their own merit but on God's good pleasure and for His glory as seen in Deuteronomy 7:7.[7]

Concurrence between individual and corporate election does not support the fallacy that God offered the kingdom to those appointed to wrath, as it was never theirs to inherit; the kingdom was the birthright of those who avowed Christ, those who were "predestined" according to Paul in Romans 8:29–20 and Ephesians 1:4–5. The NT

---

[6] Moore, "Is There a Future for Israel?"
[7] McMahon, *The Two Wills of God*, Kindle location 5857

affirms that those who had the rights to the MK avowed Christ and yet it was not consummated, which substantiates that Christ's first advent was not the appointed time of the MK. Christ's declaration that he had not come the first time to *send peace* (Matthew 10:34) reveals that Jeremiah's prophecy "Judah shall be saved, and Israel shall dwell safely" is a second advent phenomenon (Jeremiah 23:5–6). The time in which Judah and Israel/Ephraim shall dwell safely commences when the beast and false prophet come to their fiery end in Revelation 19, at the second advent. There is no true support for a first advent offer of the kingdom. All of the relevant evidence is in harmony with the NT revelation of two advents that were hidden to the prophets. Dispensationalist R. Bruce Compton unwittingly concedes the aforesaid when he acknowledged that the prophets were not allowed to see all the "implications or significance" of what they wrote. [8] The implications and significance of the two advents are revealed in the NT, such as the spiritual fulfillment of Malachi 4:5–6 by John the Baptist that confirms the widely recognized hermeneutic of Prophetic Telescoping (PT), to be dealt with presently.

Dispensationalists perceive that the offer of the MK and its postponement at the rejection of Christ (their parenthesis) was contingent upon the endorsement of the nation and is clearly a fallacy based on open theism or libertarianism, which dispensationalist Lewis Sperry Chafer attempted to harmonize.

> In the light of two determining facts, namely, (a) that Jehovah's Lamb was in the redeeming purpose slain from the foundation of the world and (b) that had Adam not sinned there could have been no need of a redeemer, why did Jehovah tell Adam not to sin? And what would have become of the redemptive purpose had Adam obeyed God? These objections to the so-called postponement theory do not take into consideration the fact of the divinely purposed

---

[8] Compton, "Dispensationalism, the Church, and the New Covenant," 44.

test involved and the necessary postponement resulting from the failure under testing, the failure itself being anticipated. These are evidently very serious problems for some Calvinists to face. If it be claimed that the birth and death of Christ were predicted and therefore made sure, it is equally true that the precross offer of the earthly Messianic kingdom to Israel by her Messiah in the days of His "lowly guise" was also made sure by prediction.[9]

Chafer's argument (b) is a fallacy, considering the idiom "the Lamb slain before the foundations of the world" in Revelation 13:8 invokes the principle of foreknowledge. The idiom conveys God's foreknowledge of Adam's fall, which Chafer concedes, but he fails to grasp that it denies the possibility of a different outcome, disregarding God's foreknowledge; Chafer's surmising is pure fallacy. For this reason, the certainty of God's foreknowledge also supports the correspondence between corporate and individual election in Romans 9:21. According to dispensationalism the Church was not anticipated, inasmuch as the MK's existence was dependent upon the endorsement of those appointed to doom, which conflicts with the idiom Christ *slain from the foundation of the world* that affirms God's foreknowledge. For these reasons the idiom does not support Chafer's argument concerning dispensationalism's perception that Christ offered the kingdom at the first advent. The notion of postponement forces the view that God's foreknowledge is limited as in the open theist's perception. No doubt Chafer's perception is an open theist's view.

Actually, Chafer never cites one example of Christ offering the kingdom to the Jews, let alone a prophecy of it being offered. He alludes to the incident where Christ fulfills Zechariah 9:9 but there is no overt account in any of the gospels where Christ offers the MK to the children of Jerusalem; if there were an overt account

---

[9] Lewis Sperry Chafer, *Dispensationalism*, (Taft Software, Inc., July 24, 2008), Kindle location 191.

it would not be necessary to rely merely on a theological dispute to sustain their assertion. Contrary to Chafer's notion, John's gospel clearly states that the disciples did not grasp the significance of Jerusalem's king riding the colt until after Christ had been glorified (John 12:16). This upholds the idea that the people could not have comprehended the significance of Zechariah 9:9 being fulfilled at the time it occurred. The contemporary dispensationalist, Michael J. Vlach, attempts to vindicate the argument that the MK was offered to Israel and which was later rejected in this comment of Matthew 11.

> The rest of Matthew 11 further discusses the rejection of the kingdom message by the leaders and people of Israel. With 11:14 Jesus states, "And if you are willing to accept it, John himself is Elijah who was to come." The conditional particle "if" (*ei*) indicates that if Israel would receive John and his message then he would be the fulfillment of the Malachi 4 prophecy concerning the coming of Elijah. Toussaint notes, "There is scarcely a passage in Scripture which shows more clearly that the kingdom was being offered to Israel at this time."[10]

But Vlach failed to grasp the significance of Christ's revelation that affirms that the prophecy of Elijah telescopes into the second advent.

> And Jesus answered and said unto them, Elias truly shall first come, and restore all things. But I say unto you, That Elias is come already, and they knew him not, but have done unto him whatsoever they listed. Likewise shall also the Son of man suffer of them. (Matthew 17:11–12)

---

[10] Vlach, "The Kingdom Program in Matthew's Gospel"

Christ's explanation conveys the Classic or General Prophecy principle of PT.[11] Simply put, God's intent concerning Malachi 4:5–6 was to illustrate that both advents have reoccurring phenomena. Like typology, the first is an image of the second advent; the consummation at the second advent accomplishes what was commenced at the first advent.[12] Avowal of "salvation" in Christ will be rewarded at the second advent, at the consummation of 2 Samuel 7:10 concerning the Davidic Covenant (Mark 9:11–13). Hebrews 9:28 affirms that Christ was offered once as the propitiation for sin at the first advent; therefore, it is easily grasped that the second appearance consummates the salvation of the elect from their temporal enemies, depicted as the separation of the wheat from the tares in the parable (1 John 2:2; Matthew 13:24–30). Such evidence also conveys that the sifting in Amos 9:9–10 corresponds to the prophecy by Christ that the tares grow along with the wheat in Matthew 13. Philippians 2:6–8 confirms that Christ "came" to lay aside his power and die for us, while Revelation 19 and other NT texts substantiate that he returns to consummate the MK, all of which renders the hypothesis that Christ offered the kingdom at his first advent a fallacy. Christ returns in power to receive the crown of David and sit upon his throne (Matthew 25:31–32). In PT there are two Elijahs but

[11] In Dr. David R. Reagan's webpage, *The Interpretation of Prophecy*, he writes: "Another peculiar feature of prophetic literature is called 'telescoping'.… the perspective of the prophet . . . looks into the future and sees a series of prophetic events" that "appear to him as if they are in immediate sequence" but they are separated by ages. *Lamb & Lion Ministries*, http://christinprophecy. org/articles/the-interpretation-of-prophecy/

[12] Commenting on Hebrews 10:1, Clarence Larkin writes: "The writer to the Hebrews tells us that the 'Types' are but the 'SHADOW OF GOOD THINGS TO COME, AND NOT THE VERY IMAGE OF THE THING.' Heb. 10:1. That is, the Old Testament 'Types' are but 'SHADOWS.' But there cannot be a 'shadow' without some 'REAL THING' to make it. And a 'shadow' is not the 'very image of the thing,' for a shadow is out of proportion, and is an imperfect representation of the thing it reveals. So the Old Testament Types are 'shadows' in the sense that they are not the 'Real Thing,' and are but imperfect revelations of it." *Dispensational Truth* (Publishers Rev. Clarence Larkin est., 1918), 133.

correspondence cannot extend to consummation; there can be only one consummation. At the consummation persecution ends and, in that day, "Judah shall be saved, and Israel shall dwell safely," but in contrast, at the sifting time "a man's enemies *are* the men of his own house" (Jeremiah 23:5–6; Micah 7:6). By nature, the consummation follows the sifting. This is also substantiated by Matthew 10:23 which affirms that persecution is contemporaneous with the commission to proclaim *the kingdom of heaven* until the return of Christ.

> But when they persecute you in this city, flee ye into another: for verily I say unto you, Ye shall not have gone over the cities of Israel, till the Son of man be come. (Matthew 10:23)

Christ prophesied that Israel's persecution would continue until his return, which also confirms that 2 Samuel 7:10, like Jeremiah 23:5–6, was intended to be consummated at the second advent, with the MK (Psalms 110:1; Matthew 10:23, 25:31; Luke 19:12–15). Christ came as a *servant of rulers*, despised by men and abhorred by the shepherds of Judah in fulfillment of Psalms 2:1–3, Psalms 118:22–24, Isaiah 49:7, Isaiah 53:1–4 and Zechariah 11:8, to name but a few. This is also corroborated in the NT by Matthew and Mark when they state that Christ came *not to be ministered unto* as a king (Matthew 20:28; Mark 10:45). Under a strict historical-grammatical hermeneutic there is no scriptural support for an offering of the MK at the first advent.

Vlach changes the meaning of "the kingdom of heaven" as an *ad hoc* in his failure to produce any real evidence that Christ offered the MK at the first advent. He believes the transition from God offering the MK and his change of mind came between Matthew 11 and 13, where Vlach also changes the meaning of the phrase "the kingdom of heaven."

Matthew 13 must be understood in light of the events preceding this chapter, especially chapters 11 and 12. The kingdom promised by the Old Testament prophets was "at hand"—its coming was on the brink. In fact, it was present in the person, words, and works of Jesus. All that needed to happen was a national recognition of the Messiah and repentance from both the people and leaders of Israel. Instead, the King and His kingdom were met with hostility and rejection and violence had been done to the kingdom program. Matthew 13 marks a dramatic shift in the kingdom program as Jesus withdraws from wide scale proclamation of the kingdom to the cities of Israel and begins to share new truths or "mysteries" concerning the kingdom with His disciples.[13]

Vlach is at odds with Christ, who declared that Malachi 4:5–6 had dual fulfillment in Matthew 17:11–12, affirming of the principle of PT. Dispensationalist David L. Larsen concedes the conveyance of PT pertaining to sections of Matthew 23 and 24, while failing to apply the hermeneutic to the prophecy of Elijah, the Day of the Lord and the good tidings in Luke 4:17–21.

A future generation of Jews would "see him again." He speaks to his listeners and by prophetic telescoping reaches forward to an end-time population. Similarly the Olivet Discourse has at points a distinctly Jewish cast ("not on the Sabbath") and a testimony which the end-time Jewish remnant would render (Matthew 24:14).[14]

---

[13] Vlach, "The Kingdom Program in Matthew's Gospel"

[14] David L. Larsen, "The Postmodern Abandonment of Israel," *Pre-Trib.com*, http://pre-trib.com/data/pdf/Larsen-ThePostmodernAbandon.pdf

Christ's explanation in Matthew 17:11–12 provides a hermeneutic in interpreting scripture and especially the phrase *the Day of the Lord* in Malachi 4:5, which is an idiom conveying *judgment* and the crucible of refinement for the elect. Christ's affirmation that "Elias is come already," in a sense conveys that judgment had commenced, but, furthermore, judgment still had to be consummated: "Judgment must begin at the house of God" (1 Peter 4:17). The judgment that commenced with the first advent rebuilds the tabernacle of David that is consummated at the second advent as the MK. What is conveyed by the Day of the Lord in Malachi and the other prophets is the refinement of the elect in the crucible of adversity, prior to any notion of presentation of the MK (2 Timothy 3:12; 1 Peter 1:6–7). This is why John the Baptist's call commenced with "repent." The gifts follow contrition and God moves us to contrition. Again, God directs Israel so as to save them; Israel does not direct herself unto salvation apart from God's regeneration, which is contrary to predestination (John 3:3; Romans 8:29–30; 1 Peter 1:2).

The principle of PT is also applied to more than just John the Baptist's mission, it is also applied to proclaiming liberty to the captives and to the opening of the prison to them that are bound. The principle is applied in Luke 4:16–21 also, where Christ recites the first part of Isaiah 61 as fulfilled and then closes the book before he states that the day of vengeance is fulfilled.

> The Spirit of the Lord is upon me, because he hath anointed me to preach the gospel to the poor; he hath sent me to heal the brokenhearted, to preach deliverance to the captives, and recovering of sight to the blind, to set at liberty them that are bruised, To preach the acceptable year of the Lord. And he closed the book, and he gave *it* again to the minister, and sat down. And the eyes of all them that were in the synagogue were fastened on him. And he began to say unto them, This day is this scripture fulfilled in your ears. (Luke 4:18–21)

Binding up the brokenhearted, proclaiming liberty to the captives, and "the opening of the prison to *them that are* bound" commenced with the first advent as the kingdom of God/heaven was developed by the spreading of the Gospel. The evidence that spreading the Gospel fulfilled the proclamation of liberty and set the prisoners free from their incarceration to the CN establishes the principle of PT concerning Isaiah 61:1–2, which destroys Vlach's perceptions of the offering of the MK at the first advent.

Christ's revelation that Malachi 4:5–6 is to be perceived as the classic prophecy or PT confirms that John the Baptist's proclamation "the kingdom of God was at hand" was not a proposal of the MK. This is also admitted by dispensationalist Thomas Ice when he acknowledged that the biological descendants had begun to obtain "everything promised them" in his interpretation of Hosea 2:23.[15] Dispensationalists fail to grasp the significance of PT in interpreting the prophecy of Elijah that led Cyrus Ingerson Scofield to fallaciously place a gap in the context of Malachi 3:1.

> The f.c. of Malachi 3:1 is quoted of John the Baptist; Matthew 11:10; Mark 1:2; Luke 7:27 but the second clause, "the Lord whom ye see," etc., is nowhere quoted in the N.T. The reason is obvious: in everything save the fact of Christ's first advent, the latter clause awaits fulfilment Habakkuk 2:20. Malachi 3:2–5 speak of judgment, not of grace. Malachi, in common with other O.T. prophets, saw both advents of Messiah blended in one horizon, but did not see the separating interval described in Matthew 13.[16]

Christ's first appearance was that of a refiner of his disciples, who in spirit fulfilled the prophecy of the refinement of the sons of Levi in Malachi 3:3 just as John the Baptist fulfilled the prophecy of Elijah

---

[15] Ice, "1 Peter 2 and Replacement Theology"
[16] Scofield's Reference Notes, s.v. Malachi 3:1

in spirit; the latter being conceded by both John Nelson Darby and Scofield.[17] Christ came to the temple of God to refine the remnant of Israel so that their offerings would become acceptable to God, while the offerings in Jerusalem became obsolete.

> Wherein ye greatly rejoice, though now for a season, if need be, ye are in heaviness through manifold temptations: That the trial of your faith, being much more precious than of gold that perisheth, though it be tried with fire, might be found unto praise and honour and glory at the appearing of Jesus Christ. (1 Peter 1:6–7)

> I beseech you therefore, brethren, by the mercies of God, that ye present your bodies a living sacrifice, holy, acceptable unto God, *which is* your reasonable service. (Romans 12:1)

> That I should be the minister of Jesus Christ to the Gentiles, ministering the gospel of God, that the offering up of the Gentiles might be acceptable, being sanctified by the Holy Ghost. (Romans 15:16)

> In that he saith, A new *covenant,* he hath made the first old. Now that which decayeth and waxeth old *is* ready to vanish away. (Hebrews 8:13)

> Be not carried about with divers and strange doctrines. For *it is* a good thing that the heart be established with grace; not with meats, which have not profited them that have been occupied therein.

---

[17] "John the Baptist had come already . . . in the spirit and power of Elijah's future ministry," *Reference Notes to the Bible,* s.v. Matthew 17:10, Ibid.; *John Darby's Synopsis:* "so John fulfilled morally and in power the mission of Elias to prepare the way of the Lord." s.v. Matthew 17

We have an altar, whereof they have no right to eat which serve the tabernacle. (Hebrews 13:9–10)

As stated, dispensationalists have conceded that the eschatological promise of Elijah was fulfilled in spirit by John the Baptist, which deviates from their parenthesis and concedes the dual fulfillment of PT as a hermeneutic in perceiving Malachi 3:1–7 as well as 5:5–6 in eschatological prophecy. Their failure to grasp the significance of PT concerning Malachi 4:5–6 led Scofield to mistakenly perceive a parenthesis where PT is called for in Malachi 3:2–5, which nevertheless accidentally acknowledges that the interval between the advents was planned and that Matthew 13 illustrates this interval. Covenantalists also see John the Baptist as fulfilling Malachi 3:1–7 also but cannot apply PT to the phenomenon of the second advent.[18]

Scofield's interpretation moves away from the parenthesis and in the direction of an acknowledgement of a planned interval and its correspondence with Matthew 13, which also sustains correspondence with the sifting of Israel in Amos 9:9–10, as stated previously. As revealed in the first chapter, Walter C. Kaiser Jr. confirmed that the object of the prepositional phrase "after these things" (Μετὰ ταῦτα) in Acts 15:16 did not pertain to how God had first visited the gentiles, which was how James prefaced his citation of Amos. It pertained to the context in Amos of "the destruction of the temple, the fact of the diaspora, and the end of Samaria," all of which led to the consequent sifting in Amos.

> Now *after these things*—the destruction of the temple, the fact of the diaspora, and the end of Samaria—warned James, with an eye to the Amos

---

[18] Malachi 3:7 was interpreted simply as a first-advent phenomenon without repeat at the second by John Gill: *"Return unto me, and I will return unto you, saith the Lord of hosts*; this message was carried to them by John the Baptist, the forerunner of Christ, and by Christ himself, who both preached the doctrine of repentance to this people, Matthew 3:2." *John Gill's Exposition of the Whole Bible* s.v. Malachi 3:7

context, God "would turn again" (*anastrepsō*) to re-establish the house of David. To obtain the dispensational view one must assume that the "first" of v 14 signified the "first [era]" (a clear interpolation) while the second reference was given a sequential meaning: "After this [gospel dispensation]"28 God would "come again" and restore Israel. But on these grounds neither phrase is a literal, grammatical or natural interpretation of James. Dispensationalism has thereby yielded any hermeneutical edge it possessed by so arguing.[19]

Dispensationalists assert that the object of the prepositional phrase pertains to how God had "first" visited the gentiles in order to maintain the sifting and rebuilding of David's tabernacle as a second advent phenomenon.[20] Essentially, Kaiser affirms the sifting as a first advent phenomenon, which constitutes the rebuilding of the David's tabernacle and God's visitation of the gentiles. In support of Kaiser, progressive dispensationalist W. Edward Glenny, affirms that James's citation from Amos used in Acts 15:16–17 conveys the re-establishment of the Davidic dynasty and the mission to the gentiles as a contemporaneous plan through Christ, commencing with the first advent, as opposed to the Classic and Revised dispensationalist's parenthesis (Glenny neglects the sifting in the article).

We can draw several conclusions from our study of Amos 9 in Acts 15. First, in contrast to the beliefs

---

[19] Walter C. Kaiser, Jr., "The Davidic Promise and the Inclusion of the Gentiles," *Journal of the Evangelical Theological Society*, vol. 20:2 (June, 1977, 97. http://thepromise.typepad.com/197706.pdf

[20] The sifting in Amos 9 is interpreted as a second-advent phenomenon by dispensationalist Les Feldick: "Amos 9:9 – 10…. In that day (When God is ready to come back and finish His work with Israel) will I raise up the tabernacle of David that is fallen…. this is Israel's future…. But it won't be until the Church is complete and we're out of the way." *Through the Bible with Les Feldick* (Book 76), Kindle location 195

of Covenant Theologians, the Church's existence is not due to God's rejection of Israel. It is a corollary of David's dynasty (and kingdom) being reestablished that the Gentile mission goes forth. Second, in the same vein, the Church is not Israel nor does it replace Israel. It is a result of God's revisiting Israel and reestablishing the Davidic monarchy and kingdom that the Gentiles can now come to God as Gentiles. (The conjunction "so that" ... at the beginning of Acts 15:17 indicates that the purpose of God in building David's fallen tent is "so that" Gentiles may be God's people. The rebuilding of the tent is distinct from the Gentile mission and is what enables it to take place. The conjunction makes no sense if the tent that is being rebuilt is the Church, or a new Israel, which includes the Gentile mission. The Gentile mission happens as a result of the building of the tent of David.) Third, in contrast to the belief of some dispensationalists, the Gentile mission is not a parenthesis in God's program and plan. It is closely connected with God's work in Israel, and it is thoroughly consistent with the OT prophets and their message.[21]

Glenny's first and third claims are viable, while his second creates tremendous tension with the NT, which will be analyzed presently. As a dispensationalist, Glenny only sees Israel as "a nation among nations", a concept which is in conflict with the OT affirmation that Israel is redeemed while in exile as "a nation scattered amongst nations", bereft of civil autonomy, recognized borders and mixed with the gentiles, when Hosea and Zechariah are considered. It is in

---

[21] W. Edward Glenny, "Gentiles and the People of God: A Study of Apostolic Hermeneutics and Theology in Acts 15," NT Resources.com, http://ntresources.com/blog/documents/Amos9inActs15b.pdf

this latter state that has a greater correspondence with the institution of the Church.

> And it shall come to pass, when all these things are come upon thee, the blessing and the curse, which I have set before thee, and thou shalt call *them* to mind among all the nations, whither the LORD thy God hath driven thee, And shalt return unto the LORD thy God, and shalt obey his voice according to all that I command thee this day, thou and thy children, with all thine heart, and with all thy soul; That then the LORD thy God will turn thy captivity, and have compassion upon thee, and will return and gather thee from all the nations, whither the LORD thy God hath scattered thee. (Deuteronomy 30:1–3)

> But now thus saith the LORD that created thee, O Jacob, and he that formed thee, O Israel, Fear not: for I have redeemed thee, I have called thee by thy name; thou art mine... Fear not: for I am with thee: I will bring thy seed from the east, and gather thee from the west.... I, even I, am he that blotteth out thy transgressions for mine own sake, and will not remember thy sins. (Isaiah 43:1, 5, 25)

> My righteousness is near; my salvation is gone forth, and mine arms shall judge the people; the isles shall wait upon me, and on mine arm shall they trust.... Therefore the redeemed of the LORD shall return, and come with singing unto Zion; and everlasting joy shall be upon their head: they shall obtain gladness and joy; and sorrow and mourning shall flee away.... The captive exile hasteneth that he may

be loosed, and that he should not die in the pit, nor that his bread should fail. (Isaiah 51:5, 11, 14)

Thus saith the LORD, The people which were left of the sword found grace in the wilderness; even Israel, when I went to cause him to rest.... For the LORD hath redeemed Jacob, and ransomed him from the hand of him that was stronger than he. (Jeremiah 31:2, 11)

And I will betroth thee unto me for ever; yea, I will betroth thee unto me in righteousness, and in judgment, and in lovingkindness, and in mercies.... And I will sow her unto me in the earth; and I will have mercy upon her that had not obtained mercy; and I will say to *them which were* not my people, Thou *art* my people; and they shall say, *Thou art* my God. (Hosea 2:19, 23)

And *they of* Ephraim shall be like a mighty *man*, and their heart shall rejoice as through wine: yea, their children shall see *it*, and be glad; their heart shall rejoice in the LORD I will hiss for them, and gather them; for I have redeemed them: and they shall increase as they have increased. And I will sow them among the people: and they shall remember me in far countries; and they shall live with their children, and turn again. (Zechariah 10:7–9)

In all the accounts above, Israel's corporate redemption is established while they are yet *a nation scattered amongst the nations* and then they are restored to being *a nation amongst nations*. Redeeming Israel in a scattered condition necessitates the development of the centrifugal worship prophesied by Christ in John 4:21–24. The first advent anticipation of centrifugal worship, in Spirit and truth, clarifies how Ephraim is redeemed, then centrifugally planted in the world as pertaining to Zechariah 10:6–9 and Hosea 2, which agrees with the parables in Matthew 13, especially that of the wheat and the tares. Judah is never portrayed as being redeemed and then sown in the earth, or as a defiled woman returned to her first husband as in Hosea 2. The destinies of Ephraim and Judah went separate paths when God influenced Jeroboam's confederation of the ten northern tribes and quelled Rehoboam's quest of using coercion to return them. Zechariah and Hosea present the greatest evidence that the sifting is synonymous with God's announcement of Ephraim's corporate redemption at the first advent and that the phenomenon is multigenerational. (Clearly the contemporary State of the Jews created from the Palestinian state is not the MK). As revealed above, Glenny believes Amos 9:11–12 was fulfilled at the first advent, but as a dispensationalist he must concede verses 13–15 remain to be consummated, which is an acknowledgement of PT. PT destroys the notion that the context supports the perception that Israel's corporate redemption is confined to the second-advent. Amos 9:13–15 pertains to the second advent, the MK, or Israel as a divinely instituted *nation amongst nations*. Nevertheless, dispensationalists maintain that the sifting is not a protracted phenomenon; they attempt to confine it to Christ's return based on the context in Amos 9, not unlike their view of the fulfillment of the NC in Jeremiah 31:31–34.[22] Even so, many dispensationalists agree, the sifting has a redemptive constituent,[23] but they fail to grasp the constituent is based upon the blotting of Israel's sins that led to the mission to the gentiles at the first advent,

---

[22] The NC is perceived as a second-advent phenomenon by R. B. Compton: "The problem with seeing the fulfillment of any of the new covenant promises in the present era with the church is that those promises without exception occur in the Old Testament in eschatological contexts." Compton, "Dispensationalism, the Church, and the New Covenant"

[23] And the sifting is also held as a second-advent phenomenon by dispensationalist Les Feldick: "not a single Jew that God has ordained to go into that Kingdom is going to miss it." *Through the Bible with Les Feldick* (Book 16), Kindle location 1032.

which is substantiated in the gospel of Luke by the witness of the Holy Spirit.

> And thou, child, shalt be called the prophet of the Highest: for thou shalt go before the face of the Lord to prepare his ways; To give knowledge of salvation unto his people by the remission of their sins. (Luke 1:76–77)

> For mine eyes have seen thy salvation, Which thou hast prepared before the face of all people; A light to lighten the Gentiles, and the glory of thy people Israel. (Luke 2:32)

The former scripture, above, pertains to John the Baptist's appointment and the latter pertains to Christ's appointment. Dispensationalists John Nelson Darby and Charles Caldwell Ryrie acknowledged that sin was remitted "once for all" at the first advent (Hebrews 10:10),[24] which deviates from the parenthesis view and rather substantiates that Israel's redemption commenced with the first advent as well as vindicating the correspondence between individual and corporate election. The sifting in Amos 9:9–10 conveys a separation between those who are redeemed and those who "die by the sword," those whom God rejects. Both dispensationalists as well as covenantalists cannot avoid the element that the blotting of sin is a constituent of the sifting, and that this substantiates Kaiser's analysis that James's citation from Amos 9 in Acts 15 was literal fulfillment and not an analogous circumstance.[25] In essence, Darby and Ryrie's concession of the blotting of sin at the first advent departs

---

[24] *John Darby's Synopsis:* "the offering is 'once for all.' It admits of no repetition." s.v. Hebrew 10:10, *The Ryrie Study Bible,* "Christ's redemption needs no repetition and no supplementation." s.v. Heb 10:1-39, 1741.

[25] The Calvinists perception of a limited atonement does not impede the argument that the blotting of sin occurred for at least all the elect at the first advent, which acknowledges individual and corporate correspondence concerning election.

from their parenthesis and concedes that the sifting commenced with the blotting.[26] Again, this agrees with Ice, who acknowledged that Israel's redemption commenced at the first advent by stating Peter's citation from Hosea 2:23 in 1 Peter 2:10 was for the benefit of "the Israel of God," as contrasted from his own brethren appointed to doom.[27] Sifting is a process of separating wheat or corn from its husk, shaft and other unwanted constituents. The OT confirms that the objective of the sifting is to winnow away those appointed to doom to preserve or save the elect (Proverbs 20:8, 26). Ice's perception of 1 Peter 2 supports the fact that Christ provoked the Jews in the manner of the sifting, which has continued unabated between the advents; it reveals Christ as the sifter. Matthew 10 supports that Christ came to sift Israel, to cause this division amongst the Jews, to winnow out the undesirable constituents appointed to doom.

> Whosoever therefore shall confess me before men, him will I confess also before my Father which is in heaven. whosoever shall deny me before men, him will I also deny before my Father which is in heaven. Think not that I am come to send peace on earth: I came not to send peace, but a sword. I am come to set a man at variance against his father, and the daughter against her mother, and the daughter in law against her mother in law. And a man's foes *shall be* they of his own household. (Matthew 10:32–36)

(The Stone, rejected by the builders also invokes the same ideas.) Acts 2 unequivocally confirms that the disciples commenced separating the wheat from the shaft, by which many were "added to the church"

---

[26] There can be no other sound conclusion to the acknowledgment that the sins of the elect were forgiven by Christ's propitiation; it not only substantiates the concurrence between individual and corporate election but substantiates the fulfillment of the NC was intended as a protracted phenomenon commencing at the first advent and being consummated by the second.

[27] Ice, "1 Peter 2 and Replacement Theology"

that they "should be saved" while those appointed to doom were winnowed away and hardened according to Paul in Romans 11, in conformity with the sifting.

> Therefore let all the house of Israel know assuredly, that God hath made that same Jesus, whom ye have crucified, both Lord and Christ.... Then Peter said unto them, Repent, and be baptized every one of you in the name of Jesus Christ for the remission of sins, and ye shall receive the gift of the Holy Ghost.... And they, continuing daily with one accord in the temple, and breaking bread from house to house, did eat their meat with gladness and singleness of heart, Praising God, and having favour with all the people. And the Lord added to the church daily such as should be saved. (Acts 2:36, 38, 46–47)

For these reasons, Kaiser has the proper perception of James's intent in citing from Amos, which perceives the sifting as redemptive and a phenomenon that commenced at the first-century and which is synonymous with the rebuilding of the tabernacle of David by Christ, as well as grasping the understanding of the mission to the gentiles. Classic and revised dispensationalism can recoil at the perception that the tabernacle of David is perceived principally as the assembling of human constituents during the inter-advent era, but the precedent for such a perception is affirmed in Peter's epistle, who perceived the individual members figuratively as stones that are built upon "a spiritual house" (1 Peter 2:5). The practice of PT by the prophets was not uncommon, which dispensationalists concede,[28] and the justification for its application to the sifting in Amos 9 is irresistible.

---

[28] Prophetic telescoping was upheld by Clarence Larkin, "The Old Testament prophet saw the future as separate peaks of one mountain. He did not see that these peaks assembled themselves in groups with the valley the "VALLEY-OF THE CHURCH," between." Larkin, *Dispensational Truth*, 20.

Justification for the application of PT in Amos 9 is also discovered in how the gentiles are possessed and called by the name of the being that moved Amos to write: "I will build it as in the days of old: That they may possess the remnant of Edom, and of all the heathen, which are called by my name" (Amos 9:12). Glenny attempts to support the progressive dispensationalist's perception that "the Church is not Israel nor does it replace Israel"[29] by reverting to the Classic and Revised perception of Amos 9:12.

> A more literal rendering of the phrase "that bear my name" (NIV) is "that are called by my name" (ASV). The phrase "denotes ownership and the act of possession," which can be accomplished by war (2 Samuel 12:28) or agreement to the requests of those desiring to be owned and possessed (Isa 3:1).... When the phrase is applied to Israel, as God's people, it is based on their covenant relationship with him (Deuteronomy 28:10; 2 Chron 7:14). Gentiles, by contrast, have not been called by the name of the Lord (Isa 63:19). Such covenant relationship, as experienced by Israel, is not explicit in the MT of Amos 9:12. Here the ownership of control, which are basic to the meaning of this phrase, appear to be as a result of military conquest, as in 2 Samuel 12:28.[30]

Glenny's perception reveals the dilemma that perceiving the gentiles as a possession acquired by war is irrelevant concerning the calling of the gentiles in Acts. Peter testified that the gentiles had received the Holy Spirit in the same power as the Jews without being circumcised; consequently, the issue of circumcision arose and inspired James to cite from Amos 9:11–12. The perception that the Edomites are

---

[29] Glenny, "Gentiles and the People of God: A Study of Apostolic Hermeneutics and Theology in Acts 15."

[30] Ibid.

subjugated by war in any context is bereft of any relevance concerning the circumstances at the first advent. The matter in Acts and the quote from Amos 9:12 concerns the mission to the gentiles who bear the name of the being who moved Amos to write; furthermore, the most relevant OT text concerning these issues is Isaiah 49:3.

> And said unto me, Thou *art* my servant, O Israel, in whom I will be glorified.... And he said, It is a light thing that thou shouldest be my servant to raise up the tribes of Jacob, and to restore the preserved of Israel: I will also give thee for a light to the Gentiles, that thou mayest be my salvation unto the end of the earth. (Isaiah 49:3, 6)

There is little controversy that the Servant, Israel, in the texts pertains to Christ, which is why revised dispensationalist Michael J. Vlach acknowledges that Christ is appointed the title of Israel in Isaiah 49.

> But what may be surprising to some is that many dispensationalists also accept Premise 2 that Jesus is identified with Israel. For instance, Craig Blaising states, "I agree with Strimple that the New Testament presents Christ as Israel."17 This author, too, believes that Christ is identified with Israel and that Matthew 1 and 2 indicates a strong connection between the nation Israel and Jesus. Jesus is the corporate Head of Israel who represents Israel.[31]

By acknowledging that Christ is appointed the title "Israel" Vlach actually affirms, the "name" of the elect gentiles in Amos 9:12 is Israel and they are graciously adopted sons and daughters, which

---

[31] Michael J. Vlach, Ph.D., "What Does Christ as 'True Israel' Mean for the Nation Israel?: A Critique of the Non-Dispensational Understanding," *The Master's Seminary Journal* 23, no. 1 (Spring 2012), 43-54.

refutes dispensationalism. Two other relevant scriptural texts that corroborate that Christ is the being that moved Amos to write are Revelation 19:10 and 1 Peter 1:10–11.

> Of which salvation the prophets have enquired and searched diligently, who prophesied of the grace *that should come* unto you: Searching what, or what manner of time the Spirit of Christ which was in them did signify, when it testified beforehand the sufferings of Christ, and the glory that should follow. (1 Peter 1:10–11)

> And I fell at his feet to worship him. And he said unto me, See *thou do it* not: I am thy fellowservant, and of thy brethren that have the testimony of Jesus: worship God: for the testimony of Jesus is the spirit of prophecy. (Rev 19:10–11)

The texts corroborate that it was Christ who moved the prophets to write, which is further supported in the opening of the Revelation.

> The Revelation of Jesus Christ, which God gave unto him, to shew unto his servants things which must shortly come to pass; and he sent and signified *it* by his angel unto his servant John: Who bare record of the word of God, and of the testimony of Jesus Christ, and of all things that he saw. (Revelation 1:1–2)

John's apocalypse conveys that God reveals his foreknowledge to Christ, who reveals it to the prophets or to the angels, and then to man. Dispensationalist Tony Garland concurs in his commentary to Revelation 19:10, which cites 1 Peter 1:11 in support, that the being who moved the prophets was Christ.

Does this verse teach that the testimony from Jesus is the spirit of prophecy? Or that the testimony about Jesus is the spirit of prophecy? Both of these statements are certainly true. For it is the Holy Spirit, the Spirit of Christ (John 14:18; Romans 8:9; 1Pe. 1:11) Who is the source of all prophecy (see below) and the primary focus of the revelation He provides concerns Jesus.... Peter indicates that it was "the Spirit of Christ who was in" the prophets that testified. Thus, the Spirit of Jesus was the empowering source of their testimony.[32]

Garland's concession that it was Christ who moved the prophets also refutes dispensationalism and rather substantiates that the "name" in Amos 9:12 is Israel, as Christ is appointed the title Israel in Isaiah 49:3, to raise "up the tribes of Jacob" and is given as a light to the gentiles, so that he may be his Father's "salvation unto the end of the earth." This was also substantiated in chapter one where it was revealed that the angel of the Lord, who declared "I will never break my covenant" (Judges 2:1), was preincarnate Christ.[33] Dispensationalists perceive the raising of the tribes of Jacob as strictly a second-advent phenomenon; however, they cannot help but conclude that sin was remitted "once for all" at the first advent, which refutes the parenthesis and actually affirms the Two House model that Israel's redemption commenced with the first advent (Hebrews 10:10). The perception that Israel's redemption commenced with the first advent is easily supported in the interpretation pertaining to Ephraim; he was redeemed corporately at the first advent by the blotting of sins and, subsequently is being sown in the earth (Hosea 2:19–23; Zechariah 10:6–9; Matthew 13:24–30). However, the dispensationalist's

---

[32] Tony Garland, "A Testimony of Jesus Christ: A Commentary on the Book of Revelation," *Bible Study Tools.com*, s.v. revelation-19-10, http://www.biblestudytools.com/commentaries/revelation/revelation-19/revelation-19-10.html

[33] Baker's Evangelical Dictionary of Biblical Theology, s.v. Angel of the Lord

perception that Israel's redemption is confined to the second advent creates tremendous tension with the former perception. This is due to the dispensationalist's failure to discern Ephraim from Judah in the inter-advent dispensation. Dispensationalists concede that the vexation and envy between Judah and Ephraim continues until the second advent (Isaiah 11:13).[34] Nevertheless, they are confronted by the historical fact that the Jews do not know where Ephraim abides, so that any such enmity between them becomes a moot issue. Yet, Two House Theology has been able to reconcile this vexation and envy by acknowledging that Ephraim is redeemed corporately at the first advent. God blots out their sins and then sows them in the earth; it is they then, who represent the nation that bears the fruit of the vineyard and they who fulfill the principal interpretation of the *tribes of Jacob* in Isaiah 49:6.

In the original quote from Glenny, above, his second claim that "the Church is not Israel nor does it replace Israel" presents numerous quandaries, the greatest being that the whole act of the redemption of Israel is to reestablish a covenant people commencing with the blotting of their sins through the ultimate sacrifice made by Christ to ensure the ultimate gift of eternal life. The blotting of sin occurred at the first-advent. The proclamation the kingdom of heaven was at hand was not an offer of the MK but was rather an offer to receive salvation in Christ that is the prelude to bringing the descendants of Israel back from being a "scattered nation amongst nations" (Deuteronomy 30:1–4; Isaiah 43:1, 5, 25, 51:5, 11, 14; Jeremiah 31:2, 11; Hosea 2:19, 23; Zechariah 10:7–9). The blotting of sin as a "once for all" (Hebrews 10:10) was a first advent phenomenon and Christ's own declarations that he had not "come to send peace on earth" and that "a man's foes *shall be* they of his own household" (Matthew 10:34, 36) confirm that his intent of the first advent was to save Israel from their sins and from their enemies at the second. This confirms PT where the prophets wrote in the eschatological

---

[34] *John Darby's Synopsis:* "The result of this intervention of God is that the dispersed of Israel, hitherto divided into two peoples, are gathered together in the earth, reunited under one Head, as one nation." s.v. Ezekiel 37.

context. An undeniable fallacy ensues in the dispensationalist's perception that Christ offered the MK at his first advent, for if that were the case it would have been necessary for Christ to come and establish peace, then subsequently vanquish Israel's enemies for those who disavowed him and were appointed to doom. It is a fallacy to maintain that God ordained the reprobate shepherds to disavow Christ and at the same time argue that their avowal to accept Christ was the prerequisite for the consummation of the MK. Even Scofield acknowledged that the OT hid the two advents in the same context,[35] which unintentionally substantiates the bifurcation of Israel's redemption and the Two House theological perception of Zechariah 10:7–9 and Hosea 2:19–23. Two House Theology affirms that Hosea and Zechariah perceive that Ephraim is corporately redeemed and then sown in the earth, and this conforms beautifully to the allusion of Ephraim as the nation bearing the fruit of the vineyard in Matthew 21:43. This perception of Ephraim as the nation bearing the fruit of the vineyard in Matthew 21:43 destroys the application of contingency used by the dispensationalists in their theory of the parenthesis, in particular in the parables of Matthew 13. When one understands that the parables of Matthew 13 pertain to the sowing of Ephraim in the earth, it becomes clear that the church is the undeniable vehicle "to raise up the tribes of Jacob, and to restore the preserved of Israel" during the entire inter-advent dispensation and not just immediately preceding the second advent as dispensationalists maintain (Isaiah 49:6).

In typical dispensationalist's fashion, through context, Vlach attempts to connect the restoration of Israel in Isaiah 49 strictly to the second advent.

> The nation Israel cannot restore itself, for it is sinful. But the Servant—who is Jesus Christ, the true Servant of Israel—can restore the nation Israel and bring blessings for the nations. Thus, this passage teaches that Jesus will restore the nation Israel

---

[35] Scofield's Reference Notes, s.v. Malachi 3:1

and bring light to the nations. He will also restore Israel to her land (Isa 49:8). The presence of the true Israelite, Jesus, does not mean that the people of Israel lose their significance.[36]

Concerning Israel, Isaiah 49:8 states "I will preserve thee, and ... cause to inherit the desolate heritages," which Vlach applied to the second advent. Yet, Isaiah 49:6 affirms that the servant is not merely meant to restore the tribes of Jacob but is given as "a light to the Gentiles" and that he is God's "salvation unto the end of the earth." Paul states that a faction of the biological descendants was appointed to disavow Christ, a consequence of the hardening of the hearts (the ESV provides a more contemporary translation).

> So I ask, did they stumble in order that they might fall? By no means! Rather through their trespass salvation has come to the Gentiles, so as to make Israel jealous. (Romans 11:11 ESV)

The only valid perception of the text is that the builders were appointed to reject Christ, so as to sow the remnant in the earth, which resulted in salvation to the gentiles, which is how Isaiah 49 must be perceived. Paul conveys two factions in Romans 11:11 concerning the biological descendants, one which stumbles on Christ (some recoverable and some doomed) and the additional faction of the gentiles. All three factions are present in Isaiah 49 when the "nation" that abhors the Servant, Christ, is grasped as Judah in contrast to Ephraim.

> And he said, It is a light thing that thou shouldest be my servant to raise up the tribes of Jacob, and to restore the preserved of Israel: I will also give thee for a light to the Gentiles, that thou mayest be my salvation unto the end of the earth. Thus saith the

---

[36] Vlach, "What Does Christ as "True Israel" Mean For the Nation of Israel?"

LORD, the Redeemer of Israel, *and* his Holy One, to him whom man despiseth, to him whom the nation abhorrcth, to a servant of rulers, Kings shall see and arise, princes also shall worship, because of the LORD that is faithful, *and* the Holy One of Israel, and he shall choose thee. (Isaiah 49:6–7)

The preserved of Israel who are restored in Isaiah 49:6 are the remnant according to the election of grace in Romans 11, while the "nation" that abhors the Servant, above, is Judah, that remains recoverable according to Paul in Romans 11 and the prophets (Isaiah 11:12–13; Jeremiah 23:5–6; Ezekiel 37:21–22); the gentiles are easily discernable. All three factions in Romans 11 are discernable in Isaiah 49. Zechariah 11, Ezekiel 34, and Micah 5 prophesy that the southern "nation" of Judah would be exiled again, and Isaiah prophesied that its consequence would be salvation to the gentiles. Darby and Scofield both unwittingly acknowledged that Zechariah 11 prophesied that the "nation" that would abhor the Servant in Isaiah 49:7 was Judah, at the first advent.[37]

In Isaiah 49 Zion cries "The LORD hath forsaken me, and my Lord hath forgotten me," which represents Ephraim (Isaiah 49:14). Zion/Ephraim is seen by the prophet as "desolate, a captive, and removing to and fro" in exile until Zion begets children to replace the others she lost to her captors (vv. 17–20), which corresponds to Hosea 2 and Zechariah 11 where Ephraim is redeemed, multiplied and then sown in the earth; the latter is conveyed by Isaiah as the children, declaring "The place is too narrow for me; make room for me to dwell in" (Isaiah 49:20 ESV). This corresponds to the fulfillment of the promise of fecundity in Genesis 48:19, 49:22 and

---

[37] *John Darby's Synopsis*: "But the shepherds of Israel arc cut off; and Christ, grieved with the wicked and corrupt people, Himself abhorred by them, leaves them to themselves to the consequences of their behaviour.", s.v. Zechariah 11; *Scofield's Reference Notes*: "The scene belongs to the first advent.... 'Beauty' (i.e. graciousness) was 'cut in sunder' . . . signifying that Judah was abandoned to the destruction foretold in Zechariah 11:1-6 and fulfilled A.D. 70." s.v. Zech 11:7.

Zechariah 10:8–9 that the nation/tribe of Ephraim would "become a multitude of nations." The blotting of sin, "once for all" (Hebrews 10:10), redeemed Ephraim/Zion and the fulfillment of the promise of fecundity is illustrated by the children who need space in Isaiah 49. This parallels with the "wife of youth," that was refused in Isaiah 54:6, who is prophesied to "break forth on the right hand and on the left" and inherit the gentiles in Isaiah 54:1–2. Paul cites Isaiah 54:1 in Galatians and connects the desolate "wife of youth that was refused" in Isaiah 54 with Jerusalem above, the mother of those who avow Christ, the Church, to include Jew and gentile.

> But Jerusalem which is above is free, which is the mother of us all. For it is written, Rejoice, *thou* barren that bearest not; break forth and cry, thou that travailest not: for the desolate hath many more children than she which hath an husband. Now we, brethren, as Isaac was, are the children of promise. (Galatians 4:26–28)

Thomas Ice acknowledged that the "Jews" dwelling in Galatia (1 Peter 1:1) had been there since the Assyrian dispersion, which would include the northern tribes of Ephraim and not merely the "Jews."

> It is clear, Peter, an apostle who was specifically called to minister to the Jews, is writing a letter to encourage Jewish believers who are in the diaspora. It makes no sense to speak of Gentile Christians as aliens living in Gentile nations. It makes good sense to speak of Jewish believers as aliens living in Gentile lands who had likely been there since their dispersion by the Assyrians and Babylonians.[38]

Like most dispensationalists, Ice fails to discern that not all Israelites are "Jews" but his acknowledgment that Peter ministered to the

---

[38] Ice, "1 Peter 2 and Replacement Theology"

descendants of the Assyrian dispersion unwittingly lends support to Paul's connection of the "Jerusalem which is above" with the "wife of youth that was refused" in Isaiah 54 as actual fulfillment and not mere allegorical circumstance. Flavius Josephus's observations that the descendants of the ten tribes were beyond the Euphrates as "an immense multitude, and not to be estimated by numbers" cannot be dismissed as irrelevant in these circumstances.[39] It was to this immense multitude that Peter ministered. They literally fulfilled the prophecy in Isaiah 49:20–21 of the children whom the woman Zion/Ephraim brings forth, ending her lamented desolation.

Dispensationalist E. W. Bullinger, like Ice, conceded that Paul addressed the Church in Galatians 4:26–28 but also omitted the historical-grammatical hermeneutic concerning the desolate "wife of youth" that was refused or divorced in Isaiah 54:6 as well as other relevant NT revelation.

> Who can read Revelation 21:10–17 without comparing its surpassing beauty and glory with Jerusalem which then was, or that now is? Those who "received the word" proclaimed by Peter (Acts 2:41; cp. 1 Thessalonians 2:13), received it by faith, and with Abraham's faith, were made blessedly free; and enjoying that wondrous liberty, they looked for "the city which hath the foundations," "Jerusalem which is above".... Jerusalem below had shed the blood of the prophets, yea, the blood of Messiah; she was in bondage to the law with all her sons; but those who received and believed the word proved themselves the true sons of the father of the faithful and looked and longed for his heavenly city, "the new Jerusalem," which the apostle could truly speak of as our mother.[40]

---

[39] Josephus, Antiquities of the Jews
[40] E W Bullinger, *The Foundations of Dispensational Truth*, (The Open Bible Trust, Kindle Edition, 2013), Kindle location 2814.

Like Ice, Bullinger sustained Paul's connection between the church and the desolate "wife of youth" that was refused in Isaiah 54 but interpreted that connection as analogous rather than literal. The allegory does not stand against the evidence that the blotting of sins of the elect of Israel also released them from the SC and made them eligible to enter into the NC.

> Know ye not, brethren, (for I speak to them that know the law,) how that the law hath dominion over a man as long as he liveth? For the woman which hath an husband is bound by the law to her husband so long as he liveth; but if the husband be dead, she is loosed from the law of her husband. So then if, while her husband liveth, she be married to another man, she shall be called an adulteress: but if her husband be dead, she is free from that law; so that she is no adulteress, though she be married to another man. Wherefore, my brethren, ye also are become dead to the law by the body of Christ; that ye should be married to another, even to him who is raised from the dead, that we should bring forth fruit unto God. (Romans 7:1–4)

Efficaciously, Christ's death, resurrection and exaltation released the descendants of the nation of Judah from the marriage to the divine being under the SC and made them eligible to be married to Christ under the NC; and in the case of the descendants of Ephraim, *the unfaithful, divorced wife,* Christ's blotting of sin made them eligible to *return to their husband* without violating Deuteronomy 24:4, which was used by the prophets to idiomatically discern Ephraim from Judah.

> Her former husband, which sent her away, may not take her again to be his wife, after that she is defiled; for that is abomination before the LORD:

and thou shalt not cause the land to sin, which the LORD thy God giveth thee for an inheritance. (Deuteronomy 24:4)

Thus saith the Lord, Where *is* the bill of your mother's divorcement, whom I have put away? or which of my creditors *is it* to whom I have sold you? Behold, for your iniquities have ye sold yourselves, and for your transgressions is your mother put away. (Isaiah 50:1)

They say, If a man put away his wife, and she go from him, and become another man's, shall he return unto her again? shall not that land be greatly polluted? but thou hast played the harlot with many lovers; yet return again to me, saith the Lord. (Jeremiah 3:1)

Consequently, Peter's ministry to the elect exiles of the dispersion commenced the fulfillment of Isaiah 54:3 that they would "break forth on the right hand and on the left" and would "inherit the Gentiles." Ephraim's desolate phase represents the time in which God pronounced them corporately divorced, proclaimed in Hosea 1 and 2 as those with "No Pity" (Lo-Ruhamah) and "Not My People" (Lo-Ammi); yet, Peter makes it clear that the reversal of their circumstance occurred at the laying of a chosen and precious cornerstone in Zion, Christ.

Wherefore also it is contained in the scripture, Behold, I lay in Sion a chief corner stone, elect, precious: and he that believeth on him shall not be confounded.... ye *are* a chosen generation, a royal priesthood, an holy nation, a peculiar people; that ye should shew forth the praises of him who hath called you out of darkness into his marvellous light:

Which in time past *were* not a people, but *are* now
the people of God: which had not obtained mercy,
but now have obtained mercy. (1 Peter 2:6, 9–10)

Peter affirms that the prophecy of the cornerstone in Zion identifies
a people, a "holy nation" that in times past were proclaimed as those
with "No Pity" (Lo-Ruhamah) and "Not My People" (Lo-Ammi).
The gentiles simply cannot be construed as "a nation" that in times
past were pronounced as such. In order to rebuke the covenantalist's
allegorical perception that Israel was replaced by the church in Hosea
2:23 and in 1 Peter 2:10, Ice maintains that the texts pertain to an
elect faction of Israel, as contrasted from those appointed to doom "to
let them know that everything promised them in the Old Testament
is being fulfilled through their faith in Jesus as their Messiah."[41] Yet,
such a perception relies upon the literal fulfillment of Hosea 2:23 as
opposed to any allegorical interpretation. Fidelity to the historical-
grammatical hermeneutic necessitates the acknowledgment that
Peter's citation of Hosea represents the literal fulfillment and is not
allegorical circumstance.

The historical-grammatical hermeneutic supports Ephraim as
the "holy nation" in 1 Peter 2:9 and the dispensationalists err in
their equivocation that the Church is not to be perceived as a nation
but as a people of all nations. Commencing with the first-century,
every biological descendant of Ephraim, saved before the foundation
of the world, and scattered throughout the world in the inter-advent
dispensation shall avow Christ and fulfill the prophecy in Isaiah
54:3 that they would "break forth on the right hand and on the
left" and that their "seed" would "inherit the Gentiles." Just as the
"seed" in Galatians 3:16, 29 conveys the plural and the singular,
the "seed" in Isaiah 54:3 conveys both the plural for the nation of
Ephraim and the singular for the Servant, Christ. It also corresponds
with the nomenclature "Israel" in Isaiah 49:3 that represents the
plural members of the nation and the singular Servant, Christ,
which even dispensationalists concede. Dispensationalists fail to

---

[41] Ice, "1 Peter 2 and Replacement Theology"

grasp that Paul's citation of Isaiah 54:1 in Galatians 4:27 pertains to Ephraim just as they fail to grasp the historical evidence that Christ inherited the gentiles at the first advent, a blessed phenomenon which fulfills Isaiah 54:3. At Christ's return, he inherits the gentiles again as witnessed in Psalms 2:8 and Revelation 11:15, which further substantiates PT in the eschatological context. The latter event accounting for "the nations of them which are saved" during the millennium in Matthew 25:31–34 and Revelation 21:24. Prior to the laying of the chosen and precious cornerstone in Zion the cities populated by the Ephraimites in Pontus, Galatia, Cappadocia, Asia, and Bithynia, are declared by God as desolate in the sense of being incapable of bringing forth the elect sons and daughters, but following Christ's advent God peopled the desolate cities with the holy nation of Ephraim in fulfillment of Isaiah 54:3. The evidence up to this juncture substantiates that no overture of presenting the MK was being made at Christ's first advent but rather, at hand was the fulfillment of the texts in Genesis, Hosea and Zechariah—an offer of salvation to go out to the gentiles and to the ends of the earth—building a multitude of nations that Christ would inherit during the inter-advent dispensation.

> And when Joseph saw that his father laid his right hand upon the head of Ephraim, it displeased him: and he held up his father's hand, to remove it from Ephraim's head unto Manasseh's head. And Joseph said unto his father, Not so, my father: for this *is* the firstborn; put thy right hand upon his head. And his father refused, and said, I know *it*, my son, I know *it:* he also shall become a people, and he also shall be great: but truly his younger brother shall be greater than he, and his seed shall become a multitude of nations. (Genesis 48:17–19)

> And *they of* Ephraim shall be like a mighty *man,* and their heart shall rejoice as through wine: yea,

their children shall see *it*, and be glad; their heart shall rejoice in the LORD I will hiss for them, and gather them; for I have redeemed them: and they shall increase as they have increased. And I will sow them among the people: and they shall remember me in far countries; and they shall live with their children, and turn again. (Zechariah 10:7–9)

The parable of the prodigal son is undoubtingly correctly interpreted by Two House theology as Ephraim returning to God, while the first born represents Judah.

And he said, A certain man had two sons: And the younger of them said to *his* father, Father, give me the portion of goods that falleth *to me*. And he divided unto them *his* living. And not many days after the younger son gathered all together, and took his journey into a far country, and there wasted his substance with riotous living. And when he had spent all, there arose a mighty famine in that land; and he began to be in want. And he went and joined himself to a citizen of that country; and he sent him into his fields to feed swine. And he would fain have filled his belly with the husks that the swine did eat: and no man gave unto him. And when he came to himself, he said, How many hired servants of my father's have bread enough and to spare, and I perish with hunger! I will arise and go to my father, and will say unto him, Father, I have sinned against heaven, and before thee, And am no more worthy to be called thy son: make me as one of thy hired servants. And he arose, and came to his father. But when he was yet a great way off, his father saw him, and had compassion, and ran, and fell on his neck, and kissed him. And the son said unto him,

Father, I have sinned against heaven, and in thy
sight, and am no more worthy to be called thy son.
But the father said to his servants, Bring forth the
best robe, and put *it* on him; and put a ring on his
hand, and shoes on *his* feet: And bring hither the
fatted calf, and kill *it;* and let us eat, and be merry:
For this my son was dead, and is alive again; he
was lost, and is found. And they began to be merry.
Now his elder son was in the field: and as he came
and drew nigh to the house, he heard musick and
dancing. And he called one of the servants, and
asked what these things meant. And he said unto
him, Thy brother is come; and thy father hath killed
the fatted calf, because he hath received him safe
and sound. And he was angry, and would not go in:
therefore came his father out, and intreated him.
And he answering said to *his* father, Lo, these many
years do I serve thee, neither transgressed I at any
time thy commandment: and yet thou never gavest
me a kid, that I might make merry with my friends:
But as soon as this thy son was come, which hath
devoured thy living with harlots, thou hast killed
for him the fatted calf. And he said unto him, Son,
thou art ever with me, and all that I have is thine. It
was meet that we should make merry, and be glad:
for this thy brother was dead, and is alive again; and
was lost, and is found. (Luke 15:11–32).

CHAPTER

FOUR

Rendering the Apocalypse of John

Before rendering the Revelation of John, the proper method of interpreting the genre of apocalyptic literature or scripture in general must be addressed. Conflict manifests in three differing methods over the "historic" rendering of Revelation: historicism, preterism and futurism. "Historic" is emphasized so as not to confuse the former three with idealism, which is an alternative method which maintains that the book does not pertain to historical phenomena; idealists interpret Revelation as representing persistent experiences common to all ages and believe it is simply symbolic.

The preterist's orientation views the Revelation as dealing with historical phenomena that took place within the first few centuries of Christ's first advent, and it must be emphasized here that they themselves are not in complete agreement with what the symbolism represents. There are endless debates on which emperors are indicated as the seven kings in Revelation 17, and rightfully so because great conflict arises when trying to reconcile any seven Roman emperors with the seven kings mentioned.

The futurist's orientation interprets the Revelation as predominately revealing phenomena that will happen just prior to Christ's return and they too have difficulty agreeing on exactly how the prophecies unfold. Their guesses as to the identity of Babylon run the gambit of the resurgent Roman Empire, the Catholic Church, Iraq, the United States, etc.

Historicism views the Revelation in the continuous-historical approach; it views the Revelation as the unfolding of historical phenomena and entities, permitting recapitulation and interludes of parenthetical matter, that stretch from John's time until the eternal estate. The variances within Preterism and Futurism were mentioned because, ironically, the greatest criticism against historicism has been that it has its own variations. As Leon Morris stated,

> Historicist views also labour under the serious disadvantage of failing to agree. If the main points of the subsequent history are in fact foreshadowed it should be possible to identify them with tolerable certainty, otherwise what is the point of it?[1]

George Eldon Ladd criticized historicism in the same manner when he stated,

> Obviously, such an interpretation could lead to confusion, for there are no fixed guidelines as to what historical events are meant.[2]

Disagreements or variances on all details over the apocalypse trouble preterists as well as futurists, so Morris's objection hardly perseveres under scrutiny. All the paradigms, including historicism, have guidelines by which they interpret fulfilled or unfulfilled prophecy; consequently, Ladd's objection to the historicism mode was clearly shortsighted. Certainly, without fixed guidelines any attempt to interpret prophecy is futile. Ladd and Morris use their own guidelines to affirm that the preterist's interpretation of the kings of Revelation 17 leads to conflict, which diminishes the preterist's guidelines.

---

[1] Leon Morris, *The Book of Revelation-An Introduction and Commentary* (Wm. B. Eerdmans Pub. Co., 1987), 19.
[2] George Eldon Ladd, *A Commentary on the Revelation of John* (Wm. B. Eerdmans Pub. Co., 1972), 11.

Preterists interpreters usually apply the verse to the succession of Roman emperors.... This interpretation makes no sense.... The problem is altogether avoided if John does not mean to designate a succession of individual kings or emperors, but a succession of kingdoms.[3]

The most significant and generally accepted guideline is that the kings in Revelation 17 persecute God's chosen people, a historical phenomenon which proponents of all paradigms agree upon, thus qualifying it as a fixed guideline to render the apocalypse. Yet, attempting to render the kings by this guideline as seven, nay, eight emperors cannot abide without *ad hoc* explanations. This unfavorable judgment of the preterist's view of the seven, nay, eight kings by Ladd and Morris is supported by historicism whether the two realize it or not, but for not quite the same reasons. In support of the historicist's guidelines, futurist E.W. Bullinger also interpreted the kings as successive dominant world powers. The nouns of Revelation 17:9-10 are meant as appositives (seven heads renamed seven mountains and etcetera).

Five are fallen, the[48] one (the sixth) is (at this stage of the Vision), the other (the seventh), is not yet come. If this be interpreted of Gentile Dominion at the future point of the Vision referred to by the Angel; then, as to the dominions, the five will have fallen: (1) Babylon, (2) Medo-Persia, (3) Greece, (4) Rome, (5) Mohammedan. The sixth will be the Kingdom of the Beast, (7) the seventh will be the Kingdom of our Lord and of His Christ.[4]

---

[3] Ibid., 229.
[4] E.W. Bullinger, *Commentary on Revelation* (Grand Rapids, MI: Christian Classics Ethereal Library), 336.

Nevertheless, Bullinger's rendition of the kings also fails to agree with other futurists. The clue that the eighth king somehow existed before John's time but did not exist in John's time and yet will exist again in the future from John's time has produced the most *ad hoc* explanations and disagreements in preterism as well as in futurism. The point being, the issue is not that guidelines do not exist in all the paradigms, but the question becomes, what are the superior guidelines that can reconcile the Revelation to harmonize with a history that will not lead to further variances?

Morris and Ladd have applied "classic prophecy" or general prophecy as a guideline, which historicist Jon Paulien defines as "contemporary perspectives" that "are mixed with a universal, future perspective" in his essay *The End of Historicism? Reflections on the Adventist Approach to Biblical Apocalyptic—Part One.*

> It was argued that general prophecy, because of its dual dimensions, may at times be susceptible to dual fulfillments or foci where local and contemporary perspectives are mixed with a universal, future perspective.[5]

Classic prophecy utilized expressions of imminence concerning impending judgment in the same context with distant eschatological phenomena, without chronological notation; the technique has come to be called prophetic telescoping.

> Another peculiar feature of prophetic literature is called "telescoping".... The reason for it has to do with the perspective of the prophet. As he looks into the future and sees a series of prophetic events, they appear to him as if they are in immediate sequence. It is like looking down a mountain range

[5] Jon Paulien, "The End of Historicism? Reflections on the Adventist Approach to Biblical Apocalyptic—Part One," *Journal of the Adventist Theological Society*, 14/2 (Fall 2003), 15–43.

and viewing three peaks, one behind the other, each sequentially higher than the one in front of it. The peaks look like they are right up against each other because the person viewing them cannot see the valleys that separate them.[6]

Ladd affirms this dual focus in the introduction of his commentary on the Revelation.

the prophets had two foci in the prophetic perspective: the events of the present and the immediate future, and the ultimate eschatological event. These two are held in a dynamic tension often without chronological distinction, for the main purpose of prophecy is not to give a program or chart of the future, but to let the light of the eschatological consummation fall on the present (II Pet. 1:19). Thus in Amos' prophecy the impending historical judgment of Israel at the hands of Assyria was called the Day of the Lord (Amos 5:18, 27), and the eschatological salvation of Israel will also occur in that day (9:11).[7]

Morris and Ladd, for the most part, interpret the Revelation through classic prophecy, as if the apocalypse focuses strictly on the circumstances in John's time and the time immediately preceding Christ's return, which conveys that the book has little relevance for the people of God living during the interim. This creates tension with the promise of blessings for those who read and "keep those things which are written therein" (Revelation 1:3). If the book has nothing to say about the lives of people who live during the interim—there is nothing to be kept. In his rejection of historicism Ladd verified

---

[6] Dr. David R. Reagan, "The Interpretation of Prophecy," *Lamb & Lion Ministries website*, http://christinprophecy.org/articles/the-interpretation-of-prophecy/,
[7] Ladd, A Commentary on the Revelation of John, 13.

that he viewed the book as classic prophecy by conflating preterism and futurism.

> Therefore, we conclude that the correct method of interpreting the Revelation is a blending of the Preterist and the Futurist methods. The beast is both Rome and the eschatological Antichrist—and, we might add, any demonic power which the church must face in her entire history.[8]

Such a view is clearly taken from classic prophecy and proves inadequate as the guidelines of preterism and futurism are irreconcilable, worlds apart. The most salient conflict comes from the failure to see that the heads/mountains/kings upon the beasts in Revelation 17 as appositives. Are the kings to represent the fall and rise of prominent worldly individual kings merely at the first and/or second advent as preterism and futurism leads us to believe—or are they intended to portray the continuous-historical approach of the rise and fall of worldly kingdoms prior to John's time and leading up onto the second advent of Christ? Clearly the former view is fraught with fallacies, one, yielding that the four kings in Daniel 7 represent successive kingdoms but, then, rendering the seven kings in the Revelation as individuals, thus, devaluing the correspondence between Daniel and Revelation. Here we have the advantage of Daniel's explanations of beasts as successive dominant world powers, which is the object of this work as it progresses (Daniel 7:17). The Revelation complements Daniel, which reveals the beasts/kings as dominant world powers and challenges the preterist and futurist guidelines that tend to interpret the mountains, renamed heads and kings, as individuals in Revelation 17. They are forced to interpret the kings as individuals because of the problems incurred by time constraints caused by their inappropriate foci of establishing these prophetic events either in the distant past or into the far future. The continuous-historical guidelines cultivate the complementary nature

---

[8] Ibid., 14.

of Daniel and Revelation without such restraints and for this reason represents the true hermeneutic in rendering the apocalypse of John as a unique genre in contrast to classic prophecy: the apocalyptic genre. The Revelation has something to say about the lives of all the people who live during the interim between the advents when the mountains, renamed heads and kings, are perceived as successive dominant world powers.

Ladd is simply in error; historicism has "fixed guidelines as to what historical events are meant," which are used to determine the identity of the five dominant kingdoms that had fallen prior to John's perspective. Morris clearly employed some of the same guidelines observed by historicism in asserting that the five kings who had fallen as: "Old Babylonian, Assyrian, Neo-Babylonian, Persian and the Graeco-Macedonian,"[9] empires. It is evident that such a rendering must be determined by some "fixed guidelines" and Ladd verbalizes such guidelines in his book when he deciphers the great harlot as one who,

> seduces the nations and persecutes the saints finds her support from the beast who appears in history in succession of secular, godless kingdoms; five belong to past history; a sixth kingdom—Rome—ruled the world when John wrote.[10]

The only conclusion that makes sense is that Ladd and Morris's criticisms against historicism are contradictory. Like historicism, they attempt to reconcile the heads/mountains/kings in the Revelation with history through a set of guidelines which are not completely different from those employed by historicism; they too see the kings as consecutive dominant world powers, some of which even coinciding with Ladd's rendition. The problem that arises concerning guidelines or presuppositions is not that guidelines do not exist in historicism or the other paradigms but that proper

---

[9] Morris, The Book of Revelation-An Introduction and Commentary, 204.
[10] Ladd, A Commentary on the Revelation of John, 229.

usage must be wisely discerned. The guidelines of Ladd and Morris are incipiently flawed because they both fail to grasp that John's perspective was not from the first-century but rather from the distant future, *the day of the Lord*, preceding Christ's return, which shall be explained presently. Ladd makes a salient mistake with his guidelines through the misapprehension that "secular" kingdoms existed in the distant past when they are a modern aberrant; his guideline is an anachronism. Consequently, the rejection of historicism and its guidelines cannot be sustained in the common objections that its proponents are not in complete agreement when the same can be confirmed concerning preterism and futurism.

An in-depth analysis of the genre of Daniel and the Revelation must conclude that both books are contrasted from classic prophecy as they prophesy phenomena during the intervening time betwixt the prophets and the eschatological consummation. Ladd, not too ironically, moves towards historicism in his assertion that the horn broken without hands in Daniel 8:9 was the historical person of Antiochus Epiphanes who lived some three-hundred plus years after Daniel;[11] such an assertion pertains to the intervening time betwixt the time of Daniel and the eschatological consummation. When we consider that Christ affirmed the abomination of desolation spoken of in Daniel as yet future (Matthew 24:15) then we have an even greater time span of events covered by Daniel and Ladd's view of Daniel 8 is called into question. Christ provided one of the guidelines upon which historicism is founded upon in Matthew 24:15; the apocalyptic genre is to be contrasted from classic prophecy as it anticipates intervening phenomena betwixt the two foci Ladd suggested. Matthew 24:15 exposes Ladd's deficiency in attempting to blend preterism and futurism and in his use of such a perverted methodology to explain the apocalypse of John. Moreover, in Daniel 9 the prophet is given additional data concerning the "vision" of Daniel 8 which would subsequently confirm that the desecration of the temple in the vision was fulfilled by the Romans and not Antiochus Epiphanes. Ladd was compelled to concede this by

---

[11] Ibid., 230

acknowledging that the desecration in Daniel 9 pertains to the Romans.

> "The people of the prince who is to come shall destroy the city and the sanctuary" may well refer to the utter destruction of Jerusalem and its temple in 70 A D by. Titus Vespasian, who later became the emperor of Rome 'To the end' of the destruction, war and desolation will continue.[12]

Ladd makes a common mistake in refusing to acknowledge that the vision of Daniel 8 is resolved through the information given in chapter 9. The common refusal to acknowledge that the vision in Daniel 8 is resolved in the next chapter has led to erroneous interpretations of these chapters by Ladd and others. Ladd, as a historical-premillennialist, rejected historicism but unintentionally held the continuous-historical perception of Daniel in his interpretation that the Romans fulfilled prophecy in Daniel 9. His interpretation concedes phenomena and entities from the prophet's time that reach down to the time when the saints possess the kingdom (Daniel 7:22), which again, supports the guidelines of historicism. This is reinforcement that the Revelation is interpreted not as classic prophecy but through the unique genre of apocalyptic literature, as is Daniel. Apocalyptic prophecy views history as the continuous unfolding of events from Daniel's or John's time until the consummation of the kingdom of God, albeit the Revelation is uniquely positioned from a future perspective to look backwards.

One of the guidelines that cannot be overlooked in understanding the apocalypse is that the perspective from which the phenomenon and entities are being viewed by John is the future. The sixth king of the beast in Revelation 17 is the kingdom ruling at the time of John's vision. If John's vision relates circumstances in the first-century then pagan Rome represents the sixth king. A fallacy results

---

[12] George Eldon Ladd, *The Last Things: An Eschatology for Laymen*, (Wm. B. Eerdmans Pub. Co., 1978), 61.

in perceiving the papacy as any king prior or during that time. Employing the guideline that the beasts persecute God's people, Egypt and Assyria are the earliest of the five kingdoms that fell if the sixth, dominant world power in Revelation 17:10 was fulfilled by pagan Rome, but Daniel is silent on these kingdoms. Here, the relevance that the beasts in Daniel are seen again in the Revelation cannot be dismissed; John's sea-beast is a composite of the beasts in Daniel. This demonstrates concurrence between the books, which has led to the reevaluation of the traditional historicist's perception of the sea-beast and the two-horned beast. By the mid-nineteenth-century Protestant disestablishment had all but succeeded in the west and the power of the papacy had all but abated which led to the reexamination of the traditional interpretation of sea-beast and two-horned beast in Revelation 13. Progressive revelation could no longer dismiss the fact that the rise of America had led to the French Revolution that ended the twelve-hundred and sixty year reign of the papacy and these facts fit precisely with the wounding prophesied in Revelation 13:3. This led to the progressive revelation that John's sea-beast was the papacy and the two-horned beast was Protestant America in place of the traditional historicist's interpretation that the former pertained to Rome's conversion to Christianity and the latter was the rise of the papacy. Noted historicist, theologian and editor of the *Review and Herald*, Uriah Smith wrote concerning this change.

> It was at the time when this beast went into captivity, or was killed with the sword (verse 10), or had one of its heads wounded to death (verse 3), that John saw the two-horned beast coming up.... Can anyone doubt what nation was actually "coming up" in 1798? Certainly it must be admitted that the United States of America is the only power that meets the specifications of the prophecy on this point of chronology.[13]

---

[13] Uriah Smith, *Daniel and Revelation*, (Review and Herald Publishing, 2009), 229.

Progressive revelation has also revealed that Daniel's little horn was also John's sea-beast, supported in their parallelism: they both came out of pagan Rome, spoke "against the most High" (Daniel 7:25) were diverse from the other beasts, had the same span of time given them to persecute the saints and both are "given to the burning flame" (Daniel 7:11; Revelation 19:20) at Christ's return.[14] Again, the relevance that the beasts in Daniel are seen again in the Revelation cannot be dismissed; John's sea-beast is a composite of the beasts in Daniel. With the realization that Daniel's beasts can be reconciled to John's the door is opened to the understanding that the five kings that had fallen in Revelation 17:10 commenced with Babylon, not Egypt, and that John's perspective was not from that of the first-century but rather, from the future eschatological phenomena of the Day of the Lord.

With the aforesaid in mind, there are four beasts in the Revelation, one of which is the image of the sea-beast (Revelation 11–20): first, the sea-beast (Revelation 13:1); second, the lamb like beast (Revelation 13:11); third, the image of the sea-beast; and the fourth, the scarlet-colored beast (Revelation 11:7: 17:8, 11). One of the beasts is resurrected, which reveals that two of the beasts are actually the same dynastic kingdom that has a "is not" span, making but three beasts to determine. Considering Daniel's little horn is John's sea-beast we are left with but two beasts in the Revelation to identify, in addition to Daniel's five beasts, which comes to seven, the exact number of kings in Revelation 17:10. The progressive historicist's rendition of the sea-beast and the two-horned beast conforms to actual history as understood by the mid-nineteenth-century and more precisely parallels Daniel, while the traditionalist's view is found wanting.

The traditional historicists' view that the sixth king was pagan Rome can only be sustained in abstracts, while Daniel and John relate observable dynastic regimes. This supports the concept that the eighth king ruled prior to the sixth king and disqualifies the notion

---

[14] "From this comparison it will appear that the little horn and the leopard beast symbolize the same power." Ibid., 226.

that the sixth king's power was interrupted, as earlier historicists had reckoned. The only determination that works is that the five fallen kings commenced with Babylon, which makes Rome the fourth king/kingdom and the papacy the fifth king/kingdom—the sea-beast in the Revelation. Certainly, the papacy followed Rome—and "was" prior to the sixth king when determining the papacy as the fifth, one of the five that were fallen. The older, traditional historicist's have attempted to hold the misapprehension that Rome qualified as the entity that "was and is not" by a wound inflicted by Christ and is not to be healed again until the papacy interacts with an international empire. It was Christ, not Rome, that suffered the deadly wound at the first advent. The traditional view pales in comparison with progressive historicism's view that the wounding of papacy occurred with the rise of America and disestablishment. The older historicist's determination that the sixth king was Rome cannot be taken seriously today. John picked-up where Daniel left-off to unveil two more kingdoms that persecute God's people, bringing the number of these kingdoms to seven, the complete, full number of the kingdoms that subjugate the covenant people of God in Revelation 17:10–11.

Contrary to the opinions of Ladd and Morris concerning historicism there is remarkable agreement within the proponents of historicism; there is overwhelming agreement concerning the fulfillment of the five beasts in Daniel, including the little horn that rises out of the fourth beast. Historicism holds that Daniel prophesied that Babylon (the lion) would fall and be succeeded by the Persian empire (the bear), which fell and was succeeded by the Greek empire (the leopard) that fell and was succeeded by the pagan Roman empire (the diverse beast) that fell and was succeeded by a fifth dominant world power/beast that persecutes the saints. Historicism holds that the fifth beast in Daniel, the little horn, was fulfilled by a loose federation of western nations under the dominion and worldly power of the papacy "over all kindreds, and tongues, and nations" (Revelation 13:7). Herbert W. Armstrong is a typical example of a historicists who wrote,

We read in history that the popes were accepted as the "Vicars of Christ," which means "IN PLACE OF Christ." The teaching was that the Second Coming of Christ had occurred — Christ had returned to earth, as KING of kings and as LORD of lords, in the person of the popes. The millennium had begun. For the entire 1260 years, the emperors accepted the popes as such, ruling the nations with a "rod of iron" as Christ is to do WHEN He really comes. Consequently they acknowledged the supreme religious power of the popes. The Church was organized as a GOVERNMENT.... It embodied CHURCH government, and it also was a STATE, or civil government, always occupying a certain amount of territory over which it, alone, ruled as an independent sovereign state— in addition to actually ruling over the vast civil kingdom.... Most nations send ambassadors to the Vatican, just as they do to the United States, or to Italy, Britain or the USSR.[15]

Details vary, but historicists hold that the papacy fulfills the little horn in Daniel 7 and through progressive revelation have come to regard it also as the sea-beast in the Revelation, which exercised power over the Western nations up until the time of the Reformation when the nations started breaking away from its authority; it suffered a deadly wound. The authority of the papacy was ultimately broken by Napoleon when he abducted the pope and confiscated his lands in 1798 AD, fulfilling the prophecy of the deadly wound in Revelation 13:3. It was the rise of the two-horned beast, the sixth king in the sequence conveyed in Revelation 17:10, that broke the power of the papacy. This is the perspective from which John saw the

---

[15] Herbert W. Armstrong, "Who is the Beast?" 1960, *Herbert W. Armstrong Library.com*, http://www.hwalibrary.com/cgi-bin/get/hwa.cgi?action=getbklet&InfoID=1325342114

harlot woman riding the scarlet-colored beast. The truth is that historicism had been the dominate method of interpreting prophecy prior to the others. It was the method used by the early reformers, such as Martin Luther, who had witnessed the iniquities of the papal institution and who viewed the Pope as the fulfillment of the prophecies of the Antichrist. Today, most people are uninformed about the history of the papacy and cannot appreciate the religious freedoms we enjoy today as the outcome of the suffering of thousands of martyrs throughout the ages who stood against the institution and were persecuted and martyred. Historicism commenced to be marginalized by the beginning of the nineteenth-century due to its abuse by some in setting times for the return of Christ, which obviously did not come to fruition. It is ironic that preterism does exactly the same thing through a hyper-allegorical method, yet it seems to be on the rise in recent times.

At this juncture it becomes unsustainable that the perspective of John was from the first-century or that the sixth king, below, was fulfilled by the pagan Roman empire. The sixth king/beast is ruling at the time John sees the vision in Revelation 17, and when Daniel and John's prophecies are reconciled the seven beasts correspond to the seven kings, of which we are told,

> And there are seven kings: five are fallen, and one is,
> and the other is not yet come; and when he cometh,
> he must continue a short space. (Revelation 17:10)

When the visions of Daniel and John are reconciled the little horn in Daniel is the same beast John perceives rising "up out of the sea", which is the fifth head/king, above. The next and sixth king is definitely the two-horned beast in Revelation 13. And as stated, above, there is universal agreement in historicism that the little horn in Daniel was fulfilled by the papacy during the dark ages; this is the *sine qua non* of historicism—which makes John's perspective our day, as the papacy's hegemony "over all kindreds, and tongues, and nations" (Revelation 13:7) has long since passed.

To lend support to this assertion that John's perspective is relatively from our time and not the first-century, we should examine the controversy over the meaning of the phrase τη κυριακη ἡμερα or "the Lord's day" in Revelation 1:10. The controversy is over John's intent in his use of "the day of the Lord"; was he using an archaic Hebrew idiom or employing a novel expression for his day referring to "the first day of the week" or Sunday? In support of the former the futurist Jerome Smith was compelled to write,

> However, such an interpretation is open to the objection that (1) such a meaning has no relevance to the context; (2) the term is never so applied in Scripture, where the day of Christian worship is uniformly called the "first day of the week"; (3) such an interpretation does not agree with the Patristic understanding of the verse; (4) the interpretation is a reading back into the text of a term subsequently applied to Sunday. The term "Lord's day" is better understood as John's way of expressing the common Hebrew term "day of the Lord," in a manner in Greek which places the emphasis upon "Lord's" (by placing it in an initial position) in the same manner as the Hebrew expression places emphasis upon "Lord" (by placing it in the final position) in "day of the Lord." Supposing the expression refers to Sunday cannot account for the presence of the Greek article "the" used in the expression. When the article is lacking, there are several possible explanations to account for the fact, but when an interpretation cannot account for the presence of the Greek article, the interpretation stands self-condemned (J. B. Smith, Comm. on Revelation, Appendix 5, p. 320). The expression "on the Lord's day" would better be translated "in the Lord's day," as a reference to this specific prophetic time period.

The Greek preposition *en* is more usually rendered "in," only once in Revelation is it translated "on," in the expression "on the earth," Revelation 5:13. Everywhere else where *en* is followed by the word "day" it is rendered "in" (Revelation 2:13. 9:6. 10:7. 11:6. 18:8). Understanding this term to refer to the "day of the Lord" emphasizes that the events which transpire in the third division of the book ("things which shall be hereafter") are events which take place during the "day of the Lord," a future time which begins at the Great Tribulation and concludes with the judgment of the Great White Throne at the end of the Millennium, and specifically ties in the prophecies of this book with the rest of Scripture relating to this coming day.[16]

There are arguments that John's intent in Revelation 1:10 was the use of the novel expression just coming into practice meaning Sunday worship, but as Smith related, such an expression has no relevance in the theme of the apocalypse, which is to reveal the eschatological Day of the Lord. The correspondence between Daniel and Revelation reveals that John's perspective is from our time, the time of the sixth king, the two-horned beast of Revelation 13:11–18, which will be substantiated in the succeeding chapter as Protestant America. Grasping that John's vision transcended time is not a great leap from grasping that Ezekiel's visions transcended space.

> And it came to pass in the sixth year, in the sixth month, in the fifth day of the month, as I sat in mine house.... Then I beheld, and lo a likeness as the appearance of fire.... And he put forth the form of an hand, and took me by a lock of mine head; and the spirit lifted me up between the earth and

---

[16] Jerome Smith, *The New Treasury of Scripture Knowledge*, (Nashville TN: Thomas Nelson Publishers, 1992), s.v. "Not Sunday."

the heaven, and brought me in the visions of God
to Jerusalem. (Ezekiel 8:1–3)

Ezekiel was transported geographically by the spirit and since
prophecy does concern the future, it is evident that John's vision was
given the additional dimension of a future perspective, which is why
it requires wisdom to discern: "And here is the mind which hath
wisdom" (Revelation 17:9). John's perspective is not from the first-
century but from the future Day of the Lord surveying events past,
and the future to come. The evidence above exposes the inadequacies
of preterism, futurism and reevaluates the interpretations of
historicism concerning the events following the wounding of the
papacy at disestablishment. In pursuing this reevaluation, the correct
rendering of the horsemen of the seven seals and the locusts of
the fifth trumpet comes to fruition. The Revelation is replete with
Hebrew idioms associated with eschatological events concerning
tribulations upon God's people by the reprobate, followed by their
deliverance and termination of their enemies. There are idioms in the
Revelation concerning the earth, sun, moon and stars that are clearly
associated with the extraordinary phenomena of the eschatological
Day of the Lord. The call for the mountains and the rocks to fall on
men who hide themselves from the wrath of God is clearly associated
with the Day of the Lord. The devastation of Babylon is clearly
associated with the Day of the Lord. The sounding of trumpets
is associated with the Day of the Lord. The conflagration of the
earth is associated with the Day of the Lord. The destruction of
sinners, the punishment of the nations, the restoration of Israel and
the consummation of God's kingdom on earth are all associated
with the Day of the Lord and, most significantly, the locusts of the
fifth trumpet are associated with the Day of the Lord. When the
locusts of the fifth trumpet are interpreted in the proper context of
the eschatological Day of the Lord, then the traditional historicist's
rendering of the seven seals fails. Under scrutiny the seven seals and

seven bowls depict eschatological events concerning trials upon God's people in the time of the end, which historicists George McCready Price affirms as our time and not John's, which is established in the following chapters.

Identifying the Two-Horned Beast

Identifying the two-horned beast that rises out of the earth can only be accomplished under the right set of guidelines, some of which were analyzed in the previous chapter. It was demonstrated that the application of only the historicist's guidelines delivers the greatest harmony when interpreting the beasts of Daniel and the beasts in the Revelation. One of those guidelines determines that the beasts in Daniel and Revelation cannot be construed as mere individuals but as successive dominant world powers.

> In ch. xvii. 9, it is said, that the seven heads are seven mountains, on which the woman sits, and seven kings. It is clear as day, that there is not a double signification ascribed here to the seven heads, but that the second only serves as an explanation of the first. Even Bengel remarks, "It is certainly no satisfactory exposition, which takes a particular symbol in two quite different significations." Now, in the symbolism of Scripture generally, and especially of the Apocalypse, mountains uniformly denote, not particular kings, but kingdoms—see on ch. viii. 8. The kings, therefore, are not individuals, but ideal persons, personifications of kingdoms, the king of

Babylon, of Rome, &c. Such phraseology occurs very frequently in the higher style of prophecy.[1]

Both preterists and futurists acknowledge that the beasts in Daniel do not represent individuals but successive regimes that go forth to conquer, but they alter the guideline when it comes to the little horn of Daniel, which kingdom they force into the past or future. Preterist Kenneth Gentry maintains that the Revelation veers from Daniel's vision of the beasts/kingdoms.

> John actually reworks and reapplies OT verses, particularly from Daniel, his second leading source (behind Ezekiel). For instance, note that Daniel's image involves four successive, distinct beasts (Dan 7:3). And these are counted seriatim: "first," "second," third (implied), and "fourth" (Dan 7:4–7). Whereas John's beast is one beast: "a beast" (Revelation 13:1). And his one beast is even a compound that employs only three of Daniel's four beasts: leopard, bear, and lion (Revelation. 13:2).... Clearly Revelation changes much regarding Daniel's imagery.[2]

The vindication that Daniel was uniform and that the little horn also represents a regime and not some individual, overthrows the preterist and futurist's paradigms. As stated earlier, both modalities must reconcile time elements in their interpretations and because they either start in the distant past or want to push things off into the far future they are forced to perceive the kings in Revelation 17 as individuals rather than being able to successfully reconcile the kings as kingdoms. The continuous-historical guidelines hold the

[1] Ernst Wilhelm Hengstenberg, *The Revelation of St John, Forgotten Books* (vol. 2, Edinburgh: T. & T. Clark, 38 George Street, 1852), 75.
[2] Kenneth L. Gentry, Jr., "Daniel's Beast and Revelation," *Postmillennialism Worldview.com*, (*PMT 2015-058*), https://postmillennialismtoday. com/2015/05/13/daniels-beasts-and-revelation/

complementary nature of Daniel and Revelation and for this reason represents the true hermeneutic in rendering the apocalypse of John. The Revelation has something to "keep" in all the lives of the people of God who live during the interim between the advents when the mountains, renamed heads and kings, are perceived as successive dominant world powers. The guidelines of preterism and futurism produce tremendous tension concerning the blessing for "he that readeth, and they that hear the words of this prophecy, and keep those things which are written therein" (Revelation 1:3) when the people of God have nothing to "keep" because the things written therein do not pertain to them, as in preterism and futurism.

The *sine qua non* of historicism is the creed that the papacy represents the antichrist and through progressive revelation it has come to view the sea-beast in Revelation and the little horn in Daniel 7 as the same entity: the papacy. Because of this view historicism is often credited to Protestantism. But under greater scrutiny historicism can be viewed as having its roots some centuries before with such men as the tenth-century bishop Arnulf of Orléans who applied the prophecy of the man of sin in 2 Thessalonians 2:3–9 to the papacy.

> Looking at the actual state of the papacy, what do we behold? John [XII.] called Octavian, wallowing in the sty of filthy concupiscence, conspiring against the sovereign whom he had himself recently crowned; then Leo [VIII.] the neophyte, chased from the city by this Octavian; and that monster himself, after the commission of many murders and cruelties, dying by the hand of an assassin. Next we see the deacon Benedict, though freely elected by the Romans, carried away captive into the wilds of Germany by the new Caesar [Otho I.] and his pope Leo. Then a second Caesar [Otho II.], greater in arts and arms than the first [?], succeeds; and in his absence Boniface, a very monster of iniquity, reeking

with the blood of his predecessor, mounts the throne of Peter. True, he is expelled and condemned; but only to return again, and redden his hands with the blood of the holy bishop John [XIV.]. Are there, indeed, any bold enough to maintain that the priests of the Lord over all the world are to take their law from monsters of guilt like these - men branded with ignominy, illiterate men, and ignorant alike of things human and divine.... What would you say of such a one, when you behold him sitting upon the throne glittering in purple and gold? Must he not be the "Antichrist, sitting in the temple of God, and showing himself as God?" Verily such a one lacketh both wisdom and charity; he standeth in the temple as an image, as an idol, from which as from dead marble you would seek counsel.[3]

Historicists agree that the beasts in Daniel 7 represent Babylon, the lion, that fell and was succeeded by the Persian empire, the bear, which fell and was succeeded by the Greek empire, the leopard, that fell and was succeeded by the pagan Roman empire, the diverse beast, that disintegrated and was succeeded by the division of its provinces depicted as ten horns upon the fourth beast in Daniel,[4] out

---

[3] Speech by Archbishop Arnulf of Orleans (+1003AD), Synod of Verzy in 991 AD; (Schaff's, *History of the Christian Church*, vol. 4), 290-292.

[4] The symbolism of the number 10 is conveyed by Jack Wellman: "The number 10 seems to reflect God's authority or God's governmental rule over the affairs of mankind. This is seen elsewhere as in the 10 elders that were placed in most of the city gates of Israel (Ruth 4:2) so the number 10 also seems to represents man's responsibility of obedience to God's law. Such a number seems to indicate the law, responsibility and a completeness of order in both divine and human structures of society. Some scholars see 10 as the number of divine perfection." Jack Wellman, "What Does the Number Ten (10) Mean or Represent in the Bible?" *Patheos.com*, (October 4, 2014), http://www.patheos.com/blogs/christiancrier/2014/10/04/what-does-the-number-ten-10-mean-or-represent-in-the-bible/,

of which the little horn, the papacy, rises. Through the *sine qua non* of historicism the dragon in Revelation 12 is easily perceived as the personification of Satan (Revelation 20:2) and of pagan Rome that bruises the heel of the seed of the woman in Genesis 3:15, Christ, and who "stood before the woman ... to devour her child as soon as it was born" who was the "man child, who was to rule all nations with a rod of iron" (Revelation 12:4–5). Christ reveals his mother in the gospel of Matthew.

> Then one said unto him, Behold, thy mother and thy brethren stand without, desiring to speak with thee. But he answered and said unto him that told him, Who is my mother? and who are my brethren? And he stretched forth his hand toward his disciples, and said, Behold my mother and my brethren! For whosoever shall do the will of my Father which is in heaven, the same is my brother, and sister, and mother. (Matthew 12:47:50)

The church is easily perceived as the woman in Genesis 3:15 according to Matthew, above, those doing the will of God at Christ's first advent, which pagan Rome immediately attempted to eradicate. Rome was in league with the seed of the serpent (John 8:44) or, in other words, those who sat upon the seat of Moses desiring to crucify Christ according to the NT, which disqualifies the latter as the woman in Revelation 12. The dragon is cast to the earth in Revelation 12, which is Christ's testimony in the gospel of Luke.

> And the seventy returned again with joy, saying, Lord, even the devils are subject unto us through thy name. And he said unto them, I beheld Satan as lightning fall from heaven. Behold, I give unto you power to tread on serpents and scorpions, and over all the power of the enemy: and nothing shall by any means hurt you. Notwithstanding in this rejoice

not, that the spirits are subject unto you; but rather rejoice, because your names are written in heaven. (Luke 10:17–20)

The power that is in Christ was taken to the nations and the pagan, demonic strongholds were cast down in fulfillment of Luke, above.

Revelation 12 also maintains that the woman/church is persecuted for a period of a thousand two-hundred and threescore days by the dragon who was cast to the earth, at which time God makes a place for her and feeds her in the wilderness. Historicist Oral E. Collins expounds on the "year-day" principle.

> One of the more controversial principles of prophetic interpretation is the "year-day" principle. This is the principle whereby chronological designations such as "day," "week," or "month" are understood to be used symbolically. This interpretation presupposes that "day" or its derivative multiples used as symbols means "year" or corresponding multiples of years, so that one "day" means one year, one "week" means seven years, and so forth. The year-day principle is explicitly indicated in several old Testament texts (cited below) and is commonly applied to the 'seventy weeks" prophecy of Daniel 9, but is often rejected in the interpretation of the Apocalypse.[5]

This is the same amount of time the sea-beast makes war with the saints, which is a thousand two hundred and threescore days, being the same as forty or two months. By the fifth-century the church had developed into five episcopal Sees with control of the churches within their dominions (Sees comes from the word *sedes*, meaning "chair"): Rome, Alexandria, Antioch, Jerusalem, and Constantinople. By the next century the Roman See ascended while the others diminished,

---

[5] Oral E. Collins, Ph.D, "The Interpretation of Biblical Prophecy," *Historicism. com*, (2001), http://www.historicism.com/Collins/interp.htm

the former provoking the monarchies that were once the Roman empire to wield their civil power against any that did not submit to its ecclesiastic authority, just as the Nicene Christianity was made the state religion of the Roman Empire.

> These ten kings should be looked for in the territory of the western empire of Rome only. "The ten horns of the fourth empire must none of them be sought for in the realms of the third, second, or first, but exclusively in the realm of the fourth, or in the territory peculiar to ROME, and which had never formed part either of the Grecian, Medo-Persian, or Babylonian empires." The master mind of Sir Isaac Newton perceived this long ago.[6]

This marriage between ecclesiastic and civil power, or the establishment of national religion is the *sine qua non* of the beasts or seven kings in Daniel and the Revelation, which is essentially one of the objects of this essay. In the sixth-century the Paulicians were one such group who fostered a pattern of dissidence, leading the way for others to depart the dominions controlled by the Roman church in remote areas outside of its control; a covert exodus which occurred for the next twelve-hundred and sixty years, until the Roman church's power was broken by the Protestant movement. Under scrutiny, the accusations of heresy by the established national church against such people as the Paulicians, Albigenses, Cathars, Waldenses and the Anabaptists do not prevail; in truth, it was these people who maintained primitive Christianity. It was these people who rejected the marriage of state and religion, the violation of their conscience, the practice of pagan rituals, the opulence of the church and numerous other defilements the Roman church had embraced by their fornication with the kings of the earth. It was these people who fulfill the prophecy of the woman in the wilderness that God

---

[6] H.Grattan Guinness, *Light for The Last Days*, (Edited by E.P. Chachmaille, London & Edinburgh: Marshall, Morgan & Scott, 1917), 72–73.

fed, and they are the saints that the beast, the papacy, made war with as revealed in Revelation 13:7.

It must be noted that the seven crowns are upon the seven heads of the dragon in Revelation 12 but are shifted to be seated on the horns when the sea-beast rises.

> And there appeared another wonder in heaven; and behold a great red dragon, having seven heads and ten horns, and seven crowns upon his heads. (Revelation 12:3)

> And I stood upon the sand of the sea, and saw a beast rise up out of the sea, having seven heads and ten horns, and upon his horns ten crowns, and upon his heads the name of blasphemy. (Revelation 13:1)

The shift of the crowns from the heads to the horns obviously represents the breakdown of Rome into numerous kingdoms, those now symbolized by horns in Daniel and John. The ten horns in Daniel parallel "all kindreds, and tongues, and nations" (Revelation 13:7). The shifting of crowns ensued when the Roman empire (the fourth beast in Daniel 7 and the fourth king in Revelation 17:10) disintegrated and was succeeded by the division of its provinces into numerous kingdoms illustrated as ten horns, out of which a little horn (John's sea-beast representing the papacy) becomes the fifth king, and which had already fallen from John's perspective. Revelation 17:10–11 expresses that the eighth king ruled prior to the sixth king and this disqualifies the notion that the sixth king's power was interrupted, as earlier historicists had interpreted. Roman civil power was shifted to the various states during the forty and two months, noted by the crowns on the horns; even so, marriage between church and state persisted until "one of his heads as it were" was "wounded to death" (Revelation 13:3). When one concedes that the beasts are dominant world powers, the wounding must be acknowledged as occurring within a considerable span of time. Upon examination of Daniel and Revelation the fifth king of Revelation 17:10 is revealed as the one who receives the wound.

Following after the model of imperial Rome, the power the papacy wielded over the ten horns did not include recognizing barriers between state and religion, which continued until the rise of the nation of America. Moreover, Daniel's little horn/beast has the same allotted power as the sea-beast and both are "given to the burning flame" just as is the eighth king in Revelation 17:11. This lends further support in correctly identifying the fifth head/king as the papacy, and it is being healed even now.

> I beheld then because of the voice of the great words which the horn spake: I beheld even till the beast was slain, and his body destroyed, and given to the burning flame. (Daniel 7:11)

> And the beast was taken, and with him the false prophet that wrought miracles before him, with which he deceived them that had received the mark of the beast, and them that worshipped his image. These both were cast alive into a lake of fire burning with brimstone. (Revelation 19:20)

The wisdom required to grasp the issue commences with accepting Daniel's determination of the first four kings as Babylon, Medo-Persia, Greece, and imperial Rome. The sea-beast in the Revelation has the body of a leopard, representing Greece, the feet of a bear, representing Medo-Persia, and his mouth was like that of a lion, representing Babylon, while the dragon, as established above, represents the personification of Satan and is imperial Rome who gives this beast its power, seat and authority as stated in the preceding chapter.

Incontrovertibly, imperial Rome gave the Roman church its power, seat and authority after almost three centuries of attempting to eradicate the church.

Persecution of Christians in the Roman Empire occurred intermittently over a period of over two centuries between the Great Fire of Rome in 64 AD under Nero Caesar and the Edict of Milan in 313 AD, in which the Roman Emperors Constantine the Great and Licinius legalised the Christian religion.[7]

The sixth king cannot be perceived as imperial Rome but rather perceived as the fourth by maintaining the historicist's guidelines. The traditional perception allows only one short lived world power after imperial Rome falls, the seventh king, which they claim will establish a national religion before the eighth king is healed and rises out of the abyss to war with Christ at his return; perceiving imperial Rome as the sixth king leads to preterism or futurism. The fourth king is none other than Imperial Rome in adhering to Daniel, which then allows for three more dominate world powers who establish national religions. Following this formulation, we can see that the papacy is the fifth king/kingdom and that the sixth sanctions, or makes the image to the beast before Christ's return, which then becomes the seventh, and this is what history actually reflects. When one grasps the *sine qua non* of the kings as the establishment of national religion and that the fifth king is the papacy, historicism is vindicated. History vindicates the papacy endured for twelve-hundred and sixty years before the Protestant Reformation enfeebled it and then mothered the sixth, the United States of America, that came up as a lamb and is even now entering its dragon stage.[8] Moreover, the fifth is gaining influence again with

<hr>

[7] Wikipedia: s.v. Persecution of Christians in the Roman Empire, last modified May 2018, https://en.wikipedia.org/wiki/Persecution_of_Christians_in_the_Roman_Empire

[8] Actually, the wall between church and state is being unwoven even now through the Faith-based Initiatives enactments by the government. Associate professor of sociology at Loyola Marymount University, Rebecca Sager, has written: "The twin processes of government desecularization and devolution—most prominent in conservative political philosophy—have significantly

the help of America. Fifty years ago, George McCready Price wrote in his book, *Time of the End*, that we are living in "the time of the deadly wound, our present age."[9]

> But, as before stated, the point of time from which the beast and its rider are seen by the apostle is our own day, the time of the end, not the time of the Roman emperors.[10]

Price correctly perceived that we live in the time of the sixth king and this work maintains that we are fast approaching the time of the seventh, whose span will be brief. Price expounds on the significance that there are no crowns to speak of in Revelation 17.

> The ten horns of the scarlet beast of chapter 17 have no crowns upon them, suggesting that this vision applies at a later period, after the ten horns have ceased to do the bidding of the Papacy, a fact further suggested by the statement that these ten kings "have not yet received royal power," or the power to oppress or lord it over the minds and lives of men; "but they are to receive authority as kings for one hour, together with the beast." (Revelation 17:12, R.S.V.) In other words, at the time here spoken of intolerance and persecution had ceased for the time being, but would again be revived, along

---

altered culture and politics in the United States. 'Desecularization' can be defined as the increasing role of religious authority in aspects of society. Most American political institutions are largely secular in nature, and this has angered conservative political and religious leaders from William F. Buckley to Jerry Falwell and Pat Robertson." Rebecca Sager, Faith, *Politics and Power: The Politics of Faith-Based Initiatives*, (Oxford University Press, 2004), 17. This will be dealt with at greater length as this work continues.

[9] George McCready Price, *Time of the End* (Southern Pub. Association; 1st edition, 1967), 31.

[10] Ibid., 34

with the power of the beast from the abyss, the bottomless pit. And how accurately this describes our own times, when the power to persecute has been quiescent for nearly two centuries, but when the ominous signs of the revival of intolerance are visible to all![11]

Price noted that the crowns are absent while the woman rides the beast, which he rightly perceived as a time running concurrent with the interlude in which the head is wounded and has not been healed, prophesied in Revelation 13:3. This is clearly affirmed in the evidence that the eighth king "is not" at the time John witnesses the woman riding the beast, but had lived prior to the "vision" and will rise and live again when the brief time of the seventh king is accomplished, to make war with Christ at his return (Revelation 17:8, 14). Moreover, Price also perceived this time as the fragile aberration of our secular society. The *sine qua non* of the beasts is easily revealed as the establishment of national religion when the Roman empire is perceived as the fourth king in Revelation 17. One must agree, history affirms this.

Please do not misunderstand me. The complete separation of church and state is a wise, good policy. Civil and religious liberty are both good. But the French Revolutionists stole these heavenly ideas from the Americans of a previous generation, and used them to camouflage their propaganda of anti-God and anti-Bible which spread so universally at that time.[12]

Many societies in antiquity had imperial cults where heads of state were worshiped as messiahs, demigods or deities. Ancient history is replete with

---

[11] Ibid., 33.
[12] Ibid., 43.

examples of political leaders who derived legitimacy through religious titles.... An important contributor to the discussion concerning the proper relationship between Church and state was St. Augustine, who in The City of God, Book XIX, Chapter 17, began an examination of the ideal relationship between the "earthly city" and the "city of God". In this work, Augustine posited that major points of overlap were to be found between the "earthly city" and the "city of God", especially as people need to live together and get along on earth. Thus Augustine held that it was the work of the "temporal city" to make it possible for a "heavenly city" to be established on earth.... For centuries, monarchs ruled by the idea of divine right. Sometimes this began to be used by a monarch to support the notion that the king ruled both his own kingdom and Church within its boundaries, a theory known as caesaropapism. On the other side was the Catholic doctrine that the Pope, as the Vicar of Christ on earth, should have the ultimate authority over the Church, and indirectly over the state. Moreover, throughout the Middle Ages the Pope claimed the right to depose the Catholic kings of Western Europe and tried to exercise it, sometimes successfully (see the investiture controversy, below), sometimes not, such as was the case with Henry VIII of England and Henry III of Navarre. In the West the issue of the separation of church and state during the medieval period centered on monarchs who ruled in the secular sphere but encroached on the Church's rule of the spiritual sphere. This unresolved contradiction in ultimate control of the Church led to power struggles and crises of leadership, notably in the Investiture Controversy, which was resolved in the Concordat of Worms in 1122. By this concordat, the Emperor renounced the right to invest ecclesiastics with ring and crosier, the symbols of their spiritual power, and guaranteed election by the canons of cathedral or abbey and free consecration.... The concept of separating church and state is often credited to the writings of English philosopher John Locke (1632–1704). According to his principle of the social contract, Locke argued that the government lacked authority in the realm of individual conscience, as this was something rational people could not cede to the government for it or others to control. For Locke, this created a natural right in the liberty of conscience, which he argued must therefore remain protected from any government authority. These views on religious tolerance and the importance of individual conscience, along with his social contract, became particularly influential in the American colonies and the drafting of the United States Constitution.[13]

Suspension of the *sine qua non* of the beasts is easily resolved as the time of the "lamblike horn" on the beast that rises "up out of the earth" (Revelation 13:11) that represents America, the sixth king in Revelation 17. The evidence that the two-horned beast makes the image proves that it is the prior beast from the sea who receives the wounding, especially when the *sine qua non* of historicism is conceded. There are those who grasp that the four heads on the leopard are subsumed or depicted as one beast by Daniel and are

[13] Wikipedia, s.v. Separation of church and state, Ancient history, Late antiquity, Enlightenment, last modified June 2018, https://ipfs.io/ipfs/ QmXoypizjW3WknFiJnKLwHCnL72vedxjQkDDP1mXWo6uco/wiki/ Separation_of_church_and_state.html

not to be counted as four in Revelation 17;[14] the horns on the beast from the earth abide in the same precedent. The beast from the earth comes up as a lamb, which represents the time of the first horn and ends when America enters the time of the dragon like horn. Price, a Seventh-day Adventist, mistakenly asserts that the horns represent "civil and religious freedom" and overlooks the precedent set by the bear-like beast.[15] The Medes held hegemony over the Persians creating Medio-Persia; but this was still perceived as one beast by Daniel, and in like manner we are to perceive the two-horned beast as successive regimes of the same sixth king. The interval between the lamblike horn and the wounded head is easily discernable as the separation of church and state when one perceives the first four beasts in Daniel as the first four heads/kings on the beast in Revelation 12:3, 13:1 and 17:3. Such a perception precludes preterism because the sixth king is not the Roman empire but one that is contemporary from our perspective. Such a perception precludes futurism because the beast in Revelation 13 is not in the far future, but rather, its narrative follows the successive unfolding of history which proves it to be the papacy. America is easily seen as the sixth king by conceding that the *sine qua non* of the beasts or kings is the marriage of state and religion.

America is also easily seen as the sixth king when one comprehends the significance of John being taken "in the Spirit on the Lord's day" (Revelation 1:10). Key in the debate is John's intent regarding the phrase "on the Lord's Day" in Revelation 1:10 (*en tē kyriakē hēmera*) that only appears once in the NT. The major evidence supports that the phrase pertains to the last judgment as opposed to the "first day of the week," the latter being anachronistic, considering the hegemony of the church was still in the hands of the

---

[14] Tony Garland: "It is apparent that the Seleucid empire—an outgrowth of the disintegration of the Greek empire under Alexander, is largely subsumed into the third leopard beast." *Spirit And Truth.org*, s.v. Revelation 17:10. http://www.spiritandtruth.org/teaching/Book_of_Revelation/commentary/htm/chapters/17.html

[15] Price, *Time of the End*, 54.

Jews who were the principal acolytes John addressed. Viewing the phrase as pertaining to the first day of the week is hardly a patristic perception. Furthermore, the context pertains overwhelmingly to eschatological events such as the introduction of the "judgment of the Harlot riding the eighth beast" by an angel in possession of one of the vials of the last plagues (Revelation 17:1). Through the syntactical evidence, futurist E. W. Bullinger maintained that John was taken in the spirit to the future Day of the Lord.

> *anthrōpinēs hēmeras*, in 1 Corinthians 4:3, is rendered "Man's judgment (margin, Greek day)". So we contend that, in Revelation 1:10, tē kuriakē hēmera should in like manner be rendered "The Lord's judgment (margin, Greek day)". In both passages the same word "day" denotes the time or period when the judgment spoken of is being carried out. In the former it is the day now present, when "man" is judging; in the latter it is the future day, when "the Lord" will be judging. Indeed, this is the exact contrast as shown by the conclusion in 1 Corinthians 4:5: "Therefore judge nothing before the time, until the Lord shall have come". This coming is the great subject of the whole book of Revelation, as is proclaimed in its opening words (Revelation 1:7). And John is taken by the Spirit into the judgment scenes of that day.[16]

John was not merely speaking in the present, but also, through the Spirit, in a future tense nearer to our time, the eschatological "Day of the Lord." Bullinger agreed that John lived during the time of the Roman empire, but was taken by the Spirit to our time, that of the sixth king, which unintentionally confirms that Rome is the fourth king in Revelation 17. It is from this future perspective, our time,

---

[16] E. W. Bullinger, "The Lord's Day," (the Open Bible Trust, Kindle Ed., 2003), Kindle locations 496–507

that John witnesses the harlot riding the beast. The fallacy that mystery Babylon is the papacy and that the sixth king was pagan Rome is exposed by the contemporary reevaluation. The papacy came into existence some four-hundred years after John's time and cannot be viewed as riding on the back of pagan Rome in any logical sense. The fallacy escalates in the evidence that the "fornication" in Revelation 17:2 is in the indicative mood which conveys the act as being prior to the indictment of the whore, before she becomes "the habitation of devils, and the hold of every foul spirit, and a cage of every unclean and hateful bird" (Revelation 17:2, 18:2). Without a doubt, one cannot render the sixth king in Revelation 17 as pagan Rome and maintain that the whore is the papacy. Nevertheless, the Revelation has long been perceived as relating to things in John's time, which is the general perception today, but only the acceptance of the future perspective, interpreting the Roman empire as the fourth king, truly represents the wisdom required to comprehend the mystery of the seven, nay eight kings of Revelation 17:10–11. The future perspective affirms the *sine qua non* of the seven kings in Revelation 17 and the beasts of Daniel as the marriage between ecclesiastic and civil power, or the establishment of national religion.

The True Structuring of the Revelation

Historicists have perceived the structure of the four septets of the seven churches, seven seals, seven trumpets, and seven vials in Revelation as considerably folding upon themselves or continually revisiting the period between the two advents of Christ.

> A second significant phase of the structure of Revelation deserves careful scrutiny. It may be called the plan of recapitulation, or better, perhaps, parallelism. What is meant is this: the chief series of visions, e. g., the Seals, Trumpets, and Vials, do not succeed each other in historical and chronological sequence, but move side by side.[1]

This was certainly the position held by the nineteenth-century historicist E. B. Elliott who interpreted the opening of the first seal as the "triumph, prosperity, and health of the Roman empire" and the opening of first trumpet as the barbarian invasion in the fifth-century, and concluded that the first vial represented "that tremendous outbreak of moral and social evil, that mixture of atheism, vice, and democratic fury, which burst forth at the French

---

[1] William G. Moorehead, *Studies in the Book of Revelation*, (The United Presbyterian Board of Pub., 1908, Kindle ed.), Kindle location 352.

Revolution."[2] Progressive revelation has certainly corrected Elliott's misapprehensions of the vials, which will be affirmed presently. Nevertheless, with centuries of progressive revelation behind him, Elliott corrected the misapprehension of the then rising preterist model that the emperor Nero fulfilled Revelation 17's eighth king, and by doing so also refuted this misapprehension by the early church, from whence preterists obtain such a notion. Elliott commences by refuting the preterist's assertion that the kings in Revelation 17 are individuals and not kingdoms.

> The *heads* then, as they assert, mean certain *individual kings*. This is not surely according to the precedent of Daniel vii. 6, where the third Beasts *four heads* would seem ... to have signified the *monarchical successions* that governed the four kingdoms into which Alexanders empire was divided at his death. – But, not to stop at this, the decisive question next recurs, What the *eighth* head of the Beast, on this hypothesis of the Præterists: *Nero* being the *sixth;* and, as they generally say, *Galba*, who reigned but a short time, the *seventh?* It is admitted (and common sense itself forces the admission) that this *eighth head* is the same which is said in Apoc. xiii. 3, 12, 14.... And, in reply, first Eichhorn, and then his copyists Heinrichs, Stuart, Davidson, all four refer us to a rumor prevalent in Neros time, and believed by many, that after suffering some reverse he would return again to power: a rumor which after his death took the form that he would revive again, and reappear, and retake the empire.[65] Such is their explanation. The *eighth head of the Beast* is *the imaginary revived Nero.* – But do they not explain the Beast (the revived Beast) in

---

[2] Tucker, Brief historical explanation of the Revelation of St. John, According to the 'Horæ Apocalypticæ' of the Rev. E.B. Elliott, 11, 103.

Apoc. xiii., and his blasphemies, and persecution of the saints, and predicated continuance 42 months, of the *real original* Nero, and *his* blasphemies and *his* three or four years persecution of the Christians, begun November, 64, A.D. and ended with Neros death, June 9, A.D. 68? Such indeed is the case; and by this palpable self-contradiction, (one which however they cannot do without,) they give to their own solution its death-wound: as much its death-wound, I may say, as that given to the Beast itself to which the solution relates.[3]

Elliot's refutation that the eighth king was Nero is founded on the perception of progressive revelation, which historicist Oral E. Collins conveyed in an essay on how to interpret prophecy.

It may be presupposed that the actual fulfillment of the prophecy in history will offer a correct alternative to previous misinterpretations. For this reason, it is to be assumed that the process of interpretation of historical prophecies is necessarily dynamic and progressive, every generation being responsible to study the prophecies and to discern the signs of its own times (Matt. 16:3).[4]

Collins credits H. Grattan Guinness for the presupposition (or hermeneutic) of progressive revelation, which was broached in the first chapter. Collins rightfully concludes that "the meaning of the prophetic text should be determined first,"[5] which is merely stating that the use of the historical-grammatical presupposition

---

[3] E. B. Elliott, *Horae Apocalypticae*, (Seeley, Jackson, and Halliday, London SEELEY, vol. 4, 1862), 582–583.

[4] Oral E. Collins, Ph.D, "The Interpretation of Biblical Prophecy," *Historicism. com*, http://www.historicism.com/Collins/interp.htm

[5] Ibid.

takes precedence in interpreting prophecy. Yet, as stated in the chapter one, the prophets were not given to see all the implications or significance of what they were inspired to write, which is irrefutably affirmed by the two separate advents of Christ; the difference of the two advents was not seen until the prophecies of the first advent were fulfilled, which affirms progressive revelation. Futurist Daniel B. Wallace concurs that "there is ample evidence of progressive revelation within the NT about several themes—that is, certain themes are not developed/recognized until after some time."[6] Thus, it was progressive revelation that exhorted Elliot to refute the notion that Nero fulfilled the wounded head in Revelation 13 and 17. Futurist Mark L. Hitchcock also exposed the fallacies that ensue when preterist, like Kenneth L. Gentry Jr., maintain that the head that the wounded in Revelation 13:3 was fulfilled by the death of the emperor Nero in 68 A.D., and Vespasian's reign represented its healing in 69 A.D., concluding that Nero was the beast in Revelation 17:14 that was destroyed at the theophany of Christ in 70 A.D.

> the mention of the eighth king seems to take the reader to the end of the list. There is no mention of a ninth or tenth king. The eighth king is the final manifestation of the beast. Speaking of the eighth and final form of the beast's rule, 17:11 says, "and he goes to destruction." Gentry says this refers to Vespasian. However, two chapters later (in 19:20) the beast and the false prophet are cast into the lake of fire, which is the same destruction of the final head of the beast described in 17:11. Yet

---

[6] Daniel B. Wallace, Th.M., Ph.D., "New Testament Eschatology in the Light of Progressive Revelation: Special Focus on the Coming Kingdom," *Bible.org*, https://bible.org/article/new-testament-eschatology-light-progressive-revelation

Gentry interprets 19:20 as a reference to Christ's providential destruction of Nero.[7]

By the same hermeneutic, progressive revelation, Hitchcock's futurist's perception is thwarted. In refuting Gentry's preterist perception of Nero, Hitchcock concurs with the historicists that the seven kings of Revelation 17:9–10 must "represent seven successive Gentile world powers or kingdoms" and cannot be interpreted as seven individual kings conterminous with the sixth king.

> The best solution to the identity of the seven kings is the view that the seven kings represent seven successive Gentile world powers or kingdoms, followed by the Antichrist as the eighth king. This interpretation is supported by the parallels between Revelation 17:9–12 and Daniel 7:17, 23, where references to kings and kingdoms are interchangeable, thus revealing that a king represents the kingdom he rules. Adopting this interpretation, the eight kingdoms are the eight Gentile world powers that encompass the sweep of history: Egypt, Assyria, Neo-Babylonia, Persia, Greece, Rome, the reunited Roman Empire in a ten-king form, and the future kingdom of the beast or final world ruler who will emerge from the reunited Roman Empire.[8]

Like so many futurists, Hitchcock mistakenly overlooks the significance that John witnessed that the eighth king "was" prior to the sixth king, and, thus, it cannot be the sixth king that suffers the deadly wound of Rev 13:3. Revelation 17:10–11 establishes the eighth king "that was" is actually of the five that were fallen, insomuch as the eighth king "is not" (v 8) at the time John witnesses

---

[7] Mark L. Hitchcock, "A Critique of the Preterist View of Revelation 17:9-11 and Nero," *Bibliotheca Sacra* 164 (October-December 2007): 472-85.
[8] Ibid.

the sixth king as the one who "is" (v. 10). Revelation 17 clearly affirms the eighth king as exercising its power prior to the time of the sixth king—and will again after the seventh's short span (Revelation 17:8, 11). If Rome is perceived as the sixth king, then Hitchcock is forced to interpret the revival of either the Egyptian, Assyrian, Neo-Babylonian, Persian, or Grecian empire as the eighth king, but not Rome. Hitchcock's futurist fallacy is only resolved by the progressive revelation that the kings/kingdoms in Revelation 17 must commence with Babylon, in correspondence with Daniel. Historicists have grasped this in more recent times,[9] by reckoning that there are two other kings that arise after John's time before the power of the eighth king is restored. Reckoning Rome as the sixth king, as Hitchcock and even some historicists have, allows for only one more king before the last, the eighth, to rise and make war with Christ at his return (Revelation 17:14, 19:20). Only the perception where Rome is the *fourth* king (of the five that were fallen) allows for the sixth king to correspond to the two-horned beast, which makes the image that becomes the seventh king, before the eighth king regains its power in correspondence with all the beasts in Revelation. Only the perception where Rome is the *fourth* king allows for correspondence between the wounding of the beast in Revelation 13:3 and that of the time the beast "is not" in Revelation 17:8–11. Only the perception where Rome is the *fourth* king allows one to grasp that the wounding, or in other words, the "is not" phenomenon is the historical fulfillment of our modern separation of church and state and the rejoining of the two as the *sine qua non* of the seven kings, nay eight. While outside the scope of this essay, the reconciliation of church and state is well on its way in America.

Returning to the issue of the structure of the four septets in

---

[9] Few Historicists commence the five fallen kings in Revelation 17 with Babylon. Here are a few websites that hold the view: Temcat at http://www.temcat.com/006-prophetic-history/Sequence-Rev17.pdf; Ulrike Unruh at http://dedication.www3.50megs.com/revelation17.html; David Barron at http://www.thethirdangelsmessage.com/the-7-kings-of-revelation-17-correcting-the-misinterpretation

Revelation, Elliott's interpretation that the opening of the first vial or plague of Revelation 16 was fulfilled in the eighteenth-century by the French Revolution has not endured the scrutiny of progressive revelation. Even the staunch historicist, Alberto R. Treiyer, has conceded that the seven vials are future, immediately preceding the return of Christ.

> While the first six trumpets were partial judgments (a third), only the last and seventh trumpet was expected to be definitive in connection with the coming of the Lord (Rev 11:18: God's wrath outpoured in the seven plagues, 16:1).[10]

Treiyer concedes the progressive revelation that the seven vials fold over the seventh trumpet, or that they are restricted to the events of the seventh trumpet and final woe (Revelation 11:14–19). An earlier nineteenth-century historicist, Uriah Smith, had come to the same conclusion that the vials were future, confined to the return of Christ.

> If these plagues are in the past, the image of the beast and his worship are in the past. If these are past, the two-horned beast, which makes this image, and all his work, are in the past. If these are past, then the third angel's message, which warns us in reference to this work, is in the past; and if this is ages in the past, then the first and second messages which precede it were also ages in the past.... Under the fifth plague, men blaspheme God because of their sores, the same sores, of course, caused by the outpouring of the first plague. This shows that these plagues all fall upon one and the same

---

[10] Alberto R. Treiyer, review of Heidi Heiks' "Satin's Counterfeit Prophecy Review," *Adventist Distinctive Message.com*, 5. http://www.adventistdistinctive messages.com/English/Documents/Heikstrumpetsreviewed.pdf

generation of men, some being, no doubt swept off by each one, yet some surviving through the terrible scenes of them all. These plagues are the wine of God's wrath without mixture, threatened by the third angel. (Revelation 14:10; 15:1.) Such language cannot be applied to any judgments visited upon the earth while Christ pleads with His Father in behalf of our fallen race. Therefore we must locate them in the future, when probation shall have closed.... Christ is then no longer a mediator. Mercy, which has long stayed the hand of vengeance, pleads no more. The servants of God are all sealed. What could then be expected but that the storm of vengeance should fall, and earth be swept with the besom of destruction.[11]

Contemporary historicist Hans K. LaRondelle also acknowledged the progressive revelation that the seven vials or plagues are folded over, or recapping, the phenomena of the seventh trumpet.

The content of the seventh trumpet is unfolded in the seven bowls of God's final judgment (chaps. 15–16). This is implied in the explicit numbering of the last three trumpets as the three "woes" on the earth dwellers (8:13).[12]

Yet, Treiyer inflexibly holds to the perception that the preceding six trumpets recap a significant part of the seven eras of the churches and that the seven seals, or in parallel recap the greater part of

---

[11] Smith, Daniel and the Revelation, 278-279.
[12] Hans K. LaRondelle, "The Trumpets in the Contexts," *Journal of the Adventist Theological Society*, 8/1–2 (1997): 82–89

the period betwixt the two advents of Christ, commencing with a judgment of the Roman empire.[13]

> On the rank of historicism were Pr. Ty Gibson (Light Bearers Ministry with James Rafferty, another panelist in the symposium), and Dr. Alberto R. Treiyer (Adventist Distinctive Messages, Ph D in the University of Strasbourg, residing in NC). The difference between them is that Gibson follows Edwin Thiele and C. M. Maxwell when he connects the first trumpet with the fall of Jerusalem, while Treiyer follows the Protestant and Adventist historicist legacy that has Rome as the target of the judgments of God, from the beginning of our Christian dispensation to the end.[14]

Treiyer's perception is described as inflexible in the consideration that the traditional Protestant historicist's perception of the seven trumpets has not surmounted the exegetical challenge of recent progressive revelation. Historicist Jon Hjorleifur Stefansson has chronicled this exegetical challenge to the traditional historicist's perception of the seven trumpets in his master thesis to Andrews University: *"From Clear Fulfillment to Complex Prophecy: the History of the Adventist Interpretation of Revelation 9, from 1833 to 1957."*[15] The challenges to the traditional historicist's rendition, according

---

[13] Alberto R. Treiyer, "review of Dr. Ekkehardt Mueller, Bri, Die Sieben Posaunen [The Seven Trumpets]," *Adventist Distinctive Message.com*, http://www.adventistdistinctivemessages.com/English/Documents/DiesiebenPosaunen-reviewed.pdf

[14] Alberto R. Treiyer, "Symposium on the Trumpets of Revelation," *Adventist Distinctive Message.com*, http://www.adventistdistinctivemessages.com/English/Documents/Symposiumtrumpets3ABN.pdf

[15] Jon Hjorleifur Stefansson, "From Clear Fulfillment to Complex Prophecy: the History of the Adventist Interpretation of Revelation 9, from 1833 to 1957," *Andrews University Digital Commons*, http://digitalcommons.andrews.edu/cgi/viewcontent.cgi?article=1053&context=theses

to Stefansson, concern the commencement of the five months of the fifth trumpet and the termination of the time conveyed in the sixth trumpet. The dates of 1299 A.D. for the commencement of the five months and 1840 A.D. for the termination have been challenged for some time with the question of their accuracy and alternative dating has resulted. This has supported the progressive revelation that the trumpets are actually contemporaneous phenomena, corresponding with our end times, in agreement with the framework of the pending judgment conveyed in the fifth and sixth seals of Revelation 6, the sealing of the 144,000 in Revelation 7, and the three angels in Revelation 14. This work will not enter into the controversy concerning the starting and ending dates of the traditional Protestant rendition of the fifth and sixth trumpets, as the controversy is not unlike the Preterist's endless arguments over which Roman emperors represent the seven, nay, eight kings of Revelation 17:10; the endless debates are evidence that the Roman emperors do not fit the prophecy any more a square peg fits into a round hole. In like manner, the debates will continue within the traditional Protestant house because the trumpets are not *historical* events, but rather end time phenomena in the framework of the judgment conveyed in the fifth and sixth seals of Revelation 6, the sealing of the 144,000 in Revelation 7 and the three angels in Revelation 14. This work uses Stefansson's thesis to vindicate the more recent progressive revelations, which refutes the traditional Protestant historicist's perception.

Considering the impending judgments conveyed in the fifth and sixth seals, Historicist Jon Paulien recognizes the significance of the framework as it pertains to the judgment scene in Revelation 8:3–5 that introduces the sounding of the seven trumpets, at the opening of the seventh seal.

> The seven trumpets, like the churches and seals before them, are preceded by a view of the heavenly sanctuary (8:2–6). The scene in verse 2 is probably based on the fact that there were seven trumpet priests in the Old Testament cultus (1 Chr 15:24;

Josh 6; cf. also 1QM 3:1–11; 7:7ff.).6 Their trumpet calls represented the prayers of God's people for deliverance in battle and forgiveness of sin (Numbers 10:8–10). Thus the prayers of the saints in Revelation 8:3–5 are probably cries for deliverance from the oppression visited by their enemies as depicted in the seven seals....

Two basic ideas are portrayed in Revelation 8:3–5, mediation and judgment....

This relationship is, perhaps, best understood by examining the apparent connection between the fifth seal and the introduction to the seven trumpets (Rev 8:3–5). In the fifth seal (Rev 6:9–11) John sees martyred souls under "the" altar crying out "How long, O Lord, the Holy and True One, do you not judge and avenge our blood upon those who live on the earth (tôn katoikountôn epi tês gês)?"11 These souls are given white robes and told to rest a short while until "the number of their fellow servants and brothers who were to be killed as they had been was completed."12

Since the question "how long" is not really answered in the fifth seal, the reader anticipates that things will be clarified later on in the book. Thus it is not surprising that there are later references to numbered groups of God's people (chapter 7), prayer (8:3–5) and those who dwell on the earth (8:13; 11:10; 13:8,14, etc.). Very significant is the reference in Rev 8:13, which stands at the structural center of the seven trumpets.13 This verse indicates that the trumpet plagues fall on "those who live on the earth," the same group which was martyring the saints, referred to in 6:9–11 as the "souls under the altar." The spiritual connection between the trumpets and the fifth seal is made in Rev 8:3–5 where incense from the golden altar is mingled with "the prayers of the saints (tais proseuchais tôn hagiôn)."14 This scene symbolizes Christ's intercession for His saints. He responds to their prayers by casting His censer to the earth, with frightful results.

This connection between the altar of 6:9–11 and that of 8:3–5 indicates that the seven trumpets are God's response to the prayers of the saints for vengeance on those who have persecuted and martyred them. The martyrs were anxious for the judgment to begin but it was delayed until all the seals had been opened.15

In verse 5 the altar which receives the prayers of the saints becomes the source from which judgments are poured out on the wicked in response (cf. 9:13–15; 14:18–20 and 16:4–7). When the fire of purification from the altar contacts the earth, it provokes disasters. The same fire which purifies can also destroy. The censer of judgment and the censer of prayer become one. Thus the seven trumpets should be understood as God's judgment-response to the prayers of the martyrs, resulting in justice being done with respect to those who persecuted the saints.[16]

Paulien's work decisively renders the prayers of the saints in Revelation 8:3–5 as corresponding to the petitions or prayers of "the souls of them that were slain for the word of God" (Revelation 6:10) and the seven trumpets as the commencement of the judgment that was entreated by the souls. This correspondence is also affirmed by

---

[16] Jon Paulien, "Interpreting the Seven Trumpets," A Paper Prepared for the Daniel and Revelation Committee of the General Conference of SDAs (March 5-9, 1986), 6-7, 11-13. http://www.thebattleofarmageddon. com/7trumpets_pdf/Interpreting%20the%20Seven%20Trumpets2.pdf

another historicist, Ranko Stefanovic, cited below, who adds that the seals and the trumpets are in the model of covenantal curses.

> The scene of the opening of the seven seals echoes the Hebrew Bible covenantal curses concept....
>
> In implementing the covenant curses, God used enemy nations, such as the Philistines, Moabites, Assyrians, and Babylonians, as instruments of his judgment (cf. Judges 2:13–14; Psalms 106:40; Isa 10:5–6). The enemy nation would come and afflict the Israelites by plundering and destroying them. In most cases, these nations, while sent by God as the executor of judgment, overplayed their part and tried to destroy God's people. In their hopeless situation, the people of Israel would turn to God for deliverance. At this point, God responded to the prayers of his afflicted people and reversed the judgments on the enemy nation(s) in order to provide deliverance for his people (cf. Deut 32:41–43)....
>
> This Hebrew Bible background clearly defines the context of the seals: the situation of the church in the hostile world. The opening of the first four seals describes in a symbolic presentation the judgments of God on the church unfaithful to the gospel (6:1–8). The scene of the fifth seal portrays the slain faithful at the base of the altar of burnt offering, crying to God for intervention and judgment on their oppressors and enemies....
>
> Thus the plea of the slain saints under the altar "must be seen as a legal plea in which God is asked to conduct a legal process leading to a verdict that will vindicate his martyred saints."[17]

---

[17] Ranko Stefanovic, "The Angel at the Altar (Revelation 8:3-5): A Case Study on Intercalations in Revelation," (University Seminary Studies, vol. 44, No. 1, Andrews University Press 2006), 89-91.

Stefanovic maintains that the four horsemen of the seals represent "the judgments of God on the church unfaithful to the gospel" and the seven trumpets as the judgments upon the wicked for exceeding their mandate and oppressing God's faithful people.

> The foregoing discussion strongly suggests that the seven trumpets are heaven's response to the prayers of God's people for deliverance from their oppressors. While the scene of the sixth seal provides the saints with an assurance that the day is coming when God's ultimate judgments will visit their adversaries, the vision of the seven trumpet plagues gives an even more direct message: God is already judging the enemies of his faithful people. This makes the trumpet plagues preliminary judgments and the foretaste of the ultimate and final judgments to fall on the wicked as portrayed in Revelation 15–16. The trumpet plagues are seen as mixed with mercy; the bowl plagues are expressed as the fullness of God's wrath unmixed with mercy (15:1).[18]

Both Paulien and Stefanovic's renditions attempt to observe a greater terminological and thematic correspondence than does the traditional Protestant interpretation concerning the seals and trumpets but continue to deny correspondence between the sealing of the 144,000 in Revelation 7 and the three angels in Revelation 14, so as not to render the seven trumpets end time events. Paulien and Stefanovic fail to consider that the covenantal judgment conveyed in the seals and the trumpets begins at the house of God *prior* to any judgment upon those who disavow Christ (1 Peter 4:17–18), and they missed the mark in noting any correspondence between the sealing of the 144,000 in Revelation 7 and the angel's messages in Revelation 14.

---

[18] Ibid., 93.

For the time *is come* that judgment must begin at the house of God: and if *it* first *begin* at us, what shall the end *be* of them that obey not the gospel of God? And if the righteous scarcely be saved, where shall the ungodly and the sinner appear? (1 Peter 4:17–18)

Paulien acknowledges the principle of 1 Peter 4:17–18 in his interpretation of the first trumpet.

> In the OT these judgments were covenant related, thus could be turned on God's own people when they broke the covenant (Deut 32:15–22). The later prophets, especially, applied the hail and fire of God's judgments more and more to Israel and Judah (Ps 80:8–16; Isa 28:2; Jer 11:16,17; 21:12–14; Ezek 15:65,7; 20:47,48)....
>
> Thus the first trumpet portrays a judgment of God, in response to the prayers of the saints, which falls on a portion of Satan's kingdom that may once have given allegiance to God's kingdom....
>
> John intended his readers to see in the first trumpet the fate of the Jewish nation that had rejected Jesus as its Messiah.[19]

Paulien rendered the first trumpet as a judgment against the "Jewish nation," which maintains that the souls under the altar were consoled by the destruction of Jerusalem; such a rendition has Revelation 8:3–5 fulfilled at the first advent in order for the judgment of the first trumpet to fall upon the Jewish nation. Yet, historicists hold that the church is the house of God and not the Jewish nation, which this work has affirmed numerous times in the first three chapters. Consequently, "God's own people" would be the church and not the Jewish nation. Again, Paulien is attempting to avoid terminological and thematic correspondence with the sealing of the 144,000 and

---

[19] Paulien, "Interpreting the Seven Trumpets," 29–31.

Revelation 14, insomuch as the judgment on the Jewish nation at the first advent is asynchronous with this correspondence. Yet, 1 Peter 4:17–18 proves Paulien wrong and specifies that oppression must originate initially from those who profess Christ, those who had "given allegiance to God's kingdom", and were envisaged that they would oppress "their brethren", which harmonizes with 2 Thessalonians 2:3–10, Daniel 7: 8–10, 21–22, 1 Timothy 4:1–2 and Revelation 17:6. The restraint of the "lawless one" in 2 Thessalonians 2:6–7 was taken out of the way when the popes usurped the place of God in his temple (Ephesians 2:19–22; Revelation 3:12) to blaspheme and "wear out the saints" and then, in the day of the son of perdition, the judgment was to be set and the books opened on the little horn of Daniel 7:10. And ultimately, Babylon cannot be omitted for its oppression of the saints, insomuch as the harlot is drunk with the blood of the martyrs, and whose merchants market the "slaves and souls of men" (Revelation 17:6, 18:11–13). The elect martyrs slain by Babylon and the eighth king of Revelation 17, candidly, cannot be omitted as they are essential constituents in the intent of the fifth seal. And, insomuch as the papacy cannot be construed as fallen from moral rectitude, as it was ordained to persecute the church, Babylon has a greater resemblance with fallen Protestantism in the latter days, in the Laodicean condition of being "wretched, and miserable, and poor, and blind, and naked" (Revelation 3:17). In acknowledging that the four horsemen of the seals represent the oppression of the church Paulien and Sefanovic unintentionally deviate from the traditional the historicist's interpretations and accord the four horsemen terminological and thematic correspondence with the sealing of the 144,000 and the messages of three angels in Revelation 14, insomuch as the martyrs slain by Babylon and the eighth king of Revelation 17 cannot be omitted as essential constituents of the intent of the fifth seal. Such correspondence supports the seven trumpets as an end-day phenomenon.

Further evidence that the trumpets have terminological and thematic correspondence with the sealing of the 144,000 and the angel's messages lies with the work of historicists Kenneth A. Strand,

Jon Paulien and Richard M. Davidson on the use of temple imagery in Revelation. In his dissertation to the University of South Africa, Johan Adraiaan Japp cites these historicists concerning John's use of the "Hebraic cultus" in the Apocalypse.

> The temple imagery also shows a definite progression that moves in the first place from the "daily" (tamid) intercession to the "yearly" (yoma), corresponding with the first and second half of the book, and in the second place from the spring festivals to the autumn festivals of the cultic year, once again corresponding with the first and second half of the book.(39)[20]

The object of Japp's use of Paulien is to maintain that the phenomena and symbolism in Revelation 8–11 pertains to the "daily intercession" and indicates, in their perception, that the seven trumpets represent the "new moon" observances between the spring and autumnal festivals (Numbers 10:1–10), which folds the seven trumpets considerably over the seven seals and the seven churches.

> The seven trumpets in Revelation are reminiscent of the seven monthly new moon festivals which form a transition between spring and autumn feasts, and climaxes in the blowing of the trumpets on Rosh Hashanah.(73) Also, just as the feast of trumpets summoned Israel to prepare for the time of judgement at Yom Kippur, so the trumpets of Revelation highlight the approach of the antitypical Day of Atonement. The Autumn festivals of Trumpets, Yom Kippur and Tabernacles, could therefore be regarded as anticipations of the

---

[20] Johan Adraiaan Japp, "The Study of Atonement in Seventh-day Adventism," (PhD dissertation, to the University of South Africa, 1994), 196, http://uir.unisa. ac.za/bitstream/handle/10500/17008/dissertation_japp_ja.pdf?sequence=3

ultimate eschaton.... It is interesting to note that the unsealing of the prophetic scroll of Revelation 10, which contains God's final message to the world (Rev. 10:7., 10), forms the dividing point for both the daily/yearly dyad, and the spring/autumn festivals dyad.[21]

In such a rendition, the seven trumpets fold over the horsemen of the seals. This allows Paulien and Japp to continue to avoid correspondence between the seven trumpets, the sealing of the 144,000 and the angel's messages; their rendition allows for the interpretation that the trumpets are past historical events, as opposed to end day phenomena. Yet, similar to the topic that judgment begins with the house of God, they overlook the evidence that the subject matter of the sounding of the seven trumpets appears for the first time in Revelation 1–3 and not in Revelation 8–11 in order to in support their assertion that the seven trumpets represent the seven monthlong religious year from Abib to Tishri (Numbers 10:10).

I was in the Spirit on the Lord's day, and heard behind me a great voice, as of a trumpet, Saying, I am Alpha and Omega, the first and the last: and, What thou seest, write in a book, and send [it] unto the seven churches which are in Asia; unto Ephesus, and unto Smyrna, and unto Pergamos, and unto Thyatira, and unto Sardis, and unto Philadelphia, and unto Laodicea. (Revelation 1:10–11)

In correspondence with 1 Thessalonians 4:26 and Isaiah 58:1, Christ's voice corresponds to the sounding of a trumpet and it is he who decrees the letters to the seven churches that rightly reveals that the seven churches represent the seven monthlong religious months from Abib to Tishri, when they are received prophetically. Historicist Clinton Wahlen maintains the view that the seven churches are

---

[21] Ibid., 206

prophetic (historical as well) and represent seven inter-advent eras and by doing so promotes the idea that the eras represent the seven months between the spring and autumnal festivals.

> The letters to the seven churches are distinctly different from the New Testament epistles in that they come from Jesus Himself and, when viewed together as a group, display a stylized structure, chiastic symmetry, and universally applicable themes. These features suggest that the letters are concerned with more than matters of merely local interest to a few particular churches. The number seven also suggests comprehensiveness in terms of their scope and application. When compared with the subsequent series of sevens in the first half of the book, i.e., the seals and the trumpets both of which culminate with the end of the world, there exists every reason to understand the seven churches in a similar way. Furthermore, the fact that the letters are permeated with apocalyptic symbols and ideas gives us reason to conclude that, like the rest of Revelation, these chapters may be intended as prophetic. Jesus Himself seems to suggest a future, as well as a present, application for them (1:19). A brief comparison of the letters with church history confirms this suggestion.[22]

Any concession that the seven churches are prophetic is an acknowledgment that they additionally represent the seven "new moon" observances between the spring and autumnal festivals that points to the phenomena of Revelation 8–11 as being coterminous with the final church era and the time of the end. Japp only mentions

---

[22] Clinton Wahlen, "Letters to the Seven Churches: historical or prophet?" *Ministry magazine* (November 2007): 12-15, https://www.ministrymagazine. org/archive/2007/11/letters-to-the-seven-churches.html

the Festival of the Trumpets twice in his dissertation, which is common for historicists of his ilk; this subset of historicism has a great deal to comment upon the antitypical Day of Atonement but are remiss concerning the antitypical Festival of the Trumpets. In the citation from Japp, above, concerning Revelation 8–11, he relates that "the seven monthly new moon festivals which form a transition between spring and autumn feasts … climaxes in the blowing of the trumpets on Rosh Hashanah." But then he proceeds to maintain the fallacy that "just as the feast of trumpets summoned Israel to prepare for the time of judgement … the trumpets of Revelation highlight the approach of the antitypical Day of Atonement." While both the seven monthly new moon festivals between spring and autumn feasts and the Festival of the Trumpets highlighted the approach of the Day of Atonement they cannot be equated as representing the same antitypical phenomenon; they *must* represent differing phenomena to avoid fallacy. More appropriately, the seven monthly new moon observances prepared the people for the seventh month festivals that represented the time of the end, judgment; the seventh month festivals included the Festival of the Trumpets. In the Hebrew cultus the seven monthly new moon rituals between the spring and autumnal festivals unmistakably prefigured the seven church eras, which proves Revelation 8–11 represents something else altogether: the final judgment. Unlike the seven monthly new moon observances, the Festival of the Trumpets (the fifth of only seven holy convocations during the year) enjoined ten days of penitence before the observance of the Day of Atonement.[23] Further, the seven holy convocations conveyed major phenomena in the plan of redemption, unlike the seven monthly new moon observances between the spring and fall feasts. Substantive scrutiny of the Hebrew cultus establishes conclusively that the seventh month of Tishri cannot be equated with

---

[23] The seven yearly festivals are conveyed on the internet by Natan Lawrence: "The seven biblical feasts are a chronological step-by-step template of YHVH's plan of redemption or salvation for mankind." Natan Lawrence, "YHVH's Plan of Salvation in the Biblical Feasts," *Hoshana Rabbah blog*, https://hoshanarabbah.org/blog/2013/02/17/plan-of-salvation-in-the-biblical-feasts/

the seven months prior in an attempt to fold Revelation 8–11 over the seven seals and the seven churches. It is the seven prophetic churches that *actually* fulfill the antitype of the "new moon" observances between the spring and autumnal festivals, which climax in the Festival of the Trumpets that is illustrated in Revelation 4:1: "After this I looked, and, behold, a door *was* opened in heaven: and the first voice which I heard *was* as it were of a trumpet talking with me; which said, Come up hither, and I will shew thee things which must be hereafter." It is this subset of historicism that tries to equate the seven trumpets with these seven months to avoid correspondence with Revelation 7 and 14. But in truth, the seven churches actually illustrate the Hebraic cultus of the blowing of the trumpets to announce the new moon observances between Abib to Tishri, establishing the correspondence they are *trying* to avoid.

The zeal to fold Revelation 8–11 over the seven churches and the seven seals results in all sorts of misrepresentations such as those seen in the work of historicist, Ekkehardt Mueller. Mueller cites from Jon Paulien in his arguments for the considerable folding of the aforementioned.

> Jon Paulien argues that the protection of certain objects from destruction in Rev 7:1–3 and Rev 9:4 "raises serious questions whether the trumpet series is to be related as an immediate sequel to the vision of chapter 7." The strongest parallel between Rev 7a and the trumpets is Rev 9:14, 16. In Rev 7a, God's people are described, "in Rev 9 their demonic counterparts." Connections between the two passages include the concept of binding and losing, the appearance of four angels, and the concept of numbering a people. "The sixth trumpet is the exact historical counterpart of Revelation 7:1–8.... The

seven trumpets, therefore, do not follow the events of Revelation 7 in chronological order."[24]

To begin, Pauline neglects the principle a "house divided against itself shall not stand.... if Satan cast out Satan, he is divided against himself; how shall then his kingdom stand?" (Matthew 12:25–26). Demonic hordes are not going to torment the rebels who refuse to repent and continue to "worship devils, and idols of gold, and silver, and brass, and stone, and of wood" (Revelation 9:20). Unquestionably, the horsemen of the sixth trumpet are a plague on those ordained to damnation and are the exact historical counterpart of Revelation 11:1–14. Fire, smoke and brimstone proceed out of the mouth of the horsemen of the sixth trumpet, in conformity with the two witnesses, that plague and kill the wicked.

> And if any man will hurt them, fire proceedeth out of their mouth, and devoureth their enemies: and if any man will hurt them, he must in this manner be killed. These have power to shut heaven, that it rain not in the days of their prophecy: and have power over waters to turn them to blood, and to smite the earth with all plagues, as often as they will. (Revelation 11:5–6)

Furthermore, it is fire and brimstone that torment the wicked who "worship the beast and his image, and receive his mark in his forehead, or in his hand" and who endure the wrath of God at the proclamations of the angels in Revelation 14.

> And I saw another angel fly in the midst of heaven, having the everlasting gospel to preach unto them that dwell on the earth, and to every nation, and kindred, and tongue, and people, Saying with a loud

---

[24] Ekkehardt Mueller, "Recapitulation in Revelation," *Journal of the Adventist Theological Society*, 9/1-2 (1998): 262.

voice, Fear God, and give glory to him; for the hour of his judgment is come: and worship him that made heaven, and earth, and the sea, and the fountains of waters. And there followed another angel, saying, Babylon is fallen, is fallen, that great city, because she made all nations drink of the wine of the wrath of her fornication. And the third angel followed them, saying with a loud voice, If any man worship the beast and his image, and receive his mark in his forehead, or in his hand, same shall drink of the wine of the wrath of God, which is poured out without mixture into the cup of his; and he shall be tormented with fire and brimstone in the presence of the holy angels, and in the presence of the Lamb. (Revelation 14:6–10)

Again, substantive scrutiny renders Revelation 11 as a counterpart to the sixth trumpet, Revelation 9:13–21, and confirms that it parallels Revelation 7 and 14. The horsemen of the sixth trumpet are merely another perspective of the two witnesses, the 144,000 and the great multitude to come out of great tribulations, who proclaim the messages of the angels in Revelation 14. Furthermore, the preceding trumpet, the fifth, is plainly perceived as a judgment upon the house of God, the church, to separate those who are sealed from those who are not, in likeness with the phenomenon in Ezekiel 9 and in correspondence with "judgment must begin at the house of God" (1 Peter 4:17–18).

And the LORD said unto him, Go through the midst of the city, through the midst of Jerusalem, and set a mark upon the foreheads of the men that sigh and that cry for all the abominations that be done in the midst thereof. And to the others he said in mine hearing, Go ye after him through the city, and smite: let not your eye spare, neither have ye pity. (Ezekiel 9:4–5)

And there came out of the smoke locusts upon the earth: and unto them was given power, as the scorpions of the earth have power. And it was commanded them that they should not hurt the grass of the earth, neither any green thing, neither any tree; but only those men which have not the seal of God in their foreheads. (Revelation 9:3–4)

Here we have the principle Paulien and Stefanovic conveyed concerning the covenantal curse concept where God used the heathen to chastise his people and refining a remnant: "In implementing the covenant curses, God used enemy nations, such as the Philistines, Moabites, Assyrians, and Babylonians, as instruments of his judgment (cf. Judges 2:13–14; Psalms 106:40; Isaiah 10:5–6)."[25] The fifth and sixth trumpet mirror the principle in 1 Peter 4:17–18; God uses those who disavow Christ to separate the wheat from the tares, the chosen from the reprobate, and then he uses his chosen as a plague upon the impenitent preceding his wrath.

Arise and thresh, O daughter of Zion: for I will make thine horn iron, and I will make thy hoofs brass: and thou shalt beat in pieces many people: and I will consecrate their gain unto the LORD, and their substance unto the Lord of the whole earth. (Micah 4:13)

Fear not, thou worm Jacob, and ye men of Israel; I will help thee, saith the LORD, and thy redeemer, the Holy One of Israel. Behold, I will make thee a new sharp threshing instrument having teeth: thou

---

[25] Stefanovic, "The Angel at the Altar (Revelation 8:3-5): A Case Study on Intercalations in Revelation," 90.

shalt thresh the mountains, and beat them small, and shalt make the hills as chaff. (Isaiah 41:14–15)

Thus saith the LORD; Behold, I will raise up against Babylon, and against them that dwell in the midst of them that rise up against me, a destroying wind; will send unto Babylon fanners, that shall fan her, and shall empty her land: for in the day of trouble they shall be against her round about.... Flee out of the midst of Babylon, and deliver every man his soul: be not cut off in her iniquity; for this is the time of the LORD'S vengeance; he will render unto her a recompence.... The portion of Jacob is not like them; for he is the former of all things: and Israel is the rod of his inheritance: the LORD of hosts is his name. Thou art my battle axe and weapons of war: for with thee will I break in pieces the nations, and with thee will I destroy kingdoms. (Jeremiah 51:1–2, 6, 19–20)

It is in the power of God's Spirit that the final warnings of judgment go forth against the ten kingdoms in Revelation 17, depicted in the sixth trumpet and Revelation 11, which causes the eighth king in Revelation 17 to rise out of the abyss to silence them.[26] And just when the beast appears to have silenced (killed) them, the seventh trumpet sounds and the dead in Christ rise first and then "we which are alive and remain shall be caught up together with them in the clouds, to meet the Lord in the air: and so shall we ever be with the Lord" (1 Thessalonians 4:16–17; Revelation 19:14).

---

[26] Paulien and Stefanovic hold the prophecy of the two witnesses in Revelation 11 was fulfilled at the French Revolution. Such a perception is untenable, as it would have the persecuting power of the papacy healed at the exact time they maintain it was wounded; they simply cannot grasp the implications that it is the completely healed papacy that overcomes the witnesses in Rev 11:7. This has been the bane of Historicists of their ilk for some time.

And they heard a great voice from heaven saying unto them, Come up hither. And they ascended up to heaven in a cloud; and their enemies beheld them. (Revelation 11:12)

Clearly, the prohibitions against harming those with the seal of God in the fifth trumpet cannot be divorced from God's use of those "who obey not the Gospel" to separate the chosen from the doomed, nor can the principle of Matthew 12:25–26 be divorced from the phenomena of the sixth trumpet. Under such scrutiny, the fifth, nay, the first five trumpets must represent God's judgment on the church before he judges the reprobate in the sixth trumpet, in conformity with 1 Peter 4:17–18.

The traditional Protestant interpretation that the fifth and sixth trumpets represent the rise and fall of the Ottoman empire falters nowhere with greater transparency than in their inability to render any coherence concerning the locust's prohibitions against harming men having "the seal of God in their foreheads" (Revelation 9:4). In analyzing the historicist Uriah Smith's interpretation of the sealing, Stefansson remarks that Smith did not go much beyond what the nineteenth-century evangelists, Josiah Litch and William Miller, had formulated concerning the seal of God in the fifth trumpet.

Though both Miller and Litch had interpreted the various elements brought to view in command given to the locusts.... neither one had interpreted the seal of God in v. 4 as being of a more specific meaning than a marker of true Christians.... Uriah Smith modified this interpretation ... that ... the seal of God in Rev 7 ... as the seventh-day Sabbath ... and that those who have the seal of God were only there "by implication," and that neither prophecy nor history taught:

"that those persons whom Abubeker charged his followers not to molest were in possession of the seal of God, or necessarily constituted the people of God. Who they were, and for what reason they were spared, the meager testimony of Gibbon does not inform us, and we have no other means of knowing; but we have every reason to believe that none of those who had the seal of God were molested, while another class, who emphatically had it not, were put to the sword."

If Smith had had historical sources that had shown that Sabbath-keepers were especially spared by the Arab invaders, he would probably have dropped his caution. But since this did not appear to be the case, he warned against interpreting more than was explicitly stated in the text.[27]

Smith added his own interpretation of the seal of God as "the seventh-day Sabbath," but there is no historical evidence that the Muslims withheld any such torments from Sabbath-keepers. Such recanting and lack of historical evidence is to the discredit of the traditional historicist's rendition of the trumpets.

The historicist's hermeneutic that the seven churches represent seven eras between the advents maintains that the Laodicean church epitomizes the "end of this age" and that the following three septets must also arrive at the end of this age, in order to sustain recapitulation as the structure of the Revelation; this work concedes that. The object of this work is to vindicate the concept that the placement of the "start" of the following three septets is at the seventh part of the antecedent septet, which was conceded by Alberto R. Treiyer concerning the vials or final plagues; the start of the seven vials or final plagues is concurrent with the seventh trumpet. This work agrees with the testimony of Paulien, Stefanovic and Japp that the trumpets are the response to the petitions of the

---

[27] Stefansson, "From Clear Fulfillment to Complex Prophecy: the History of the Adventist Interpretation of Revelation 9, from 1833 to 1957."

souls under the altar, but comes to a different conclusion that the trumpets cannot fold considerably over the seven churches and seven seals, insomuch as the martyrs slain by Babylon and the eighth king of Revelation 17 cannot be omitted as essential constituents of the meaning of the fifth seal. In support of this different conclusion, this work has shown that the trumpets cannot fold considerably over the churches and seals, insomuch as the seventh month of Tishri cannot be equated with the seven months prior; it is the seven churches that actually represent the "new moon" observances between the spring and autumnal festivals. In support of said conclusion, this work has shown the trumpets *cannot* fold considerably over the churches and seals, inasmuch as the prohibitions against harming those with the seal of God in the fifth trumpet establishes judgment upon God's house (in correspondence with Ezekiel 9:4–5 and 1 Peter 4:17–18). Furthermore, the principle of Matthew 12:25–26 must be observed in interpreting the sixth trumpet; under such scrutiny, the fifth, nay, the first five trumpets must represent God's judgment on the church *before* he judges the reprobate in the sixth trumpet. All the evidence supports that the historical phenomena depicted by the seven trumpets commence with the seventh seal, and, in like manner, the blowing of the seventh trumpet kicks off the seven vials or last plagues. In that view, the trumpets maintain terminological and thematic correspondence as end day phenomena with the sealing of the 144,000 and the messages of the angels.

In continuing to observe the conformity of the structure established above, the historical phenomena depicted by the seven seals must commence during the time of the seventh church; the seals represent the oppression of the church by those who profess allegiance to God's kingdom (in congruity with 2 Thessalonians 2:3–10; Daniel 7: 8–10, 21–22; 1 Timothy 4:1–2 and Revelation 17:6). Conformity to this structure reveals that the seals and trumpets relate to Laodicea's fallen condition of self-indulgence and prodigal material concerns, a condition which spawned persistent provocation for God's punishment under the Old Covenant (Isaiah 5:8–9, 10:2; Jeremiah 34:8–17; Ezekiel 22:29, 45:9; Amos 2:6–8, 8:2–7). This explains the symbolism of the white horse which a great number of historicists attempt to apply to the church;[28] the church goes forth "conquering, and to conquer", but not in the first-century and certainly not for the gospel—but rather it goes forth "conquering, and to conquer" at the time of the end, the nineteenth-century. For it is by their *commerce* that the Protestants oppressed their brethren in order to enrich themselves, and this is the shameful depiction of the spirit of the Laodicean church. The symbolism in the seals represents the provocation for covenantal judgments in the OT that Japp, not too ironically, defined in his dissertation.

> Because the Jews did not keep either the letter or the spirit of the sabbath year, which demanded the freeing of all Jewish slaves, without compensation, every seventh year, and the resting of the land from all agricultural activities, the principle of the sabbath year became the basis of punishment for Judah and Jerusalem (81). The principle of the Jubilee year prescribed that in addition to the freeing of all Israelite slaves and the resting of the land, the full restoration of all property to their original owners or their descendants.(82) In Daniel 9, the Jubilee, encapsulated in the prophetic number of 490 days, becomes the basis for a Messianic promise of release from the enslavement of sin, rest from the works of unbelief and complete restoration of the land to Israel.[29]

---

[28] *Seventh-day Adventist Bible Commentary*: "Thus the first horseman is taken to represent a time when the people of God lived in a world characterized by military conquest and dominion, when Rome, going forth "conquering, and to conquer," maintained the leading world power. Seventh-day Adventists have generally held that the first horse represents the church in the apostolic age." vol. 7, s.v. A white horse, 776.

[29] Japp, "The Study of Atonement in Seventh-day Adventism."

James's prophesy of the last days, below, conveys the self-indulgent and the prodigal materialist condition of the final Laodicean era, which was ordained to oppress their brethren as depicted in the seals; Paulien, Stefanovic, and other historicists of their ilk concede that the seals represent the oppression of the church, but mistakenly attribute it to those who disavow Christ, which does not withstand examination. God uses those who disavow Christ to *refine* the church under the trumpets.

> Go to now, ye rich men, weep and howl for your miseries that shall come upon you. Your riches are corrupted, and your garments are motheaten. Your gold and silver is cankered; and the rust of them shall be a witness against you, and shall eat your flesh as it were fire. Ye have heaped treasure together for the last days. Behold, the hire of the labourers who have reaped down your fields, which is of you kept back by fraud, crieth: and the cries of them which have reaped are entered into the ears of the Lord of sabaoth. Ye have lived in pleasure on the earth, and been wanton; ye have nourished your hearts, as in a day of slaughter. Ye have condemned and killed the just; and he doth not resist you. Be patient therefore, brethren, unto the coming of the Lord. Behold, the husbandman waiteth for the precious fruit of the earth, and hath long patience for it, until he receive the early and latter rain. (James 5:1–7).

The oppression of the elect conveyed by the fifth seal followed the Protestant reformation depicted in the era of Sardis, that sold "the poor for silver, and the needy for a pair of shoes" (Amos 8:6).

> The wool trade was a major driver of enclosure (the privatization of common land) in English agriculture, which in turn had major social

consequences, as part of the British Agricultural Revolution.[30]

Enclosure evicted masses of the peasantry from the land so as to build large scale production farms that sold their produce as commodities during the first attempt at globalism. The peasantry, including the women and children, had no choice but to work the large farms for wages that barely sustained them or to become the cheap labor that prompted the industrial revolution: "And I saw the woman drunken with the blood of the saints, and with the blood of the martyrs of Jesus." Historian Alfred J. Toynbee wrote about this transition that fostered the modern industrial and commercial societies of today. Concerning the early transition Toynbee wrote,

> When we turn to investigate the industrial organisation of the time, we find that the class of capitalist employers was as yet but in its infancy. A large part of our goods were still produced on the domestic system. Manufactures were little concentrated in towns, and only partially separated from agriculture. The manufacturer, was, literally, the man who worked with his own hands in his own cottage. Nearly the whole cloth trade of the West Riding, for instance, was organised on this system at the beginning of the century. An important feature in the industrial organisation of the time was the existence of a number of small master-manufacturers, who were entirely independent, having capital and land of their own, for they combined the culture of small freehold pasture-farms with their handicraft.... This system, however, was no longer universal in Arthur Young's time. That writer found at Sheffield a silk-mill employing 152 hands,

---

[30] Wikipedia, s.v. Medieval English Wool Trade, last modified December 2017, https://en.wikipedia.org/wiki/Medieval_English_wool_trade

including women and children; at Darlington "one master-manufacturer employed above fifty looms"; at Boyton there were 150 hands in one factory. So, too, in the West of England cloth-trade the germs of the capitalist system were visible. The rich merchant gave out work to labourers in the surrounding villages, who were his employes, and were not independent.[31]

According to economic and theological Historian, Richard Henry Tawney, the matter of election was corrupted by Puritanism during the seventeenth-century, which was the underlying cause of the oppressed at issue.

For, since conduct and action, though availing nothing to attain the free gift of salvation, are a proof that the gift has been accorded, what is rejected as a means is resumed as a consequence, and the Puritan flings himself into practical activities with the demonic energy of one who, all doubts allayed, is conscious that he is a sealed and chosen vessel. Once engaged in affairs, he brings to them both the qualities and limitations of his creed in all their remorseless logic. Called by God to labor in his vineyard, he has within himself a principle at once of energy and of order, which makes him irresistible both in war and in the struggles of commerce. Convinced that character is all and circumstances nothing, he sees in the poverty of those who fall by the way, not a misfortune to be pitied and relieved, but a moral failing to be condemned, and in riches, not an object of suspicion—though like other gifts they may be abused—but the blessing which

---

[31] Arnold J Toynbee, "The Industrial Revolution in England," (Beacon press, 1956), 25, https://archive.org/details/industrialrevol00toyngoog

rewards the triumph of energy and will. Tempered
by self-examination, self-discipline, self-control,
he is the practical ascetic, whose victories are won
not in the cloister, but on the battlefield, in the
counting-house, and in the market.[32]

The Reformation had removed the stigma from wealth. But
Puritanism did a complete turnabout to place the stigma on poverty
as if it were a curse from God "a moral failing to be condemned" that
gave them license to exploit and oppress their brethren.[33] Toynbee
and Tawney wrote about the era of the church of Sardis, who was
warned to repent or Christ would come upon them like a thief in the
night (Revelation 3:1–6). Covenantal curses require a warning before
judgment (Amos 3:7), and the warning was fulfilled by the era of the
Philadelphian church, which is expounded upon fairly accurately by
the historicist, Austin Cooke.

At what time, then, did the Philadelphian period
commence? The timeframe covered by Sardis, the
fifth church, was that of the Reformation and post-
Reformation churches, concluding in approximately
1750. This position has been generally held by most
scholars through the years.[34]

---

[32] R.H. Tawney, *Religion and the Rise of Capitalism* (Transaction Publishers
April 1, 1998), 230.

[33] Historicist Ellen G. White conveyed the same mindset concerning the
Pharisees: "Their hearts were full of avarice and selfishness.... When the
poor had presented their affliction to them, they had turned away as unfeeling
as though the afflicted had no souls to save. They had pointed the finger of
scorn at them, speaking vanity, and charging the poor with sin, declaring
that their suffering and poverty was a curse from God on account of their
transgressions." (*Manuscript 37, 1894*, paragraph 12), https://m.egwwritings.
org/en/book/7065.2000001#0

[34] Austin Cooke, "The evangelical revival of Philadelphia," *Heidiheiks.
com*, http://heidiheiks.com/pdf/Revelation/Cooke_Austin-Exposition_of_
Revelation-Topic_5-Philadelphia.pdf

Cooke has the Philadelphian era commence with the time of the Great Awakenings, and with the time of men like John Wesley who,

> attacked the legal, political and religious corruption of the day....
> They abolished child slavery—the cruel system of child labour. The individual prominent in this reform was Lord Shaftesbury, a product of the Revival....
> They attacked bribery and smuggling—the curse of English life—and engaged in a remarkable ministry to the poverty-stricken, who were the vast majority of the population.[35]

Yet, the Great Awakenings abated, while the Protestant penchant for exploiting their brethren did not and became the spirit of the final church era, the Laodicean era. All one has to make is a cursory investigation into the abuses of child labor that continued well into the twentieth-century in America, to find that its horrific practice was upheld by a Supreme Court decision under the right to contract in 1918.[36] Again, the rider of the white horse represents how the Protestants went forth conquering and to conquer the world to expand their markets, where they were compelled to exploit labor

---

[35] Ibid.

[36] William Carey Jones: "Now, after exhaustive investigation,12 displaying an intensity of interest in the subject and a thoroughness of preparation unusual in our legislative methods, Congress passed the Child Labor Law of 1916. An especial effort was made to keep the terms of the statute within strictly constitutional bounds.... the United States Supreme Court and a decision thereon was rendered on June 3, 1918.13 The decision of the lower court was sustained by a vote of five to four, and the act was thus by final authority declared null and void.... the act is not an act to regulate commerce among the states, but is an attempt to regulate the hours of labor of children in factories and mines within the states, and is therefore an unlawful interference with powers reserved to the states." *Child Labor Decision*, 6 Cal. L. Rev. 395 (1918), 399. http://scholarship.law.berkeley.edu/cgi/viewcontent. cgi?article=4050&context=californialawreview

in foreign fields when at home labor began to dissent violently, as they would in America, also. Colonialism ensued, fomented wars and rumors of wars, as characterized by the rider of the red horse. The use of markets and national banks to control the prices of goods and services is characterized by the rider of the black horse and the rider of the pale horse follows when fluctuations, such as depressions and recessions, result in famine and death: "And I saw the woman drunken with the blood of the saints, and with the blood of the martyrs of Jesus" (Revelation 17:6). The scope of this book is not to provide the minutiae on such events, but to show that the events are easily discernable as the apocalyptic four horsemen when the seven seals are properly placed on the Hebraic cultic calendar.

One final issue must be attended to; the apparent conflict with the time constituents in the fifth and sixth trumpets, which causes heated debates when they are synchronized with the 144,000 and the three angels of Revelation 14. Uriah Smith broached the issue some time ago concerning Revelation 10:6.

> "Time No Longer." What is the meaning of this most solemn declaration? It cannot mean that with the message of this angel, time, as computed in this world, in comparison with eternity, should end. The next verse speaks of the days of the voice of the seventh angel, and Revelation 11:15–19 gives us some of the events to take place under this trumpet in the present state. It cannot mean probationary time, for that does not cease until Christ closes His work as priest, which is not until after the seventh angel has begun to sound. (Revelation 11:15, 15:5–8.) It must therefore mean prophetic time, for there is no other to which it can refer....
>
> In other words, prophetic time shall be no more not that time should never be used in a prophetic sense, for the "days of the voice of the seventh angel" spoken of immediately after, doubtless mean the

years of the seventh angel. It means, rather, that no prophetic period should extend beyond the time of this message.[37]

Smith was correct that prophetic time comes to an end at the uttering of the seven thunders, prior to the seventh trumpet, which signifies that the year-for-a-day principle is no longer viable at this junction for determining the time of the seven trumpets. Two witnesses have concluded that the gentiles were given forty Jubilee cycles, or nineteen-hundred and sixty years from the time of Christ, inasmuch as prophetic time is calculated prior to the pronouncement of the seventh angel.

> The types and shadows of Scripture seem to indicate that the Pentecostal Age was meant to last for about 40 Jubilee cycles, or 1960 years (49 x 40). A Jubilee time cycle is 49 years. The Jubilee year was the fiftieth year, but that was also the first year of the next Jubilee cycle. God measures time in sevens, and so 40 Jubilees of time would be 1960 years. It may be, then, that the Pentecostal Age, which began in 33 AD, began to come to a close in 1993 in preparation for a greater Age to come under the anointing of Tabernacles.[38]

> God raised up a brilliant young Jew, Saul of Tarsus, and made him an apostle to the Gentiles in A.D. 34. As a result, the Christian church soon had more Gentile believers in it than Jewish converts. Because there is a New Covenant, the Christian church did not displace Israel; it replaced Israel as trustee.

---

[37] Smith, Daniel and Revelation, 209.
[38] Stephen Jones, "The Millennial Question," *God's Kingdom Mysteries. net*, http://gods-kingdom-ministries.net/teachings/books/creations-jubilee/chapter-1-the-millennium-question/

God abolished the Old Covenant by creating a New Covenant. This redefined Israel. Believers in Jesus are now the heirs of Abraham.[14] History confirms that God granted forty Jubilee cycles to the Gentiles! (A.D. 34 to 1994)[39]

One must conclude that this present age represents the "times of the Gentiles" in Luke 21:24 and Romans 11:25. While the calculations of the theorists differ by one year, 1994 appears to be the most plausible date. As a result, the time constituents in the fifth and sixth trumpets can be calculated with some assurance, but which, as stated above, for the sake of brevity, will be dealt within our examination of Revelation 9.

---

[39] Larry Wilson, "Appendix A-The Importance of 1994," *Wake Up America Seminars*, (March 2014), https://www.wake-up.org/jesus-final-victory-book/importance-of-1994.html

CHAPTER

SEVEN

The Folding of the Seals, Trumpets and Vials

In the previous chapter it was concluded that the historicist's interpretations have progressed as each new generation has learned from the mistakes of the past and corrected their errors; this was chiefly conveyed in the case of the seven vials. Historicist E. B. Elliott held that the first vial or the commencement of the final plagues was fulfilled at the French Revolution,[1] but more recent historicists have concluded that Elliott was in error and that and the vials or final plagues are an end time phenomena at the close of probation, just prior to Christ's return.[2] As a result, the seven vials cannot fold over the eras pertaining to the six earlier churches but must commence within the era of the seventh church; the seventh church encloses the seventh trumpet or the seven final plagues, just prior to Christ's return.

No equivocation can prevail against the truth that past historicists have blundered in interpreting the seals, the trumpets and their structuring, which is even now being brought to light.

---

[1] Tucker, Brief historical explanation of the Revelation of St. John, According to the 'Horæ Apocalypticæ' of the Rev. E.B. Elliott, 103.

[2] The confinement of the seven plagues to the time of the seventh trumpet was sustained by Treiyer: "the last and seventh trumpet was expected to be definitive in connection with the coming of the Lord (Rev 11:18: God's wrath outpoured in the seven plagues, 16:1)." Treiyer's review of Heidi Heiks': *Satin's Counterfeit Prophecy,*" 5.

The contemporary historicists Jon Paulien and Ranko Stefanovic have challenged the traditional historicist's interpretations of the trumpets in connection with the fifth seal and the opening of the trumpets,[3] by which they refuted the traditional views of the fifth and sixth trumpets as representing the rise and fall of the Ottoman empire.[4] Even so, Paulien and Ranko's omissions undermine their own interpretations; for example, the victims of the harlot Babylon (Revelation 17:6) cannot be omitted as an essential constituent of the fifth seal, which establishes that the trumpets maintain terminological and thematic correspondence with the sealing of the 144,000 and the three angels of Revelation 14. The souls under the altar in the fifth seal cry out for the final deliverance from oppression against the saints, in contradiction to the traditional interpretation of the ongoing oppression for two millennia; i.e., claiming that the deliverance is from the Jewish nation, or the Romans and so on, rather promotes a protracted period of oppression. While God delivered his people from such oppression in past ages the adverbial phrase (ἕως πότε) "how long" in Revelation 6:10 expresses finality, an end, as in Psalms 94. Ἕως πότε appears in Psalms 94:3 of the Septuagint to express finality concerning the oppression of the house of Israel in the corporate sense, until its ultimate deliverance, which

---

[3] The traditional perception of recapitulation in Revelation was challenged by Ranko Stefanovic: "It thus appears that the clue to the full theological meaning of Rev 8:3-5 lies in the scene of the fifth seal." *The Angel at the Altar (Revelation 8:3-5): A Case Study on Intercalations in Revelation*, 86; Paulien also states: "Very significant is the reference in Rev 8:13, which stands at the structural center of the seven trumpets. This verse indicates that the trumpet plagues fall on 'those who live on the earth,' the same group which was martyring the saints, referred to in 6:9-11 as the 'souls under the altar,'" *Interpreting the Seven Trumpets*, 6-7. In both cases the sixth seal becomes a flash-forward and thwarts the traditional perception of recapitulation.

[4] In the sixth chapter of this work Stefansson was cited to vindicate the traditional historicist's interpretation of the trumpets, specifically the fifth and sixth, is under assault and cannot withstand the contemporary historic evidence that exposes its fallacies.

is precisely how the adverbial phrase is used in the fifth seal. The use of the phrase to convey a protracted phenomenon is an inconsistency.

It must be noted that the prophesied judgment depicted in the fifth seal must, by precedent, also represent, in the words of historicist William H. Shea, a "judgment which distinguishes between the righteous and the wicked in Israel."[5] An indication that this is the particular judgment applicable to the souls under the altar is seen in the response to them; they are given gifts of white robes and a favorable decision is rendered on their behalf as saints of the most High as in Daniel 7. Shea makes just such a connection with his perception that the judgment in Daniel 7 pertains to the church and the little horn in the booklet, *Selected Studies on Prophetic Interpretation*.

> For if the little horn stands for the papacy (as various interpreters in this school of interpretation have held), then this judgment has to deal, among other matters, with a professedly Christian entity.... Thus a judgment of the little horn would appear to involve a judgment of the millions of people who have attempted to follow God through allegiance to this alleged earthly representative of His. Any investigation by this judgment of the little horn should therefore involve an investigation into the cases of those professed Christian individuals who have made up and followed this corporate group.... The results of the judgment described in Daniel 7 cut both ways. An unfavorable decision is rendered in the case of the little horn: Its dominion is taken away and it is destroyed (vs. 6). On the other hand, a favorable decision is rendered in behalf of the saints of the Most High: They receive the kingdom (vs. 22).[6]

---

[5] William H. Shea, *Selected Studies on Prophetic Interpretation*, (Biblical Research Institute, 1992, printed by Review and Herald Publishing Association), 145.
[6] Ibid.

Shea's passage is from a composition about Divine judgments that were connected to the sanctuary, which surely concerns the anticipated judgment of the fifth seal that is consummated by the events of the trumpets. The applicability of Shea's conclusion is confirmation that the judgments anticipated in the fifth seal cannot commence asynchronously with the sealing of the 144,000 and the decrees of the three angels in Revelation 14; they must be contemporaneous. Shea did not go on to elaborate that the judgment "of the millions of people who have attempted to follow God" must conform to the principle of 1 Peter 4:17–18; the little horn cannot be judged until God judges his house, first. Historicist Ellen G. White stumbled on the synchronicity between the judgment in Daniel 7 and the sealing of the 144,000 and the decrees of the three angels in a publication intended for evangelists.

> No one has yet received the mark of the beast. The testing time has not yet come. There are true Christians in every church, not excepting the Roman Catholic communion. None are condemned until they have had the light.... the loud cry of the third angel shall warn men against the worship of the beast and his image, the line will be clearly drawn between the false and the true. Then those who still continue in transgression will receive the mark of the beast.[7]

White is unequivocally addressing the judgment of the little horn that must be preceded by calling out God's people, which is the same judgment that Shea wrote about in the passage from his composition. Shea found that there is a minority of judgments connected to the sanctuary, some of which pertain strictly to heathen nations; this is not the case concerning the trumpets, conveyed in the imagery of the gift of the white robes. The trumpets must initially represent

---

[7] Ellen G. White, *Evangelism* (Washington, DC: *Review and Herald Pub. Assn.*, 1946), 234.

the precedent of a "judgment which distinguishes between the righteous and the wicked in Israel" that pertains to the church, which contrasts it from the prototypes pertaining strictly to the nations. The judgments depicted in the trumpets must commence with the church, in correspondence with 1 Peter 4:17–18, as conveyed in chapter six. This was also unintentionally confirmed by White in other publications.

> The events to transpire under the fifth seal are, the crying of the martyrs for vengeance, and giving to them white robes. This represents the work of the reformers, and covers the period of the great reformation. In reference to the souls under the altar, Dr. Clarke says: 'A symbolical vision was exhibited in which he saw an altar. And under it the souls of those who had been slain for the word of God—martyred for their attachment to Christianity—are represented as being newly slain, as victims to idolatry and superstition. *The altar is upon earth, not in Heaven.*'[8]

> When the fifth seal was opened, John the Revelator in vision saw beneath the altar the company that were slain for the Word of God and the testimony of Jesus Christ. After this came the scenes described in the eighteenth of Revelation, when those who are faithful and true are called out from Babylon.[9]

The historicists discussed at present represent the Seventh-day Adventists, who are a significant group within historicism. They are

---

[8] White is delineating her interpretation of the seals in the citation, which was written down by her husband James. James White, *The Sign of the Times*, 20.1, (Seventh-day Adventist Publishing Association. Battle Creek, Mich., 1865) https://m.egwwritings.org/en/book/1535.28#92

[9] Ellen G. White, Manuscripts 39 (Silver Spring, MD: Ellen G. White Estate, 1906), paragraph 3

committed to agreeing with White and cannot avoid her conclusion that the oppression referred to in the fifth seal includes that imposed on the reformers in the sixteenth- and seventeenth-centuries,[10] and her thematic and terminological correspondence with the call to come out of Babylon in Revelation 18. Her concessions support the understanding that the trumpets cannot represent judgments prior to that time, insomuch as the souls of the fifth seal are admonished to wait until an appointed time when more of their brethren must be killed before said judgments materialize. Adventists Jon Paulien and Ranko Stefanovic correctly maintain that the trumpets represent the punishment of those who oppress the souls depicted in the fifth seal;[11] yet they err on the timing, proposing that the trumpets represent judgments prior to the "Great Reformation." If one concedes Ellen G. White was correct above, the punishments depicted by the trumpets are yet future.

> The prophecies in the eighteenth of Revelation will soon be fulfilled. During the proclamation of the third angel's message, "another angel" is to "come down from heaven, having great power," and the earth is to be "lightened with his glory." The Spirit of the Lord will so graciously bless consecrated human instrumentalities that men, women, and children will open their lips in praise and thanksgiving, filling the earth with the knowledge of God, and with his unsurpassed glory, as the waters cover the sea.[12]

---

[10] In her book, *The Great Controversy*, pages 249-64, White has the opening of the "Great Reformation" commence with Luther and Tyndale (circa sixteenth century) and then expiring by the eighteenth century and having to be rekindled by men such as Charles and John Wesley.

[11] Paulien, "Interpreting the Seven Trumpets," 6–7; Stefanovic, "The Angel at the Altar (Revelation 8:3-5): A Case Study on Intercalations in Revelation," 90.

[12] *Seventh-day Adventist Bible Commentary*, vol. 7, s.v. chapter 18 (Review and Herald Pub., 1980), 983–984.

White maintained that the fifth seal conveyed the oppression of the reformers in the sixteenth- and seventeenth-centuries, which substantiates that the events depicted by the trumpets cannot commence prior to this, which agrees with her passages, above, and makes the traditional historicist's interpretation of the trumpets, imbibed by the Adventists, steeped in contradictions and errors. Furthermore, White's rendition of the fifth seal represents the same judgment in Shea's extract, above, which indisputably establishes that the judgments depicted by the trumpets cannot possibly be interpreted as commencing until the reformation abated, after the phenomenon in Daniel 7:10. No gainsay will prosper against the conclusion that the victims of the harlot Babylon (Revelation 17:6) are an essential constituent of those who are martyred in the fifth seal, and such establishes terminological and thematic correspondence between the trumpets, the sealing of the 144,000 and the decrees of the three angels.

The traditional historicist's interpretation of the harlot woman in Revelation 17, Babylon, is that she represents the papacy. White held this view.

> In Revelation 17, Babylon is represented as a woman, a figure which is used in the Scriptures as the symbol of a church. A virtuous woman represents a pure church, a vile woman an apostate church.... The Babylon thus described represents Rome, that apostate church which has so cruelly persecuted the followers of Christ.[13]

Yet, the Adventists developed the notion that in other passages in the Revelation, Babylon cannot be construed as such because the papacy can hardly be described as fallen from moral rectitude at the time of

---

[13] Ellen G. White, The Spirit of Prophecy: The Great Controversy Between Christ and Satan from the Destruction of Jerusalem to the End of the Controversy, vol. 4 (Battle Creek: Steam Press, 1884), 233.

the pronouncement to God's people to come out of her (Revelation 14:8; 18:1–4). White conceded this reflection.

> The message of Revelation 14, announcing the *fall* of Babylon, must apply to religious bodies that were once pure and have become corrupt. Since this message follows the warning of the judgment, it must be given in the last days; therefore it cannot refer to the Roman Church alone, for that church has been in a fallen condition for many centuries. Furthermore, in the eighteenth chapter of the Revelation the people of God are called upon to come out of Babylon. According to this scripture, many of God's people must still be in Babylon.[14]

A contemporary of White in the Advent movement, Edward S. Ballenger, contended with her over the issue of viewing Babylon as disconnected entities in Revelation.

> There is but one Babylon of the book of Revelation and any one who attempts to teach otherwise is ignorant, stupid, or blinded by a creed. My brother, if you contend that Babylon of Rev. 17 represents Rome, and Babylon of Rev. 14:8 represents Protestant churches that fell morally in 1844, how can you meet the Sunday Sabbath advocate if he contends that "Sabbath" of the book of Acts, or "the Lord's day" of Rev. 1:10 means Sunday? One is no more inconsistent than the other. To contend that Babylon of the second angel's message represents fallen Protestantism one is obliged to ignore God's

---

[14] Ellen G. White, *The Great Controversy*, (Review and Herald pub., 1911), 383.

definition of Babylon and violate one of the most fundamental rules of sound interpretation.[15]

Ballenger was correct in one sense; there are good reasons to consistently perceive Babylon as the same entity throughout the book of Revelation, but he failed to grasp that Babylon cannot be equated to the revived eighth king in Revelation 17. There is a juxtaposition between the woman and the kings. The kings were ordained or chosen to oppress the people of God; however, the woman, who this work maintains represents the people of God, was not ordained as such but is allowed to fall from moral rectitude in the time of the end to oppress or exploit her children. Although displeasing to God, he allowed her unsanctified behavior to fulfill his plan. Again, in contrast, the kings were ordained to oppress God's people while the woman, unlike the kings, is allowed to have her way and fall from moral rectitude to oppress her children, just as the Israel under the OT.

> Son of man, cause Jerusalem to know her abominations.... thou hast taken thy sons and thy daughters, whom thou hast borne unto me, and these hast thou sacrificed unto them to be devoured. *Is this* of thy whoredoms a small matter, thou hast slain my children, and delivered them to cause them to pass through *the fire* for them? (Ezekiel 16:2, 20–21)

There is no juxtaposition between the harlot in Revelation 14, 17 and 18, insomuch as she is indicted in Revelation 17, which links her to her fall in Revelation 14 and 18. White unwittingly stumbles on this by maintaining that the "image" to the papacy represents the time when "the Protestant churches shall seek the aid of the

---

[15] Edward S. Ballenger, "The Second Angel's Message or the Fall of Babylon," 5-6, https://archive.org/details/BallengerEdwardStroud.TheSecond AngelsMessageOrTheFallOfBabylon

civil power for the enforcement of their dogmas."[16] But White's view of Protestantism as becoming apostate in her time was not unprecedented and Revelation makes it plain that the beast and the false prophet (Revelation 13–19) represent persecuting ecclesiastic and civil powers on judgment day. Protestantism and Roman Catholicism play a part in judgment day. The history of Romanism and Protestantism make a case for John being taken by the Spirit into the future and from that viewpoint, then, the woman represents apostate Protestantism that is on the verge of steering America into making the "image" that will enforce religious dogmas through civil authority. The traditional Protestant interpretation that the sixth king in Revelation 17 represents imperial Rome cannot withstand the evidence in verses 8–11 that the eighth king "was" prior to the sixth king, and not that the sixth king "was" and "is" at the time John is witnessing the indictment of the harlot woman Babylon. Further, the view that the sixth king is Rome only allows for one more king before the eighth king, the papacy, becomes clothed in the civil power it once had prior to the rise of America. But in rendering imperial Rome as the fourth king (one of the five that had fallen) the sequence correctly allows for three more kings to rise after Rome before the eighth is once again clothed in civil power. Rendering imperial Rome as the fourth king allows the two-horned beast in Revelation 13, America, to be the sixth king and the image it makes becomes the seventh that rules for a short space before the eighth is once again clothed in the civil powers it had before the rise of America; all the beasts in Daniel and the Revelation are accounted for as the seven, nay eight kings in Revelation 17. Obviously White failed to grasp that the viewpoint in which John saw the woman was from the future, with the consequence being that the woman of Revelation 17 cannot then be interpreted as the papacy at any time, but must rather consistently represent the same entity of apostate Protestantism.[17] This makes Ballenger correct in his

---

[16] White, The Great Controversy, 445.

[17] Ironically, White grasped the concept of being taken into the future and viewing events from that perspective but never applied it to interpret

assessment that Babylon is not the papacy in one place and apostate Protestantism in another, even though he was wrong in stating that she represents the papacy, whatsoever. There is an indication that the woman is indicted as Babylon at the time the two-horned beast makes the image in Revelation 13 and this supports she cannot be the papacy, but must represent apostate Protestantism, which somewhat substantiates what White stumbled onto: that the one who steers America to make the image is apostate Protestantism.

The woman riding the beast in Revelation 17 cannot be perceived as Babylon until she is indicted for exercising the "the aid of the civil power for the enforcement of her dogmas," which means that prior to her fall she is merely an ecclesiastical entity. This is supported when the *sine qua non* of the kings in Revelation 17 is grasped, conveyed in *Identifying the Two-horned Beast*: the marriage of state and religion. The kings must exercise civil as well as ecclesiastical authority or ultimately sanctioning that power again, as in the two-horned beast, in any proper interpretation by a historicist, or error results, such as in the failure of some who have construed the kings as mere ideologies.[18] While the Protestant churches experimented with the marriage of state and religion as they broke from the papacy, the Spirit moved them to realize that the Roman church had been responsible for infamous and horrendous atrocities only because of this church and state relationship; thus, they ultimately established secular states in the Protestant nations. In command of the previous evidence, the woman that is indicted in Revelation 17

Revelation 17: "At times I am carried far ahead into the future and shown what is to take place. Then again I am shown things as they have occurred in the past." *Spiritual Gifts*, vol. 2, (Battle Creek, MI: Seventh-day Adventist Publishing Association, 1860), 292, http://text.egwwritings.org/publication. php?pubtype=Book&bookCode=2SG&pagenumber=292

[18] George McCready Price mistakenly rendered the sixth king as, "the anti-Genesis apostasy of our time," a mere ideology, instead of maintaining the historicist's guideline that the kings are *successive dominant world powers*, which conveys tangible civil as well as ecclesiastical power. (Price, *Time of the End*, 45); other historicists have followed him and have mistakenly rendered the sixth king as a mere ideology.

is easily equated to the woman that is helped in the "wilderness" in Revelation 12: the Jerusalem which is above (Galatians 4:26). She is the only woman in the Revelation that is able to mother daughters capable of falling from moral rectitude, to be fulfilled when the Protestants steer America to make the image to the papacy.

> What constitutes the fall of Babylon? Those who contend that the Babylon of Revelation is the city of Rome, answer that the fall of Babylon is the burning of Rome; while those who make Babylon a symbol of the church of Rome only, answer that this fall is the loss of her civil power-the fall of the woman from the beast. We dissent from both these positions, believing that the fall of Babylon is a moral fall, and that it denotes her rejection as a body, by God.[19]

History actually confirms that it was the work of groups like the Paulicians, Albigenses, Cathars, Waldenses and the Anabaptists, to name a few, who "birthed" the Reformation and the Protestants, while the papacy was actually attempting to kill the reformation, which exposes the traditional Protestant interpretation of Babylon as a warped perception of motherhood. It was the "Jerusalem which is above" in Galatians 4:26 that mothered the Paulicians, Albigenses, Cathars, Waldenses and the Anabaptists and it was their work that led to the Reformation and the several groups that became the Protestants, which affirms that the woman of Revelation 12 is the same woman of Revelation 17. Further evidence lies in the precedent where God's people are personified as Jerusalem and then at times they are indicted as a harlot for fornicating with the kings of the earth, as in Ezekiel 16. The Revelation simply does not support

---

[19] J. N. Andrews, *The Three Angels of Revelation 14:6-12*, (Advent Review Office, Rochester, N. Y., 1855), 52, http://www.centrowhite.org.br/files/ebooks/apl/all/Andrews/The%20Three%20Angels%20of%20Revelation%20 14:6-12.pdf

that the papacy represents Babylon; unquestionably the papacy is the beast that rises from the sea, the fifth and revived eighth king in Revelation 17, that is ordained to persecute the woman of Revelation 12. The woman, first observed in heaven in Revelation 12, represents the era of Ephesus, who subsequently is seen in the wilderness during the era of Thyatira, and who later represents Babylon in the final Laodicean era, when John sees her indicted and seated upon the scarlet colored beast in Revelation 17:3.

Only upon the establishment of the ancient city of Jerusalem did the city become the personification of a woman and the people of God, as in Galatians 4:26 (Isaiah 2:3, 51:17, 52:1, 2, 9; Jeremiah 51:35, 52:1–2, 17; Ezekiel 5:5, 16:2). In the OT the people of God were personified as a woman, Jerusalem, and Jerusalem becomes "the city set upon a hill," which is the source of Christ's theological perception in Matthew, below.

> Ye are the light of the world. A city that is set on an hill cannot be hid. Neither do men light a candle, and put it under a bushel, but on a candlestick; and it giveth light unto all that are in the house. (Matthew 5:14–15)

The term hill (ὅρους) and woman are theological perceptions representing Jerusalem.

> Son of man, cause Jerusalem to know her abominations. (Ezekiel 16:2)

> Thus saith the LORD; I am returned unto Zion, and will dwell in the midst of Jerusalem: and Jerusalem shall be called a city of truth; and the mountain of the LORD of hosts the holy mountain. (Zechariah 8:3)

This personification and theological perception hinder Egypt and Assyria from being counted as the kings in Revelation 17; God had not set his people on any mountain in any association with Egypt or Assyria. The personification is an anachronism while the descendants of Jacob abide in Egypt, insomuch as the personification abides in Judah when the northern tribes are deported to Assyria. Only upon the deportation to Babylon did the personification have justification (Isaiah 52:1–2; Zechariah 1:14–17, 2:7), but she had no more independence than did the Byzantine state as an Ottoman vassal. As established above, it was the woman depicted in the wilderness in Revelation 12 that "birthed" the Reformation and the Protestant daughters, who finally broke from the papacy and formed independent states in Europe and most significantly in America, which is why White and Adventists maintain that America, at the influence of apostate Protestantism, will form the "image" to the papacy. The woman in Revelation 12 had no power to steer any state during the twelve-hundred and sixty years of Papal persecution and only gained such power when American arose; this becomes the justification for why she sits and steers the beast during the reign of the sixth king, America. It is America that developed the greatest Protestant influence upon the state in the Laodicean era, from the event when the papacy suffered its deadly wound. It is America, the sixth king in Revelation 17, that represents the two-horned beast that enforces the "image" to the papacy. The personification of the woman in Revelation 17 has no fulfillment in the papacy.

The evidence in Revelation points to the woman in Revelation 12 as being the woman who is indicted as Babylon in Revelation 17 when she inaugurates the "image" to the papacy. A significant part of the evidence is the denunciation of the woman for fornicating with the kings of the earth, which reveals that the woman was obligated to maintain a spiritual, monogamous and marital covenant relationship with God. This also substantiates that the woman in Revelation 17 can only refer to the woman in Revelation 12 (2 Corinthians 11:2; Ephesians 5:26). The fornication is in the indicative mood that qualifies the action to the past, in relation to the indictment that she has become "the habitation of devils, and the hold of every foul spirit, and a cage of every unclean and hateful bird" (Revelation 18:2). The evidence that the woman is denounced for her past fornication with the kings of the earth also substantiates that she once wrestled against the powers of evil, which is by definition the "church militant."

> CHURCH MILITANT: the Christian church on earth regarded as engaged in a constant warfare against its enemies, the powers of evil — distinguished from *church triumphant*.[20]

> CHURCH TRIUMPHANT: members of the church who have died and are regarded as enjoying eternal happiness through union with God — compare CHURCH MILITANT, CHURCH SUFFERING[21]

The idioms are not found in the scriptures and have their origins in theological doctrines early in Christendom, evidenced by the Roman Catholic and traditional Protestant's perceptions, above, that militant obligations end when individuals die and go to heaven. While the militancy of the church in this age is based on sound doctrine, through texts such as Ephesians 6:12, the traditional Protestant concept of the "triumphant church" is not founded as such and requires correction, which was undertaken by an author for Wikipedia.

> Thus, the Seventh-day Adventist view is unique in that the church is the Church Militant until the general resurrection at the end of the present age.

---

[20] *Merriam-Webster Dictionary.com*, s.v. church militant, accessed October 27, 2018, https://www.merriam-webster.com/dictionary/church%20militant
[21] Ibid., s.v. church triumphant, accessed October 27, 2018, https://www.merriam-webster.com/dictionary/church%20triumphant

> The church becomes the Church Triumphant only
> after the second coming of Christ.[22]

We wrestle against the satanic powers of this world as the "church militant" until Christ's return, at which time the church shall triumph over them. Texts such as Ephesians 6:12 are foundational to the doctrine of the "church militant,"[23] while texts such as Matthew 25:21, 23 support the notion of the "church triumphant." But Adventists have unfortunately perverted the doctrine to such a degree that they believe that a faction of the church becomes the "church triumphant" before Christ returns and coexists with the "church militant." This perversion stems from one of White's statements pertaining to the doctrine.

> The members of the church triumphant—the
> church in heaven—will be permitted to draw near
> to the members of the church militant, to aid them
> in their necessity.[24]

This is an obvious distortion of the doctrine of the "militant church." The distortion has led to the persistence by a small faction of historicists, such as Ron Beaulieu, to maintain that the two groups coexist in this age.

---

[22] Wikipedia, s.v. Churches Militant, Penitent, and Triumphant, last modified May 2018, https://en.wikipedia.org/wiki/Churches_Militant,_Penitent,_and_Triumphant

[23] *Seventh-day Adventist Bible Commentary*: "Paul did not mean that Christians would find no enemies among men, for the church has always suffered at the hands of wicked men. He refers to those spirits and powers that are superior to men in intelligence as well as in evil cunning, the satanic forces arrayed in open rebellion against God and against His children." vol. 6, s.v. Flesh and blood, 1044.

[24] Ellen G. *White, The Southern Watchman*, (Washington, D.C.: Review and Herald Publishing), https://m.egwwritings.org/pt/book/489.452

Ellen White says that the church triumphant co-exists with the church militant in order to come to the aid of the church militant.[25]

Nevertheless, as long as there are powers of evil, the church has an obligation of militancy against evil; she still represents the "church militant" by definition. White's statement that "the church in heaven" will be permitted to engage those who are members of the church militant actually concedes the existence of evil that maintains power in this age and the obligation to wrestle against it. The noun phrase "the church in heaven" does not appear anywhere in scripture and is based on a fallacious theology of a faction within the church that perceives they have triumphed against evil and by implication are no longer obligated to wrestle against it, which is in actuality the condemnation of the women in Revelation 17.[26]

> And there came one of the seven angels which had the seven vials, and talked with me, saying unto me, Come hither; I will shew unto thee the judgment of the great whore that sitteth upon many waters: With whom the kings of the earth have committed fornication, and the inhabitants of the earth have been made drunk with the wine of her fornication. (Revelation 17:1–2)

As long as there are principalities, powers, rulers of the darkness, and spiritual wickedness in high places the church is obligated

---

[25] Ron Beaulieu, "The Real Church That Appears as About to Fall But Does Not!" *Omega Countdown Ministries*, http://omega77.tripod.com/churAATFall.htm

[26] Beaulieu cites Hebrews 12:22-24 to assert: "Mount Zion in the heavenly Jerusalem city, is the general assembly and church of the FIRSTBORN, [FIRSTFRUITS] that are written in heaven, and it consists of the spirits of just men made perfect. This is the church triumphant. This is the heavenly kingdom church from which and by which sinners are shaken, (Matthew 13:41-49)." Ibid.

to wrestle against them according to Ephesians 6:12 and by definition represents the "church militant" even as she can also be perceived, theologically, as "the church in heaven" in such places as Galatians 4:26, Ephesians 2:6 and Hebrews 12:22–24. The woman of Revelation 17 is condemned because she fails to maintain her obligation to remain militant against the kings of the earth, which is personified as fornication with the kings of the earth.

In review, Shea maintained that the judgement of the little horn in Daniel involves "a judgment of the millions of people who have attempted to follow God through allegiance to this alleged earthly representative,"[27] and that earthly representative is the papacy according to Adventists and historicists in general. Considering those same people, White maintained they would pay this allegiance until "the loud cry of the third angel,"[28] which reveals that the judgment in Daniel 7 begins with the house of God in conformity with 1 Peter 4:17–18 and exposes the judgment as covenantal in nature. Said conformity affirms that the first five trumpets, the first woe, must uphold the precedent of past judgments "which distinguish between the righteous and the wicked in Israel."[29] The condemnation for fornicating with the kings of the earth, regarding the woman riding the beast in Revelation 17, refers to her obligation of militancy, as she was to wrestle against the kings of the earth; thus, the woman cannot be said to be the papacy, insomuch as the papacy was ordained to oppress the woman in Revelation 12 up until the time of the sixth king, when it was wounded (Revelation 13:3, 7). White agreed with the latter, which substantially supports the point that the woman in Revelation 17 represents the fallen state of the women of Revelation 12 and is the mother of harlot daughters. The papacy was not obliged to wrestle against evil; it was ordained as an evil power and for this reason cannot be condemned for fornicating with the kings of earth. Mastering this evidence renders the woman in Revelation 17 as apostate Protestantism, not the papacy, who is drunk with the

---

[27] Shea, "Selected Studies on Prophetic Interpretation"
[28] White, *Evangelism*, 234.
[29] Shea, "Selected Studies on Prophetic Interpretation"

blood of the saints and the martyrs. The Protestant's fornication with the kings was occurring at the time of White and the advent movement, but this history was for another time, for succeeding generations to uncover. The history of how the Protestants exploited their brethren and made their lives miserable and short was meant for this generation, the final generation, to unveil: "And I saw the woman drunken with the blood of the saints, and with the blood of the martyrs of Jesus" (Revelation 17:6). This revelation unveils the four horsemen of the seven seals as representing the exploitation of the saints by apostate Protestants, insomuch as the martyrs slain by Babylon, apostate Protestantism, cannot be omitted as an essential constituent of the intent of the fifth seal. Mastering the aforesaid, unveils the four horsemen of the seals as representing apostate Protestantism's exploitation of their own brethren to enrich themselves.

As revealed in chapter six, the evidence that the opening scene of the trumpets represents the response to the pleas of the saints in the fifth seal for judgment against those who have oppressed them establishes that the seals represent their oppression and the trumpets represent said judgment. What the traditional historicists and Adventists have failed to grasp concerning this is that the trumpets represent covenant judgments, which must begin at the house of God (1 Peter 4:17–18), and, consequently, the oppression represented by the seals must be interpreted as originating from those who profess "allegiance to God's kingdom" before judgment falls on those who have never avowed such allegiance. Precedent establishes that the most common covenantal provocation for God's judgments was the exploitation of the poor by the affluent.

> Woe unto them that decree unrighteous decrees, and that write grievousness *which* they have prescribed; To turn aside the needy from judgment, and to take away the right from the poor of my people, that widows may be their prey, and *that* they may rob the fatherless! And what will ye do in the day of

visitation, and in the desolation *which* shall come from far? to whom will ye flee for help? and where will ye leave your glory? (Isaiah 10:1–3)

Thus saith the LORD; For three transgressions of Israel, and for four, I will not turn away *the punishment* thereof; because they sold the righteous for silver, and the poor for a pair of shoes; That pant after the dust of the earth on the head of the poor, and turn aside the way of the meek. (Amos 2:6–7)

Such compounding evidence revealing that apostate Protestantism exploited their poor brethren with the first attempt at globalism leads us to confirm another shocking conclusion—the fallen woman, apostate Protestantism, also represents Babylon in the Revelation. She is not the papacy, and this suggestion was eradicated in chapter six. This can be supported by looking at the history of the struggle between the Anglican church and Puritanism in England. The Anglican church still held vestiges of the Medieval concept that the obligations of society were based upon a spiritual endeavor, which married state and religion, while the Puritans championed "individualism" that diminished "obligations imposed by social institutions (such as the state or religious morality)";[30] the latter led to the separation of church and state. The historical evidence overwhelmingly vindicates that the Puritan doctrine of "individualism" triumphed and that this led to an exploitation of the lower masses in agriculture and industry at a magnitude never before witnessed in history. The alteration from an agrarian society to a wage earning one is just one element that vindicates the aforesaid.

---

[30] Wikipedia: "Individualists are chiefly concerned with protecting individual autonomy against obligations imposed by social institutions (such as the state or religious morality)." s.v. Individualism, modified May 2018, https://en.wikipedia.org/wiki/Individualism

Go to now, *ye* rich men, weep and howl for your miseries that shall come upon *you*. Your riches are corrupted, and your garments are motheaten. Your gold and silver is cankered; and the rust of them shall be a witness against you, and shall eat your flesh as it were fire. Ye have heaped treasure together for the last days. Behold, the hire of the labourers who have reaped down your fields, which is of you kept back by fraud, crieth: and the cries of them which have reaped are entered into the ears of the Lord of sabaoth. Ye have lived in pleasure on the earth, and been wanton; ye have nourished your hearts, as in a day of slaughter. Ye have condemned *and* killed the just; *and* he doth not resist you. Be patient therefore, brethren, unto the coming of the Lord. Behold, the husbandman waiteth for the precious fruit of the earth, and hath long patience for it, until he receive the early and latter rain. Be ye also patient; stablish your hearts: for the coming of the Lord draweth nigh. (James 5:1–8)

Theologian and economic historian Richard Henry Tawney was cited in chapter six for his analysis that the early Calvinists had subdued the medieval onus of wealth that was ultimately placed on poverty by the Puritans.[31] We discovered this shift under the heading of THE NEW MEDICINE FOR POVERTY, where we observed that during the earlier Elizabethan Tudor dynasty "statesmen had little mercy for idle rogues" but had to concede "pauperism primarily as a social phenomenon produced by economic dislocation," which still triggered "social compunction" with indictments of "at whose handes shall the bloude of these men be required?" by the English clergy, such as William Harrison.[32] Harrison fulfilled the apolitical obligation of the "church militant" and exposed the mischief

---

[31] Tawney, *Religion and the Rise of Capitalism*, 230.
[32] Ibid., 270.

produced by the unregenerate who exploited their impoverished brethren to enrich themselves (James 5:1–8). Harrison concluded that the church's failure to expose such mischief would place the blood of the victims in her hands: "And I saw the woman drunken with the blood of the saints, and with the blood of the martyrs of Jesus" (Revelation 17:6). Another social, historical author, Richard F. Hamilton, chronicles the very same account.

> Calvinism, however, is best seen as a social movement. As such, it was subject to many impulses and, accordingly, was continuously changing. The movement had its greatest impact over nearly two centuries, beginning in the 1540s. It began as an aggressive radical force, as a "church militant," the phrase culminating in the Thirty Years' War, a devastating struggle to determine among other things, the position of Calvinism within Europe.... In England, Calvinism was represented by the Puritans, a reform movement within the Church of England that began in the Elizabethan period. The struggle between the orthodox Anglicans and the reformers centered on questions of ritual, church governance, moral standards, and the royal prerogative. The attempted repression of this movement under Charles I and Archbishop William Laud led to the English Civil War (also called the Puritan Revolution), 1642–1648, and to the deposition and execution of the monarch. The short-lived Commonwealth followed; it was the period of Calvinist triumph. In 1660, Parliament ended that experiment and the monarchy was restored. The Puritanism of the Restoration period

differed from its predecessors—sober, temperate, and restrained, it was no longer a "militant" church.[33]

Hamilton chronicled that the Puritans during the Elizabethan era fulfilled their "militant" obligations, which Tawney conveyed in one sense was to apolitically expose the fallen moral standard of the state pertaining to its obligation to provide relief for the pauperism it created because of "economic dislocation," which was merely another way of expressing that the state had fostered the circumstances due to its economic policies. Some century and a half later the situation had changed and the Puritans no longer fulfilled their obligations to remain "militant" and act as the apolitical conscience of the state, to act as a city set on a hill to be a light, but became a political force to further their own ambitious aims of "individualism" to exploit the poor; Hamilton cites from other authors such as Baxter and Essen and continues.

> The doctrine of the calling existed before and after the Civil War, but before, the Puritan writers counseled "activism, warfare, vigilance, and intolerance," whereas afterwards the emphasis was on "meekness, humility, chastity, tolerance, etc." The earlier attempt to "transform the earthly order" gave way to an encouragement of the "lower class" in the "obedience to the new order by then produced." Baxter's ideal type, Eisen writes, "cannot be Weber's, for the personality moulded is different: in place of mastery, we find resignation, and in place of the accountable believer, a belittling of man's ability to decide the right for himself." Weber picked up and emphasized (Eisen says he "exaggerated") the denial of pleasure, the asceticism of Puritanism.

---

[33] Richard F. Hamilton, The Social Misconstruction of Reality: Validity and Verification in the Scholarly Community (Yale University Press, April 24, 1996), 69-70.

But the portrait of driven men aiming to master the world is a "distortion" of the later formulations. Puritanism, in the second half of the seventeenth-century, had adopted the quietism Weber attributes to Lutheranism.[34]

Hamilton chronicled that the Puritans began to "encourage" (more in the order of control) the "poor" to be obedient to the new order, which completely conflicts with his criticism of Weber's analysis that the Puritans were "driven men aiming to master the world." Hamilton's former analysis is rather in harmony with Weber and is what history actually affirms, especially when it affirms that the Puritans became the bourgeois of the era. Hamilton affirms that the Puritans encouraged the "lower class" to be obedient to the new order, but as history affirms, for themselves, they continued to champion "individualism" which diminished "their obligations imposed by social institutions (such as the state or religious morality)." Hamilton unsuccessfully attempts to nitpick the German sociologist, philosopher, jurist, and political economist, Max Weber, who also wrote about the era. Here Weber writes,

As far as the influence of the Puritan outlook extended, under all circumstances – and this is, of course, much more important than the mere encouragement of capital accumulation – it favoured the development of a rational bourgeoisie's economic life; it was the most important, and above all the only consistent influence in the development of that life. It stood at the cradle of the modern economic man. To be sure, these Puritanical ideals tended to give way under excessive pressure from the temptations of wealth, as the Puritans themselves knew very well. With great regularity we find the most genuine adherents of Puritanism among

---

[34] Ibid., 70.

the classes which were rising from a lowly status, the small bourgeois and farmers, while the *beati possidentes*, even among Quakers, are often found tending to repudiate the old ideals. It was the same fate which again and again befell the predecessor of this worldly asceticism, the monastic asceticism of the Middle Ages. In the latter case, when rational economic activity had worked out its full effects by strict regulation of conduct and limitation of consumption, the wealth accumulated either succumbed directly to the nobility, as in the time before the Reformation, or monastic discipline threatened to break down, and one of the numerous reformations became necessary.[35]

According to Weber, the monasteries had accumulated wealth that had influenced them to fraternize with the nobility and in like manner the Puritans also succumbed to the same thing when they became wealthy in their temporal enterprises, which resulted in their fornication with the kings of the earth; they became the object of what E. J Hobsbawm wrote about in his work, The Age of Capitalism.

"Buttressed by clothes, walls and objects, there was the bourgeois family, the most mysterious institution of the age. For, if it is easy to discover or to devise connections between puritanism and capitalism, as a large literature bears witness, those between nineteenth-century family structure and bourgeois society remain obscure. In deed the apparent conflict between the two has rarely even been noticed. Why should a society dedicated to an economy of profit making competitive enterprise,

---

[35] Max Weber, *The Protestant Ethic and the Spirit of Capitalism* (Merchant Books; abridged edition, October 12, 2013), 103.

> to the efforts of the isolated individual, to equality
> of rights and opportunities and freedom, rest on an
> institution which so totally denied all of these?[36]

Of course, there really was no general "equality of rights and opportunities and freedom" under the circumstances where the bourgeois held the wealth and the lower classes had no recourse but to submit to their regimentation. (At this juncture, it must be conveyed that this work is not an endorsement of socialism; neither capitalism or socialism will be the models for Christ's kingdom. Such notions are foolishness and if one wants to conjecture about the model for the kingdom to come, all they would have to do is study the economy of ancient Israel, which was an agrarian society and is the only true model for what is coming!) Hobsbawm wrote about the"unfettered" capitalism during the years 1848 and 1875 and observed that there should have been conflict between a chaste Puritan home and the infidel example but noted rather that conflict all but disappeared in the era. All of the above vindicates that the woman in Revelation 17 is apostate Protestantism that extracts the blood of the saints and "of the martyrs of Jesus" (Revelation 17:6). The historical evidence affirms that the domineering body of Protestantism failed to maintain their obligation to remain apolitical and militant in the era and became the Laodicean church.

> Because thou sayest, I am rich, and increased with
> goods, and have need of nothing; and knowest not
> that thou art wretched, and miserable, and poor,
> and blind, and naked: I counsel thee to buy of me
> gold tried in the fire, that thou mayest be rich; and
> white raiment, that thou mayest be clothed, and
> *that* the shame of thy nakedness do not appear; and
> anoint thine eyes with eyesalve, that thou mayest
> see. (Revelation 3:17–18)

---

[36] E. J. Hobsbawm, *The Age of Capital 1848-1875* (New American Library, Inc., New York, N.Y., 1979), 261.

England and then America truly became wretched and miserable in their exploitation of the poor, especially with the weakest of all: women and children.

> Since the Industrial Revolution was so new at the end of the 18th century, there were initially no laws to regulate new industries. For example, no laws prevented businesses from hiring seven-year-old children to work full time in coal mines or factories. No laws regulated what factories could do with their biohazard waste. Free-market capitalism meant that the government had no role in regulating the new industries or planning services for new towns. And those who controlled the government liked it that way—only a small minority of people, the wealthiest, could vote in England at this time. So during the first phase of the Industrial Revolution, between 1790 and 1850, British society became the first example of what happens in a country when free-market capitalism has no constraints.... for starters, the working class—who made up 80% of society—had little or no bargaining power with their new employers. Since population was increasing in Great Britain at the same time that landowners were enclosing common village lands, people from the countryside flocked to the towns and the new factories to get work. This resulted in a very high unemployment rate for workers in the first phases of the Industrial Revolution.... only wealthy people in Great Britain were eligible to vote, workers could not use the democratic political system to fight for rights and reforms. In 1799 and 1800, the British Parliament passed the Combination Acts, which made it illegal for workers to unionize, or combine, as a group to ask for better working conditions....

working conditions were very tough, and sometimes tragic. Most laborers worked 10 to 14 hours a day, six days a week, with no paid vacation or holidays. Each industry had safety hazards too; the process of purifying iron, for example, demanded that workers toiled amidst temperatures as high as 130 degrees in the coolest part of the ironworks (Rosen 155). Under such dangerous conditions, accidents on the job occurred regularly.... During the first 60 years of the Industrial Revolution, living conditions were, by far, worst for the poorest of the poor. In desperation, many turned to the "poorhouses" set up by the government. The Poor Law of 1834 created workhouses for the destitute. Poorhouses were designed to be deliberately harsh places to discourage people from staying on "relief" (government food aid). Families, including husbands and wives, were separated upon entering the grounds. They were confined each day as inmates in a prison and worked every day.... One of the defining and most lasting features of the Industrial Revolution was the rise of cities. In pre-industrial society, over 80% of people lived in rural areas. As migrants moved from the countryside, small towns became large cities. By 1850, for the first time in world history, more people in a country—Great Britain—lived in cities than in rural areas.... The densely packed and poorly constructed working-class neighborhoods contributed to the fast spread of disease.... Child labor was, unfortunately, integral to the first factories, mines, and mills in England. In textile mills, as new power looms and spinning mules took the place of skilled workers, factory owners used cheap, unskilled labor to decrease the cost of production. And, child labor was the cheapest labor of all.... The Industrial Revolution completely transformed the role of the family. In traditional, agricultural society, families worked together as a unit of production, tending to fields, knitting sweaters, or tending to the fire. Women could parent and also play a role in producing food or goods needed for the household. Work and play time were flexible and interwoven. Industrialization changed all that. The same specialization of labor that occurred in factories occurred in the lives of working-class families, and this broke up the family economy. Work and home life became sharply separated.... In difficult circumstances, mothers struggled to make ends meet and keep the family out of the poorhouses.[37]

In conclusion, the evidence, above, explains the symbolism of the white horse of the first seal that many historicists attempt to apply to the early church;[38] even so, the church goes forth "conquering, and to conquer", but not in the first-century and not for the gospel—but rather it goes forth "conquering, and to conquer" in the time of the end, the nineteenth-century. For it is by their *commerce* that the Protestants oppressed their brethren in order to enrich themselves, and this is the shameful depiction of the spirit of the Laodicean church. Colonialism ensued, which fomented wars and rumors of wars, which is characterized by the rider of the red horse. The use of the markets and national banks to control the prices of goods and services is characterized by the rider of the black horse and rider of the pale horse follows when fluctuations, such as depressions and

---

[37] *Effects of the Industrial Revolution*, BCP.org, http://webs.bcp.org/sites/vcleary/modernworldhistorytextbook/industrialrevolution/ireffects.html

[38] E. G. White: "The opening of the first seal reveals a white horse.... This is a fit image of the triumphs of the gospel in the first centuries of this dispensation." *Sings of the Times* (Seventh-day Adventist Pub. Association, Battle Creek, Mich., 1865), 186.

recessions, result in famine and death: "And I saw the woman drunken with the blood of the saints, and with the blood of the martyrs of Jesus." The symbolism in the seals represents the provocation for the covenantal judgments depicted by the trumpets. All discord in historicism is resolved in structuring the events of the seven-seals as conterminous with the last era of the seventh church, the events of the seven-trumpets as conterminous with the seventh seal and the events of the seven vials as conterminous with the seventh trumpet. This is the recapitulation and structure that John intended.

EIGHT

Babylon, the Mother of Harlots

In analyzing the Revelation through the historicist's lens in the previous chapter we saw that it was the twelve-hundred and sixty-year-old papacy that received the wounding of its head in fulfillment of Revelation 13:3. The conclusion was also reached that the metaphor of the woman in Revelation 12 and 17 represent the same entity. In support, the church is anthropomorphized corporately as a virtuous woman in 2 Corinthians 11:2, Matthew 25:1–4 and Revelation 14:4, which was the illustration of the OT covenant wife before she apostatized herself (Isaiah 62:5; Jeremiah 14:17, 31:4, 13). Further, the woman Babylon is prophesied to fall in Revelation 12 and 14, which is also conveyed concerning the corporate church in the last days in such NT texts as Matthew 24:12, 2 Thessalonians 2:2–3 and 1 Timothy 4:1–3. The woman in Revelation 12 is initially observed in heaven but afterwards falls to the earth in flight, enveloped by the wilderness of the earth to escape persecution from the dragon—which some historicists have rendered as the early flight of militant groups like the Paulicians, Albigenses, Cathars, Waldenses and Anabaptists from the coercive and apostatizing penchant of the union of state and religion developed particularly through the Roman bishopric, who dwelt "in the seat of Satan" and became the papacy. The historicist's lens also parallels the woman's wilderness experience with the era of the church of Thyatira, that was warned of the apostatizing penchant of the false prophetess Jezebel, who historicists have also interpreted as the papacy during the Dark

Ages.[1] Consequently, the historicist's lens conveys two women in the message to the church in Thyatira: the woman Jezebel and the woman who fled into the wilderness during the era of the fourth church, Thyatira. Historicists have blundered on who mothered Protestantism; they mistakenly have held that Jezebel mothered Protestantism.

So too does John's description of the woman herself. For she is no more the virgin bride of Christ of which the Church of Rome was once a part, prior to the rise of Papal Vaticanism. No! By the time reflected in John's description, in much the same way that the Older Testament's Israel degenerated into a veritable Sodom also the Early-Christian Virgin had now degenerated into a mediaeval "Whore" or a painted Jezebel. This Whore had been unfaithful, constantly, to the heavenly Bridegroom to Whom she owed loyalty. For she had fornicated with the Kings of the Earth. Thereby she had also intoxicated the inhabitants of the Earth with the wine of all this fornication all this immoral commerce going on between an apostate ecclesiastical power and international political leaders. The great Whore, then, is Rome. Thus Tertullian, Eusebius, Jerome, Ambrose, Augustine, Bede, Berengaud, and many others. Specifically, she is the Romish Papacy. Thus Waldo and the Waldensians, Joachim of Floris, Eberhard of Salzburg, Pierre d'Olivi, Dante

---

[1] Jezebel is interpreted as the papacy by historicists such as Reid: "It is supposed that the church of Rome is described in the epistle to the church of Thyatira, under the name of that woman, 'Jezebel.' And it must be confessed, even by those who reject this theory, that the similarity is wonderful." William J. Reid, *Lectures on the Revelation*, (Stevenson, Foster & Co., No. 48 Fifth Avenue 1878), 87.

Alighieri, Petrarch, Wycliffe, Huss, Savanorola, and all of the Protestant Reformers.[2]

But upon further analysis only the woman of Revelation 12 meets the criteria as the mother of the Protestant denominations.

The woman in Revelation 12 appears first in heaven in the representation of a chaste state in the metaphor. The twelve disciples, filled with the Holy Spirit, comprised the nascent church in its chaste state. This same corporate abstract is conveyed by the phrases "Jerusalem which is above" in Galatians 4:26 and "heavenly Jerusalem" in Hebrews 12:22. These images convey the inaugural corporate abstract. Nevertheless, the woman of Revelation 12 falls from her position in heaven signifying that the chaste state does not endure, which agrees with numerous NT texts that prophesies corporate apostasy and a final judgment prior to Christ's return (Matthew 5:13, 24:12; Romans 14:10; 2 Corinthians 5:10; 2 Thessalonians 2:1–12; 1 Timothy 4:1–3).[3] It is written that "in the last days" there will be corporate apostasy and mystery Babylon in Revelation 17 is symbolic of this apostasy.[4]

In the corporate abstract, from whence did Babylon fall? Ancient Babylon never attained moral rectitude; the city's origin was pagan. This perception is also applicable to Jezebel in the OT. In juxtaposition, the OT expressed a fall from moral rectitude in

---

[2] Dr. Francis Nigel Lee, *John's Revelation Unveiled* (Ligstryders 1999), 211.

[3] Meaning, few that profess actually worship in spirit and truth (John 4:23-24).

[4] (Acts 2:17; 2 Timothy 3:1; Hebrews 1:2; Jas 5:3; 2 Peter 3:3) Preterists hold the "last days" commenced with the first advent. What they fail to grasp is Prophetic Telescoping. To the prophets the two advents appeared in immediate sequence, like looking down a mountain range and viewing peaks than appear adjacent but instead are a great distance apart. Even so, PT conveys that both advents inaugurate new beginnings at the end of the previous age or dispensation. The end of the Mosaic age ended in reformation and salvation for a remnant, which will be repeated at the inauguration of the Messianic Kingdom. The reformation is a trial or hardship that inaugurating this age or dispensation will be repeated at its end. The Baptism of fire at the first advent was also seen on the last mountain peak, which is not grasped by Preterism. It helps to explains their misapprehension about temporal indicators.

Israel's marriage metaphor (Isaiah 50:1; Jeremiah 3:1, 8; Ezekiel 16:15); in the corporate abstract, a great falling away was prophesied by the song of Moses in Deuteronomy 31–32. The fall of the woman in Revelation 12 is analogous to the OT motif of "the unfaithful, divorced wife returned to her first husband" (Hosea 2; Isaiah 50:1, 54:4; Jeremiah 3:12–14), conflated with chastisement and the trial by fire or adversity in Malachi and Paul's epistles (Malachi 3:1–5; 1 Corinthians 3:9–15).

Again, it was through the historicist's lens that the aforementioned transition was rendered as the fall of Protestantism when it fornicated with the kings of the earth at the time the Reformation had all but dwindled away and capitalism rose. It was broached in chapter four that John was taken by the Spirit into the future to witness the harlot women in Revelation 17 entering the final judgment, and from this perspective, the sixth king of verse 10 "is." From this future perspective, the sixth king is easily reconciled as the two-horned beast in Revelation 13 and the image it makes of the previous beast becomes the seventh that rules for a short space before the eighth, the revived papacy is once again clothed in the civil powers it had before the rise of America; all the beasts in Daniel and the Revelation are accounted for as the seven, nay eight kings in Revelation 17. America cannot be overlooked as the sixth king that "is," who makes the image to the papacy under the direction of apostate Protestantism, Babylon. The woman in Revelation 17 represents apostate Protestantism during the prophetic era depicted by the last church, the final era of Laodicea (Revelation 3:14–22). The woman is depicted as highly attached to her affluence and to her corrupt merchants during this era, which is easily seen as the Protestant's far-reaching corrupt influence of capitalism in the nineteenth through twenty-first centuries. The fallen commerce associated with the church/woman falls right into place with the exploitation of the poor to enrich the merchants at the height of the Industrial Revolution, foreseen also by James.

Go to now, *ye* rich men, weep and howl for your miseries that shall come upon *you*. Your riches are corrupted, and your garments are motheaten. Your gold and silver is cankered; and the rust of them shall be a witness against you, and shall eat your flesh as it were fire. Ye have heaped treasure together for the last days. Behold, the hire of the labourers who have reaped down your fields, which is of you kept back by fraud, crieth: and the cries of them which have reaped are entered into the ears of the Lord of sabaoth. Ye have lived in pleasure on the earth, and been wanton; ye have nourished your hearts, as in a day of slaughter. Ye have condemned *and* killed the just; *and* he doth not resist you. (James 5:1–6)

Apostate Protestantism is fulfilling the prophecy of the woman riding the scarlet beast in Revelation 17 and when it elects to reestablish religion again with the aid of the state it will have inaugurated the image, that is, when looking through the historicist's lens.

Revelation 17:10–11 expresses that the eighth king ruled prior to the sixth king and not that the sixth king's power was interrupted, as earlier historicists had resolved. The traditional historicists attempted to maintain the misapprehension that it was Rome that "was and is not" and who received a wound inflicted by Christ, not to be healed again until the papacy interacts with an international empire.

That is the same Beast already described in earlier chapters. That Beast "was" before Calvary. It "is not," ever since it was "slain" through Christ's resurrection. "And yet [it] is," even thereafter. For its deadly wound was inflicted by Christ's death and resurrection (and further by Constantine's resultant accession). Yet later, it was to be healed (particularly by the Papacy) so that it would even thereafter continue to live on. Explained the Angel to John: "The seven Heads are seven Mountains, on which the Woman keeps on sitting. And there are seven Kings [or Kingdoms]. Five are fallen; and one is; and the other has not yet come. And when he [or it] comes, he [or it] must remain for a short age" meaning: keep on ruling for a time.[5]

It was Christ, not Rome, who suffered a deadly wound by his crucifixion (Genesis 3:15; Psalms 22; Isaiah 49:7, 52:14, 53:1–3; Zechariah 11:8). The traditional view pales in comparison with a progressive historicist's view that the wounding of the head in Revelation 13:3 occurred with the rise of America and disestablishment. The traditional historicists' determination that the sixth king was Rome cannot be taken seriously in light of progressive revelation. John picked-up where Daniel left-off to unveil two more kingdoms that persecute God's people, bringing the number of these kingdoms to seven, the complete, full number of the kingdoms that persecute the covenant people of God in Revelation 17:10–11.

The previous chapter postulated that modern capitalism is a secular phenomenon, mothered by Puritan dissidents. The early twentieth-century sociologist Max Weber posited that the "spirit of capitalism" was the Protestant work ethic and their ascetic habits, but his thesis has not withstood the critics that point out that these mindsets existed previously in medieval monasteries and throughout the Italian Renaissance. Even so, critics have not been able to adequately explain why "business leaders and owners of capital, as well as the higher grades of skilled labor, and even more the higher technically and commercially trained personnel of modern enterprises" were overwhelmingly Protestant at the time Weber wrote his thesis.[6] Weber's "spirit" concerns a mindset that embodied modern capitalism, which cannot be separated from disestablishment with a modicum of scrutiny.

---

[5] Lee, *John's Revelation Unveiled*, (Ligstryders 1999), 215.
[6] Max Weber, *The Protestant Ethic and the Spirit of Capitalism* (Merchant Books; abridged edition, October 12, 2013), 1.

Weber's first task was to define the spirit of capitalism. The first thing I want you to notice is the word spirit. Weber is concerned with showing that a particular cultural milieu or mindset is required for rational capitalism to develop. This culture or mindset is morally infused: the spirit of capitalism exists as "an ethically-oriented maxim for the organization of life" (Weber, 1904–1905/2002, p. 16). This culture, then, has a sense of duty about it, and its individual components are seen as virtues.[7]

Professor of early American literature at Santa Clara University, Michelle Burnham, wrote about the "modern notion of selfhood" that emerged in colonial New England that is coterminous with disestablishment and the modern capitalistic mindset.[8] This "modern notion of selfhood" is conveyed as "one's outward behavior was not necessarily tied to the state of one's soul" in an article on Anne Hutchinson in Wikipedia.[9] Burnham merely uses the expressions of "invisible self" in place of "one's soul" and "visible self" in place of "one's outward behavior." In Burnham's book, *Folded Selves*, the "modern notion of selfhood" represented the mindset of the dissident Puritan merchants, as far as their profession could *not* be separated from their mindset. She maintains that the dissident Puritan

---

[7] Kenneth Allan, *Explorations in Classical Sociological Theory* (SAGE Publications, Inc; 3 edition, April 30, 2012), 188.

[8] Michelle Burnham, *Folded Selves: Colonial New England Writing in the World System* (Published by University Press of New England, 2007), Kindle location 2511.

[9] Wikipedia: "Her ideas that one's outward behaviour was not necessarily tied to the state of one's soul became attractive to those who might have been more attached to their professions than to their religious state, such as merchants and craftsmen." s.v. Anne Hutchinson, modified July 2018, https://en.wikipedia.org/wiki/Anne_Hutchinson

attitudes typified the modern-day perception of the individual in relation to society and traces it back to their doctrine of Free Grace.[10]

> Hutchinson and her followers challenged dominant social, economic, and spiritual authority in New England by invalidating the significance of visible evidence, undercutting the covenant of works preached by authorized Puritan ministers as well as the organic social and economic models subscribed to by the ruling authorities in Massachusetts. By locating authority instead in an internal and invisible self, and by insisting and demonstrating that this self could be inconsistent with and misrepresented by the visible self (as would some of those accused of witchcraft in Salem several decades later), Anne Hutchinson performed in her trials a very early and extremely modern notion of selfhood—one crucially linked with the relations of mercantile capitalism and one that provoked panic among the orthodoxy perhaps especially because they were, in fact, "infected" with precisely the "disease" whose symptoms they so urgently projected onto Hutchinson. As Stephen Innes and others have observed, the attitudes and practices of seventeenth-century New Englanders reflected a profound ambivalence toward emergent capitalist relations. Indeed, economic practice in Puritan New England tended to disable the social order whose stable hierarchy it was meant to support, thus producing the very things many orthodox Puritans most feared (Creating 101). The hostility aimed at

---

[10] "By the multitude of thy merchandise they have filled the midst of thee with violence, and thou hast sinned.... By thy great wisdom *and* by thy traffick hast thou increased thy riches, and thine heart is lifted up because of thy riches" (Ezekiel 28:16, 18).

the Hutchinsonians by dominant magistrates and ministers was thus a function at least as much of the likenesses—including economic similarities—between the two groups as it was of the differences between them....

The orthodoxy's exile of Hutchinson aimed to banish the "monstrous" possibilities set loose by the world of trade and commerce in which colonialism necessarily situated them, even while repeating the gesture of venting, which they otherwise sought to curtail.[11]

Locating authority in an invisible self is the "modern notion of selfhood" that developed out of the Puritan philosophies of Individualism and Free Grace,[12] which led to the Second Great Awakening as well as to the "rationalism and individualism ... that would be elaborated by nineteenth-century revivalists" according to a professor of sociology George M. Thomas in his book, *Revivalism and Cultural Change: Christianity, Nation Building, and the Market in the Nineteenth-Century United States.*

Much of this approach was shared with the European pietistic tradition and was built on Protestant themes. For example, "revival" is a Protestant and especially a Puritan concept. The First Great Awakening developed a focus on an

[11] Burnham, *Folded Selves: Colonial New England Writing in the World System,* Kindle Location 2506-2511.

[12] Wikipedia: "Free Grace theology is a Christian soteriological view teaching that everyone receives eternal life the moment that they believe in Jesus Christ as their personal Savior and Lord. "Lord" refers to the belief that Jesus is the Son of God and therefore able to be their 'Savior'.[1] The view distinguishes between (1) the 'call to believe' in Christ as Savior and to receive the gift of eternal life and (2) the 'call to follow' Christ and become obedient disciples. [1]" s.v. Free grace theology, last modified May 2018, https://en.wikipedia.org/wiki/Free_grace_theology

"experimental religion" which was fully integrated into the Puritan system. The focus on revival during the First Great Awakening certainly laid the groundwork for the rationalism and individualism of the revolutionary period and articulated elements that would be elaborated by nineteenth-century revivalists. However, nineteenth-century revivalism was centered on rational self-determination within a mechanical universe. It shifted its base from the action of a sovereign God and from the moral authority of community to autonomous rational human action in nature. These revivalists parted company with most of European and American Reformed theology including mainstream eighteenth-century revivalism. For example, Berthoff (1982) and Ellah (1975, 16–20) describe the nineteenth-century transformation of the communal nature of Puritan individualism. Hofstadter (1962), who takes great care in pointing to continuities with the First Great Awakening (e.g., pp 58, 64), describes the Evangelicalism and revivalism of the nineteenth-century as "a new and distinctive Christianity" (p,81).[13]

The modern notion of individual rights is easily seen as elemental to Burnham's perception of modern selfhood. This chapter will substantiate that the "spirit" of Max Weber's capitalism is the same thing as Burnham's selfhood, when regarded through the scope of the dissident Puritanical zeitgeist. Incontrovertibly, the Puritans established some of the first secular communities by disestablishing religion. The "monstrous" possibilities, according to Burnham, concerned economic practices that were denounced

---

[13] George M. Thomas, Revivalism and Cultural Change: Christianity, Nation Building, and the Market in the Nineteenth-Century United States (University of Chicago Press, January 19, 1998), 67-68.

by the church-state, colonial authorities. This is also suggested in Bernard Bailyn's book on the merchants of colonial New England. Bailyn introduces his comments on the dangers of untrammeled traffic with the pre-capitalistic Puritan communitarian principles that had, prior to that time, suppressed the "monstrous" possibilities in Burnham's book.

> Despite such differences all of the first generation Puritan merchants agreed that religious considerations were highly relevant to the conduct of trade, that commerce, being one of the many forms of human intercourse, required control by moral laws. But some of the newly arrived merchants, as they assumed power over the exchange of goods, felt the restrictive effect of these ideas when acted upon by a determined ministry and magistracy. In their confused reaction to ethical control as well as in the progress of their business enterprises lay seeds of social change....
>
> Of all private occupations trade was morally the most dangerous. The soul of the merchant was constantly exposed to sin by virtue of his control of goods necessary to other people. Since proof of the diligence he applied in his calling was in the profits he made from precisely such exchanges, could a line be drawn between industry and avarice? The Puritans answered, as had Catholics for half a millennium, that it could, and they designated this line the "just price"....
>
> Equally treacherous to the soul of the businessman and the good of the public was the fact that the merchants came into control of the available supply of money and charged interest on debts. One

who controlled supplies of cash or credit held a knife over a vital vein in the social body.[14]

Bailyn defines the monstrous possibilities that Burnham addresses in her book as the merchant's penchant for untrammeled avarice in commerce. Bailyn also substantiates the connection between Free Grace and Antinomianism that defiled the traffic of the dissident Puritan merchants according to the communitarian hierarchy at that time, which triggered the trial of Anne Hutchinson.

> The "Antinomian schism" of 1636–1637 which rocked the Bay Colony to its foundations turned on the relative importance of inner, direct religious experience and conformity to the Calvinist laws of behavior in the attainment of a Christian life. The magistracy steadfastly maintained that conformity to the letter of the law, careful performance of religious duties, was essential discipline and that it should be evident in one before he was to be admitted to church membership. To them the dissenters were dangerous mystics whose belief in the prior importance of spiritual illumination was not only a doctrinal heresy but also a threat to civil and ecclesiastical polity. The merchants, with striking uniformity, backed the dissenters.[15]

Again, Bailyn agrees that the dissident Puritan merchants attempted to shift authority to the inner self, which is Burnham's "modern notion of selfhood." This is incontrovertibly the modern mindset, insomuch as disestablishment demolished the authority of the church and relocated that authority in an invisible self, which wrought the "rationalism and individualism of the revolutionary

---

[14] Bernard Bailyn, *The New England Merchants In The Seventeenth Century* (Porter Press, April 16, 2013), Kindle location 329-428.
[15] Ibid., Kindle location 784.

period" as Thomas emphasized previously. Returning to Weber's spirit of capitalism, it was the dissident Protestant mindset that supplanted that of the authoritarian regimes, which also led to the untrammeled capitalism that Burnham maintains as being elemental to her "monstrous possibilities." This relocation of authority led to disestablishment, which is the true "spirit of capitalism" when the communitarian tyranny held by the ridged hierarchy of church and state is considered. Medieval society had been a religious autocracy and was rigidly stratified, the religious autocracy offering little possibility of change for anyone's status. Disestablishment is the "ethically colored maxim for the conduct of life" that Weber sought,[16] which liberated those from the religious autocracy that limited their ability to worship freely, pursue wealth and advance in society. Their new-found wealth brought them greater status, through which they fornicated with the kings of the earth (Revelation 17:2).

Reformed theologian, Mark A. Noll, acknowledges that disestablishment was beneficial as well as injurious. (The knowledge of good and evil was set in Genesis 3:22).

> This combination of revivalism and disestablishment had effects whose importance cannot be exaggerated. Analyzed positively, the combination gave the American churches a new dynamism, a new effectiveness in fulfilling the Great Commission, and a new vitality in bringing the gospel to the people. Analyzed negatively, the combination of revivalism and disestablishment meant that pragmatic concerns would prevail over principle.[17]

The list of benefits to individualists is as long as the list of reproaches by tyranny in the forms of exploitation of the poor and class stratification; the latter is what Burnham is driving at in her

---

[16] Weber, The Protestant Ethic and the Spirit of Capitalism, 14.
[17] Noll, The Scandal of the Evangelical Mind, 66.

expression "monstrous possibilities." Noll addresses these monstrous possibilities as untrammeled or "liberal economic practices."

> By "liberal" in the context of the nineteenth century, historians mean the tradition of individualism and the market freedom associated with John Locke and especially Adam Smith....
> The point again is not whether evangelicals should have embraced liberal economic practice, for a case can be made for the compatibility between evangelical Christianity and moderate forms of market economy. The point is rather how evangelical embraced liberal economic practice. Again this was done without a great deal of thought.... The most important economic questions of the day dealt with the early growth of industrialization. How would the growth of large industries, first in textiles and then in railroads, affect community life or provisions for the disabled, aged, and infirm? Each of these questions, and many more like them, posed a potential threat to Christian witness and to public morality. Each of them was also the sort that could be answered only by those who had thought through principles of Scripture, who had struggled to see how the truths of creation, fall, and redemption applied to groups as well as to individuals. Unfortunately, there was very little of such thinking. These problems developed pretty much under their own steam and received little specific attention from Christians wrestling with the foundations of economic thought and practice.[18]

The benefits of liberal economics were touted by those who gave little thought about their injurious effects. Noll maintains that

---

[18] Ibid., 75-76

the injurious effects could have been avoided "by those who had thought through principles of Scripture;" even so, history affirms that they were not avoided because secular capitalism disregarded the "principles of Scripture." Historian, Eric J. Hobsbawm expresses a number of "injurious" observations regarding the consequences of the disestablishment in his book, *The Age of Capitalism*. Hobsbawm held that one of those "negative" effects was the demotion of the wife in the Puritan family at the beginning of the nineteenth-century.

> Buttressed by clothes, walls and objects, there was the bourgeois family, the most mysterious institution of the age. For, if it is easy to discover or to devise connections between Puritanism and capitalism, as a large literature bears witness, those between nineteenth-century family structure and bourgeois society remain obscure. Indeed the apparent conflict between the two has rarely even been noticed. Why should a society dedicated to an economy of profit-making competitive enterprise, to the efforts of the isolated individual, to equality of rights and opportunities and freedom, rest on the institution which so totally denied all of these?
>
> Its basic unit, the one-family household, was both a patriarchal autocracy and microcosm of the sort of society which the bourgeoise as a class (or its theoretical spokes-men) denounced and destroyed: a hierarchy of personal dependence.... Below him— to continue quoting the Proverbial Philosophers Martin Tupper, there fitted "the good angel of the house, the mother, wife and mistress" whose work, according to the great Ruskin, was:
>
> I "To please people
> II To feed them in dainty ways
> III To clothe them

IV   to keep them orderly

V   To teach them"

A task for which, curiously, she was required to show,
or to possess, neither intelligence for knowledge
("be good sweet maid and let who will be clever,"
as Charles Kingsley put it). This was not merely
because the new function of the bourgeois wife,
to show off the capacity of the bourgeois husband
to keep her in leisure and luxury, conflicted with
the old functions of actually running a household,
but also because her inferiority to the man must be
demonstrable.[19]

Hobsbawm was correct; religion lost ground to secularism
commencing late in the eighteenth-century, and has wreaked havoc
on family values since. Hobsbawm associated this change with the
demotion of the Puritan wife. He obviously alludes to decadence—
affluence corrupted the Puritan family man as well as the Puritan
wife. Here, Hobsbawm inadvertently stumbled onto one of the themes
in ancient goddess worship, which depicts the plight of the church
in the hands of Protestantism, especially the dissident Puritans,
which will be analyzed presently. The demotion of the Puritan wife
illustrates the dissident Puritans' success in having the woman-
church demoted at disestablishment. The church meretriciously
cooperated with her demotion, in that she was consoled with leisure
and luxury; viz., the dissident Puritans successfully changed the
perception that the church contributed knowledge and intelligence
in running civil society into one in which she was kept in leisure and
luxury for her cooperation with their economic enterprises. This is
depicted in Revelation 17 by the fornication of the woman with the
kings of the earth and her compensation of leisure and luxury.

---

[19] Hobsbawm, The Age of Capital 1848-1875, 261-262.

And the woman was arrayed in purple and scarlet colour, and decked with gold and precious stones and pearls, having a golden cup in her hand full of abominations and filthiness of her fornication. (Revelation 17:4)

Hobsbawm also observed the papacy resisted "progress," and that disestablishment was Protestant progress.

Anti-clericalism was militantly secularist, in as much as it wanted to deprive religion of any official status in society ("disestablishment of the church", "separation of church and state"), leaving it a purely private matter. It was to be transformed into one of several purely voluntary organizations, analogous to clubs of stamp-collectors only doubtless larger. But this was based not so much on the falsity of the belief in God or any particular version of such belief, but on the growing administrative capacity, scope and ambition of the secular state—even in its most liberal and *laissez-faire* form—which was bound to expel private organizations from what was not considered its field of action. However, basically anti-clericalism was political, because the chief passion behind it was the belief that established religions were hostile to progress. And so indeed they were, being both sociologically and politically very conservative institutions. The Roman Catholic Church indeed, had nailed hostility to all that the mid-nineteenth century stood for firmly to its mast.... And, in so far as the masses—especially the rural masses—were still in the political reaction, their power had to be broken, if progress was not to be in jeopardy.[20]

---

[20] Ibid., 301.

Hobsbawm validated that disestablishment, anti-clericalism, secularization and liberal economics are Protestant in nature, while history affirms that anti-liberal Roman Catholic mindsets dominated Latin America, Spain and Portugal. This vindicates the principle that the "spirit of capitalism" is disestablishment, insomuch as it promoted religious freedom, liberal economics, capitalism and then the Industrial Revolution, while the anti-liberal mindset kept the Roman Catholic societies economically staggering behind the Protestant nations for some time.

Returning to the relevance of goddess worship, the lascivious Babylonian goddess Ishtar (Inanna was her Sumerian counterpart) was depicted riding a beast in myth, along with other parallels that have moved many scholars to support her relevance in determining the woman of Revelation 17. One such scholar is the director of biblical studies at the Reconstructionist Rabbinical College, Tikva Frymer-Kensky. In her book *In Wake of Goddess*, Frymer-Kensky's research revealed other parallels, one of which Hobsbawm accidentally stumbled upon in his account of the demotion of Puritan wife at disestablishment. Frymer-Kensky affirms that "the relationship between the gods" was "both mirror of and model for human social relationships."[21]

> The eclipse of the goddesses was undoubtedly part of the same process that witnessed a decline in the public role of women, with both reflective of fundamental changes in society that we cannot yet specify. The existence and power of a goddess, particularly of Ishtar, is no indication or guarantee of a high status for human women. In Assyria, where Ishtar was so prominent, women were not.... The world by the end of the second millennium was

---

[21] Tikva Frymer-Kensky, In the Wake of Goddess: Women, Culture and the Biblical Transformation of Pagan Myth, (Ballantine Books, 1993), 147.

a male's world, above and below; and the ancient goddesses have all but disappeared.[22]

Frymer-Kensky found that Israel's marriage metaphor (or the Church's for that matter), did not mirror the Israelite marriage, as the goddess myth mirrored the "patriarchal autocracy" of the heathen.

> The question must be asked whether this relationship of God to Israel is intended to serve as the paradigm for Israelite marriage. After all, in polytheism, the relationship between the gods is both mirror of and model for human social relationships. Can this be true in the Bible? Does the metaphor itself give men the right to be jealous of their wives, and to punish them when they do not live up to their husbands' expectations.... Marriage in Israel was certainly not "egalitarian" in the modern sense of the world. At the same time, it was not the hierarchy of master and servant, but a bond between loving intimates. As such it was an exact paradigm of the biblical conception of the proper relationship of people and God.[23]

Yet, Frymer-Kensky also found that in exile the Israelites were overwhelmed by heathen autocratic, patriarchal pressure. While in exile, Israel's conquers wreaked havoc with their family values, just as disestablishment and secularism did with the Puritan household according to Hobsbawm. Finding a vacuum of "gender talk" in Torah, Frymer-Kensky held that this vacuum was filled by the "patriarchal autocracy" of their conquerors.

---

[22] Ibid., 80.
[23] Ibid., 147-148.

After the exile, as Israel encountered other cultural traditions, the vacuum became more noticeable; it was ultimately filled by the introduction of Hellenistic misogyny and sexual phobia into the biblical tradition. The influence of these ideas on the newly emerging Christianity was very powerful.... promotion of the patriarchal household and the power of the paterfamilias ... became more patriarchal; as it became Roman, the process intensified. Emerging Christianity incorporated these misogynistic and antierotic themes and made them central to its ideas about human existence.[24]

Is it an accident that Hobsbawm's meretricious account of the demotion of the Puritan or Protestant wife, due to financial success—following disestablishment and secularization—mirrors the prophet's motif of the "unfaithful, divorced wife returned to her first husband" (Hosea 2; Isaiah 50:1, 54:4; Jeremiah 3:12–14)? The woman in Revelation 17 represents corporate apostasy—the Great falling away prophesied in 2 Thessalonians 2:3 and 2 Timothy 3:4 (Luke 8:11–13; 1 Timothy 4:1–4; Hebrews 3:12–14). Through anthropomorphism, Hosea 2 and Ezekiel 16 prophesied of Israel's initial chastity and subsequent fall from fidelity, her condemnation and punishment for corporate harlotry, and that there would yet be redemption for a contrite remnant (Deuteronomy 30:1–10).[25]

---

[24] Ibid., 213-214.

[25] "The Torah's use of this imagery may have been influenced by the prophetic development of the marital metaphor. It may also be the source of it.... This bond of love and commitment between marital partners provides the positive note in a marriage that might otherwise be called disastrous. The marriage is not a 'happily ever after' affair. The wife of Hosea/God is a wanton, and does not give God the steadfast exclusive loyalty that is expected of her. God-as-husband is not forbearing. He is angry, and punishes. Nevertheless, the marriage does not end, for the marital metaphor emphasizes the commitment of God to Israel. The repudiation will only be temporary, and God will come again to woo his bride, and re-espouse her. After the disaster comes

This is easily seen in the narrative of the Revelation; viz., the woman is witnessed in heaven, representing her chastity, falls to the earth's wilderness, representing her fall in leaving her first love (Revelation 2:5–6), and is seen later in "leisure and luxury," after having fornicated with the kings and during the supremacy of the sixth king. In the last illustration the woman finds refinement in persecution, a "trial by fire" (vv. 16–17), fulfilling Malachi 3:1–5 and 1 Corinthians 3:9–15, fire being a metaphor for a trial, an ordeal or judgment (Psalms 66:12; Isaiah 43:2; 1 Peter 1:7, 4:12, 17). In similitude, the Babylonian goddesses Ishtar abides in heaven and her fornication engenders a lurid fall into hell and death, ending with her resurrection and restoration to heaven. Both employ the "mortification will only be temporary" motif, which corresponds with the "unfaithful, divorced wife returned to her first husband" in scripture (Isaiah 54:4–8).

Inanna/Ishtar was ultimately used to promote the societal acceptance that prosperity could be obtained through religion, empire, raising the status of the merchants and facilitating war; her symbolism conveyed the sophistication of an ideology. This is substantiated in Daniel Timmer's book: *Cultural Imperialism and American Protestant Missionaries: Collaboration and Dependency in Mid-Nineteenth-Century China*. Trimmer held that there was a symbiosis of "religion, warfare and economic activity" in the goddess myth that mirrored the society of the Assyrian empire.

> The threat in 3:4–7 describes Nineveh in terms of prostitution and sorcery. Given Assyria's strong interest in various deities and mode of divination, the emphasis on sorcery is understandable. The parallel characterization of a harlot draws in part on Nineveh's attractiveness (טוֹבַת חֵן 'charming'), and

---

the reconciliation; after the destruction, the renewal; after the violence, the lovemaking." Ibid.,151.

both comparisons probably reflect the symbiosis of Assyrian religion, warfare, and economic activity.[26]

The "economic activity" is easily seen as the "multiplication of the merchants" of the harlot in Nahum, representing the Assyrian Empire.

> Because of the multitude of the whoredoms of the wellfavoured harlot, the mistress of witchcrafts, that selleth nations through her whoredoms, and families through her witchcrafts. Behold, I *am* against thee, saith the LORD of hosts; and I will discover thy skirts upon thy face, and I will shew the nations thy nakedness, and the kingdoms thy shame.... Thou hast multiplied thy merchants above the stars of heaven: the cankerworm spoileth, and fleeth away. Thy crowned *are* as the locusts, and thy captains as the great grasshoppers, which camp in the hedges in the cold day, *but* when the sun ariseth they flee away, and their place is not known where they *are*. (Nahum 3:4–5, 16–17)

Professor at the Department of Theology and Religious Studies at the University of Botswana, Laurel Lanner, also ties merchants with the goddess of the Assyrian empire through the book of Nahum.

> I see no reason why a motif—in this case "locusts"— cannot be used in different metaphors and similes successively. In fact, given the identification of the locusts as the officials, merchants and scribes of the imperial power in 3:16 and 17, 15bA offers a neat reversal of situations; "as you the Assyrians scythed

---

[26] Daniel Timmer, *The Non-Israelite Nations in the Book of the Twelve: Thematic Coherence and the Diachronic-Synchronic Relationship in the Minor Prophets* (Brill, 2015), 130-31.

us with your oppressive regime, so we shall return the favor."[27]

Lanner also researched Inanna/Ishtar as the goddess referred to in Nahum 3:4 "that selleth nations through her whoredoms," which symbolized Neo-Assyrian's promotion that prosperity could be obtained through religion, empire, raising the status of the merchants and facilitating war.

> Eaton considers that כְּשָׁפִים בַּעֲלַת is a reference to Ishtar, "who was represented in Mesopotamia as a harlot, beautiful and gracious, but sometimes destructive." Watts notes that Ishtar, the goddess of sex and war, was savage, destructive and seductive; "With lustful visions of riches and power Ishtar had beguiled nations into the war of conquest." Van der Woude also has little doubt that the harlot imagery of 3:1–4 refers to Ishtar. This passage is religious as well as political.[28]

In relation to the symbol of Ishtar, there has been no dearth of information in recent times exposing Protestantism's part in Anglo-American imperialism, even after disestablishment—broadening the parallelism. The disestablishment of the church only demoted the women-church; this is illustrated by the woman riding the beast, which mirrors disestablishment, as disestablishment did not end the church-woman's usefulness to Anglo-American imperialism according to many historians. Professor of sociology at Georgetown University, José Casanova, is one who maintains that evangelism increased with disestablishment.

---

[27] Laurel Lanner, Who Will Lament Her?: The Feminine and the Fantastic in the Book of Nahum (Bloomsbury Publishing USA, 2006), 159.
[28] Ibid., 146.

The first disestablishment, the constitutional one, constructed the still disputed "wall of separation" between Protestant churches and the American state. This disestablishment brought about the separation of the state from ecclesiastical institutions and the dissociation of the political community of citizens from any religious community. But the secularization of the state did not bring in its wake either the decline or the privatization of religion. On the contrary, as is widely recognized today, the constitutional protection of the free exercise of religion created the structural framework for the emergence and the unprecedented expansion of what Martin Marty has called "the crazy quilt of Protestant denominationalism." At the time when continental European Christianity was mostly retreating, unable to withstand the waves of industrial, political, and cultural revolution, American Christianity was "awash in a sea of faith." Evangelical revivalism became the organizational principle and the common denominator of all the religious groups competing in the Protestant denominational religious system. By the 1830s, evangelical Protestantism had become established de facto as the American civil religion, that is, as the public religion of American civil society. The homogenization of the main Protestant denominations made possible the launching of transdenominational evangelical crusade to "Christianize" the people, the social order, and the republic.[29]

[29] José Casanova, *Public Religions in the Modern World*, (University of Chicago Press; 1 edition, 2011), 135-136.

The Protestants usefulness in Anglo-American imperialism is what is illustrated in Revelation 3:17 and 17–18 and also parallels the four horsemen of the seven seals. Professor of World Christianity and History of Mission, and Director of the Center for Global Christianity and Mission, Dana L. Robert, has researched the contemporary and highly controversial issue of Protestant missionary imperialism. She maintains that "since the 1960s, public opinion has been severely divided over the meaning of missionary visions," and that "flaws emerged" in the paradigm of missionary involvement, and that it did not account for "missionary efforts to 'convert' it."[30] (The pronoun "it" refers to imperialism.) Even so, two other professors, Lalsangkima Pachuau (the John Wesley Beeson Professor of Christian Mission and Dean of Advanced Research Programs) and Max Lynn Stackhouse (the *Rimmer and Ruth de Vries Professor of Reformed Theology and Public Life Emeritus* at Princeton Theological Seminary), account for "missionary resistance" to imperialism and concluded that "modernization" or imperialism still succeeded up to World War I and was facilitated by a good number of missionaries for sundry reasons.

> Christian missions were both allies and critics of colonialism. It was widely recognized that the missionary movement often spread with the extension of colonialism in the nineteenth and early twentieth century. The military, administrative, and business leaders who dominated the colonized regions of the world were sometimes admired and imitated but often also deeply resented—especially by the indigenous elites who found themselves socially displaced, and also by masses of people who found it difficult to adapt to "foreign" influences. The wrenching experience of "modernization" was not easy and many treasured practices, skills, aspects

---

[30] Dana L. Robert, Converting Colonialism: Visions and Realities in Mission History, 1706-1914, (Eerdmans, 2008), 1-4.

of life-style, and conventions were made obsolete. While it is true, as already suggested, that many missionaries resisted the exploitation of indigenous peoples at the hands of colonialists or imperial administrators, and tried both to protect the people to whom they ministered and prepare them for some inevitable changes, their efforts were often seen as simply another part of the paternalistic problem. And, some missionaries were clearly supportive of colonial establishment, since it was believed to bring "Christian civilization" to the world.[31]

It is clearly viable that John, knowing Nahum's use of Ishtar "marveled," in part, due to this parallelism. The final analysis cannot be avoided, the Protestant's part in Anglo-American imperialism is supported, even after disestablishment, establishing the parallelism between the harlot in Revelation 17 and the goddess Ishtar. The parallelism between Ishtar and apostate Protestantism accentuates imperial Protestant's marketing of prosperity through religion, empire, the raising of the status of the merchants, and ultimately, the facilitation of war.

The marriage metaphor of the harlot in Nahum 3:4 corresponds with the metaphor of Jezebel in Revelation 2:20—in contrast with the metaphor of the harlot in Revelation 17. Whence did Nineveh fall; the city's origin was pagan. The noun translated "harlot" in Nahum 3:4 has been hotly contested in recent years, just like the same idea related in Revelation 17; when applied to the pagan deities the metaphor of the prostitute cannot refer to covenantal infidelities (Isaiah 54:6; Hosea 2:5; Jeremiah 3:1–11). Two professors and one associate, Carol A. Newsom, Sharon H. Ringe and Jacqueline E. Lapsley, authored: *The Woman's Bible Commentary*. They agree "there is no underlying sense that the woman belongs to Israel's God," in Nahum 3:4.

---

[31] Lalsangkima Pachuau, Max L. Stackhouse, *News of Boundless Riches*, (ISPCK, 2007), xiii.

Yet the metaphor of the prostitute functions differently here than in most other biblical passages. Elsewhere the prostitute is God's own people ... the underlying image is that of marriage between God and his people.... In the case of Isa. 23:15–18 regarding Tyre and Nahum 3:4–7 regarding Nineveh, however, there is no underlying sense that the woman belongs to Israel's God.... Thus it is not unfaithfulness to God—or to any husband—that is in view here but rather habitual promiscuity with a variety of nations ... she was perceived as a brazen, mercenary predator out solely for her own gain and loyal to no one but herself.... In Nahum's patriarchal imagination Nineveh had seduced and then deceived many political and military allies, including Judah.... her seduction had brought nothing but trouble to her allies, presumably because, after she made treaties with them, she either failed to deliver the promised help or perhaps even worked against them (Second Chronicles 28:16–21 exemplifies Nahum's attitude toward Assyria's "help") ... Nahum's use of the metaphor against Nineveh not only reveals the patriarchal fear of the power of women's sexuality but also recalls the accusation of witchcraft.[32]

There is no dearth of research in affirming that Ishtar's harlotry, depicted in the Great Epic of Gilgamesh, pertained to her infidelity to her husband, Dumuzi-Tammuz, in affirmation of Ringe and Lapsley's commentary. It is untenable to interpret Ishtar's harlotry as spiritual adultery in the covenantal sense; instead, Ishtar's relevance concerns her perception "as a brazen, mercenary predator out solely for her own gain and loyal to no one but herself," that she "had seduced and then deceived many political and military

---

[32] Carol A. Newsom, Sharon H. Ringe, *Women's Bible Commentary*, (Westminster John Knox Press, 1998), 234.

allies, including Judah," and "her seduction had brought nothing but trouble to her allies, presumably because, after she made treaties with them, she either failed to deliver the promised help or perhaps even worked against them." Without any inconsistency, this supports what Pachuau and Stackhouse relayed concerning the missionary impact on Anglo-American imperialism, above; it was highly unreliable but it ultimately succeeded. Again, this establishes a parallelism between Ishtar and the woman in Revelation 17, considering that both represent a prosperity that could be obtained through religion, empire, the raising of the status of the merchants, and, ultimately the facilitation of war.

The raising of the status of the merchants at the end of medievalism with the first attempt at globalism cannot be examined in entirety without considering the influence of apostate Protestantism upon the times nor the parallelism with the harlot in Revelation 17. It requires only a modicum of reckoning to determine that Burnham, Thomas Bailyn, Noll and Hobsbawm substantiate apostate Protestantism as the driving force in the raising of the status of the merchants in modern times. Frymer-Kensky, Lanner, Timmer and Newsom substantiate the parallelism with Ishtar's defiled traffic and apostate Protestantism, which, coupled with the former set of authors, confirms that disestablishment and secularism are easily resolved to the illustrations of the four horsemen and the harlot Babylon. The result of ending the church-state influence in commerce unleashed the "monstrous possibilities" that Burnham wrote about and those which Catholicism had opposed.

> Of all private occupations trade was morally the most dangerous. The soul of the merchant was constantly exposed to sin by virtue of his control of goods necessary to other people. Since proof of the diligence he applied in his calling was in the profits he made from precisely such exchanges, could a line be drawn between industry and avarice? The Puritans answered, as had Catholics for half a

millennium, that it could, and they designated this line the "just price."[33]

Try as they as they may, Max Weber's critics cannot surmount the principle that the spirit of capitalism lies in Protestantism; Protestantism ended establishment and secularized society. Success with disestablishment raised the status of "the merchants of the earth" recounted in Revelation 18, which essentially accompanied the first attempt of globalism and the mass exploitation of the poor at their being wrenched from the land to become wage earners. Even unbelievers, such as the historian Niall Ferguson, confirm the massive exploitation at the first Anglo attempt of globalism.

> Globalization ... is not a new phenomenon.... Over a century ago, enterprising businessmen in Europe and North America could see that there were enticing opportunities throughout Asia.... Capital was abundantly available and, as we shall see, British investors were more than ready to risk their money in remote countries.... the promise of Victorian globalization went largely unfulfilled in most of Asia, leaving a legacy of bitterness towards what is still remembered to this day as colonial exploitation....
>
> Moreover, the last globalization had anything but a happy ending. On the contrary, less than a hundred years ago, in the summer of 1914, it ended not with a whimper, but with a deafening bang, as the principal beneficiaries of the globalized economy embarked on the most destructive war the world had ever witnessed....
>
> If a foreign trading partner decided to default on its debts, there was little that an investor situated

---

[33] Bailyn, The New England Merchants In The Seventeenth Century, Kindle location 407.

on the other side of the world could do. In the first era of globalization, the solution to this problem was brutally simple but effective: to impose European rule....

This vulnerability of early globalization to wars and revolutions was not peculiar to China. It turned out to be true of the entire world financial system....

The origins of the First World War became clearly visible—as soon as it had broken out.[34]

Furthermore, Ferguson also confirms that American imperialism is alive and well in the continuation of our present and final attempt at globalism through America's International Monetary Fund and the World Bank.

Yet the days had gone when investors could confidently expect their governments to send a gunboat when a foreign government misbehaved. Now the role of financial policing had to be played by two unarmed bankers, the International Monetary Fund and the World Bank. Their new watchword became "conditionality": no reforms, no money. Their preferred mechanism was the structural adjustment programme. And the policies the debtor countries had to adopt became known as the Washington Consensus, a wish-list of ten economic policies that would have gladdened the heart of a British imperial administrator a hundred years before.... To some critics, however, the World Bank and the IMF were no better than agents of the same old Yankee imperialism. Any loans from the IMF or World Bank, it was claimed, would simply be used to buy American goods from

---

[34] Niall Ferguson, *The Ascent of Money*, (Penguin Books; 1 edition, 2009), 287-305.

American firms—often arms to keep ruthless dictators or corrupt oligarchies in power. The costs of "structural adjustment" would be borne by their hapless subjects. And Third World leaders who stepped out of line would soon find themselves in trouble.[35]

Financial journalist, Nicola Walton, concurs in her book: *How to Report Economic News.*

Like the IMF, the World Bank is said by its critics to be an agent of Western and in particular US imperialism, imposing faulty development policies on poor third world countries. The World Bank then becomes part of the set of international institutions designed to keep people of the third world in poverty.[36]

Again, the raising of the status of the merchants at the end of medievalism and the first attempt at globalism cannot be examined in entirety without considering the influence of apostate Protestantism upon the times nor the parallelism with the harlot in Revelation 17. It is the evidence that determines that the first horsemen in the seven seals represent Protestantism's missionary imperialism.

The traditional historicist's perception that the harlot of Revelation 17 must be interpreted as the corrupt Church is not contested; what is contested is that the harlot of Revelation 17 is the papacy, as the papacy represents Jezebel during the era of the church of Thyatira (Revelation 2:18–24). Those who were not seduced by Jezebel represented the chaste woman of Revelation 12, the church, sheltered in the wilderness for twelve-hundred and sixty years. Jezebel was ordained to persecute the church as the sea-beast of

---

[35] Ibid., 309-310.
[36] Nicola Walton, *How to Report Economic News*, (Routledge; 1 edition, 2017), 182.

Revelation 13 and the scarlet colored beast in Revelation 17. As John was taken to the wilderness in Revelation 17 he marvels at witnessing the same woman, now in leisure and luxury, which represents the corrupt Church in the final days. This is supported in NT texts such as Matthew 24:12, 2 Thessalonians 2:3, 2 and 1 Timothy 4:1–3.

> Now we beseech you, brethren, by the coming of our Lord Jesus Christ, and *by* our gathering together unto him, That ye be not soon shaken in mind, or be troubled, neither by spirit, nor by word, nor by letter as from us, as that the day of Christ is at hand. Let no man deceive you by any means: for *that day shall not come,* except there come a falling away first, and that man of sin be revealed, the son of perdition. (2 Thessalonians 2:1–3)

It is the woman in Revelation 12 that daughters the Protestants as only the mother and daughters can fall from moral rectitude, which is the judgment of the "great whore that sits on many waters." Protestantism sits on many waters, when the waters are defined as peoples, and multitudes, and nations, and tongues in Revelation 17:15 by way of its missionary imperialism.

Focus on the Seals

The previous chapter substantiated that the first horseman of the seven seals in John's apocalyptic vision represents Protestant missionary imperialism (PMI) during the first and post-modern attempts at globalism. In the traditional historicist's view fulfillment of the seven seals started at the first advent, with the trumpets maintaining the same mode of recapitulation. The greater part of the occurrences of the seals and trumpets have already taken place, according to traditionalists. Looking through the traditionalist's lens, the seven seals or the seven trumpets lack terminological and thematic correspondence with end day phenomena, such as the sealing in Revelation 7 and the end day proclamations in Revelation 14. Nevertheless, this work, commencing with chapter six, has established a terminological and thematic correspondence between the seven trumpets, the sealing in Revelation 7 and the end day proclamations in Revelation 14. In continuing to substantiate this correspondence it must be noted that there is a symbolic theological connection between PMI and the symbolism of the bowman on the white horse. Scripturally, white is associated with righteousness (Daniel 7:9; Matthew 17:2; Mark 9:3; Luke 9:29; Revelation 1:12–14, 6:11, 19:8, 20:11), while horses predominantly represent apostasy for reliance upon illicit power (Isaiah 2:6–7, 30:15–17; Amos 2:15), which is indicative of the end day covenant apostasy prophesied of in the NT (Matthew 5:13, 24:12; 2 Thessalonians 2:1–12; 1 Timothy 4:1–3; Romans 14:10; 2 Corinthians 5:10). In Jeremiah "horsemen and bowmen" represent God's agent Babylon in judging Jerusalem because "as a cage is full of birds, so *are* their houses full of deceit: therefore they are become great, and waxen rich" (Jeremiah 4:29, 5:27). This combination of symbols fits PMI when it is also accepted that the term *Babylon* fulfills the NT prophecy of corporate apostasy and the *final* judgment prior to Christ's return. Furthermore, PMI maintains the *sine qua non* of historicism in that the papacy-beast-king is a dynastic world power that persecutes God's elect within the inter-advent age. Moreover, the interpretation that the first seal represents PMI forensically maintains the chronological correspondence between the trumpets and the autumnal festivals in the Hebraic cultus, the final harvest or second advent. Two great wars, market driven exploitation of the poor and death is the legacy of PMI, which is easily seen in the illustrations accompanying the red, black and pale horses. And most importantly, we cannot forget that the judgments illustrated by the trumpets must commence with God's house, in agreement with 1 Peter 4:17, which substantiates that the exploitation illustrated by the four horsemen—the oppression the souls lamenting in the fifth seal—develops from within God's house in correspondence with OT precedent and NT prophecy (Isaiah 5:8–9, 10:2, 33:15; Jeremiah 34:8–17; Ezekiel 22:29, 45:9; Amos 8:2–7; Micah 2:2; Matthew 23:4; James 5:1–6). God's people will be judged prior to the judgment that falls upon the little horn, according to 1 John 4:17.

> Thus saith the LORD; For three transgressions of Israel, and for four, I will not turn away *the punishment* thereof; because they sold the righteous for silver, and the poor for a pair of shoes. (Amos 2:6)

> But there were false prophets also among the people, even as there shall be false teachers among you, who privily shall bring in damnable heresies.... And through covetousness shall they with feigned words make merchandise of you. (2 Peter 2:1, 3)

And after these things I saw another angel come down from heaven, having great power.... And he cried mightily with a strong voice, saying, Babylon the great is fallen, is fallen.... And the merchants of the earth shall weep and mourn over her; for no man buyeth their merchandise any more: The merchandise of ... slaves, and souls of men. (Revelation 18:1–2, 11–13)

As substantiated in the previous chapter, the traditional historicist's lens establishes that it was the "primitive church" who represented God's house in the wilderness for twelve-hundred and sixty years. In juxtaposition, the woman Jezebel attempted to seduce God's "servants to commit fornication" during the era of Thyatira, which identifies the "servants" with the woman of Revelation 12 and Jezebel as the fifth beast-king in Revelation 13:1–10 and 17:10 that makes war with the saints. Even the traditional historicists maintain that the papacy was ordained to seduce the ten kings in order to oppress the church during the era of Thyatira, while the woman in the wilderness was elected to treasure her children. Yet history affirms, exploitation arose among the brethren at the end of the twelve-hundred and sixty years, which has been the object of this work commencing with chapter six. Further evidence is pending.

This work presents a progressive historicist's rendition of the apocalyptic horsemen that commences with the correlation between the prayers of the saints in Revelation 8:3–5 and with the petitions of "the souls of them that were slain for the word of God" in the fifth seal—a correlation which progressive historicists like Jon Paulien have indorsed.[1] Babylon's intoxication with the blood of the martyrs

---

[1] The connection between the sixth seal and Revelation 8:3-5 is sustained by historicist Jon Paulien: "This connection between the altar of 6:9-11 and that of 8:3-5 indicates that the seven trumpets are God's response to the prayers of the saints for vengeance on those who have persecuted and martyred them. The martyrs were anxious for the judgment to begin but it was delayed until all the seals had been opened." *Interpreting the Seven Trumpets*, 12.

and her merchants' enrichment through the merchandising of the "slaves, and souls of men" are illustrations of the essential crimes that inspired the outcry and caused the petitions of the souls under the altar in fifth seal (Revelation 18:13). These correlations also lend to a chronological agreement with the sealing in Revelation 7, and the final warnings in Revelation 14. The blood of the saints shed by Anglo-American imperialism, predominately PMI, simply cannot be overlooked in rendering the fifth seal, insomuch as it also promotes the *sine qua non* of historicism—the identity of the papacy as the antichrist and the year-for-a-day precept. The progressive historicist's lens champions the concept that the first horseman of the seven seals is PMI as established in the history of the first and post-modern attempts at globalism.

In the sixth chapter it was presented that the seven "new moon" observances between the spring and autumnal festivals in the Hebraic cultus prefigured the seven prophetic church eras that are dictated to the angels by Christ, whose voice is that of a trumpet: "I was in the Spirit on the Lord's day, and heard behind me a great voice, as of a trumpet, Saying, I am Alpha and Omega, the first and the last" (Revelation 1:10–11). The object being that the new moons between the spring and the autumnal festivals were announced in the Hebraic cultus by the sounding of a trumpet (Numbers 10:10). Said evidence substantiates the synchronism between the last Laodicean church era, the opening of the seven seals, the subsequent blowing of the seven trumpets, the sealing in Revelation 7 and the final messages in Revelation 14. The traditional historicists have overlooked this synchronism to assert the erroneous belief that the "seven trumpets" represent the seven new moon observances between the spring and autumnal festivals and the ministration of the *Tamid*, the "daily" worship between the two advents, folding the trumpets over the seven seals and seven church eras. The *Tamid* concerns the "daily" ministration of the temple, as opposed to the *Yoma* ministration or Day of Atonement that occurred but once, yearly, and designated Yom Kippur in the Hebrew. Johan Adraiaan Japp conveyed the traditionally held historicist's perception.

The third vision is introduced with angels ready to blow trumpets (Rev. 8:2) and an angel with a golden censer (Rev. 8:3), as mentioned before, the trumpets were associated with the "daily" during the religious year of Israel between Passover and the Blowing of the Trumpets (today called Rosh Hashana), but was not mentioned in connection with the day of atonement in Leviticus 16 or in the tractate Yoma of the Mishnah. Rev. 8:2–6 is modelled on the Tamid rather than the Yoma liturgy. In the Mishnah, according to Paulien, the incense alter was the main event of the Tamid as in Rev. 8:3, but was bypassed during the Yoma. Secondly, in the Tamid liturgy of the Mishnah, the officiating priest is given the incense, as in Revelation 1:3, while he had to gather it for himself during the celebration of Yoma. Thirdly, the incense of the Tamid is ministered on the incense altar, as in Revelation 8:3, while the incense of Yoma is ministered on the Ark of the Covenant.(57)[2]

Japp overlooked the fact that the blowing of the jubilee trumpet connects the seven trumpets in the Revelation with the Day of Atonement; they meet the terminological and thematic correspondence between the last Laodicean church era, the opening of the seven seals, the sealing in Revelation 7 and the final messages in Revelation 14.

Then shalt thou cause the trumpet of the jubilee to sound on the tenth *day* of the seventh month, in the day of atonement shall ye make the trumpet sound throughout all your land. (Leviticus 25:9)

---

[2] Japp, The Study of Atonement in Seventh-day Adventism, 200-201.

He also overlooked the significance of the theological placement of the golden altar of incense within the Holy of Holies in Hebrews 9:2–3, which is commented upon by Harold S. Camacho in his dissertation published by Andrews University Seminary.

> In conclusion, the ritualistic importance and theological significance of the altar of incense in the sanctuary of ancient Israel were derived, not merely from its location in the Holy Place, but also and perhaps more importantly—from the ministry of its incense in the Most Holy Place. Thus, the description in Hebrews 9:3–4, rather than showing ignorance of the Hebrew ritual, would appear to indicate familiarity and knowledge of that ritual's most minute particulars and subtle meanings. That is to say, these seemingly problematical verses do not reveal either a textual corruption or any inconsistency or error on the part of an uninformed author, but suggest instead a precise theological interpretation of the function of the altar of incense in the sanctuary services. This fact becomes even clearer when one remembers the context of the passage in question. The concern there is a spiritual and theological one, expressing the divine reality of Christ's work as High Priest in "the greater and more perfect tabernacle, not made with hands" (Heb 9:11).... In short, when the Holy of Holies is described in that passage, the golden altar of incense is mentioned because of the sacral, ritualistic, and intercessory significance of the special incense ascending into the presence of Yahweh enthroned upon His mercy seat.[3]

---

[3] Harold S. Camacho, "The Altar of Incense in Hebrews 9:3-4," *Andrews University Seminary Studies*, vol. 24, No. 1 (1986), 5-12.

The "sacral, ritualistic, and intercessory significance" that Camacho proposes is the golden alter in Revelation 8:3–5.

> In this connection, it is interesting to compare another NT reference to the altar of incense— Rev 8:3–4. In this apocalyptic vision, precisely the theological concept we have just noticed is illustrated: As the angel offers "much incense" on that altar "before the throne," the smoke of the incense mingles with the prayers of the saints in going "up before God."[4]

Furthermore, there is a precedent that the appellation of *angel*, which means "Messenger of Yahweh," is applied to Christ as in Judges 2:1, which Matthew Henry affirms.

> Judges 2:1 It was the great Angel of the covenant, the Word, the Son of God, who spake with Divine authority as Jehovah, and now called them to account for their disobedience.[5]

No common angel is given the authority to intercede for the petitions of the souls depicted in the fifth seal, which affirms that the angel in Revelation 8:3–5 is Christ, just as in Judges 2:1. Consequently, the presence of Divinity and of the incense are features that show us that the scene takes place in the second compartment of the sanctuary, the Holy of Holies, where the Israelites were to meet God only once a year for the ministration of the *Yoma*, or Yom Kippur; the daily was performed in the first compartment and so the offering in Revelation 8:3–5 is substantiated as the *Yoma*, or Yom Kippur (Exodus 25:22; Leviticus 16:12–14). Here *Yoma* represents the antitypical Day of Atonement and the actions of the angel with the golden censer

---

[4] Ibid.
[5] *Matthew Henry's Concise Commentary*, s.v. Judges 2:1, *Study Light.org*, accessed October 27, 2018, https://www.studylight.org/commentaries/mhn.html

terminologically and thematically link the opening of the seven trumpets with the sealing in Revelation 7 and the final messages in Revelation 14. Things coalesce even further when the locusts of the fifth trumpet are considered. In answer to the petitions of the souls under the altar, the locusts who are "likened unto horses" (Revelation 9:7, 9), are no longer able to hurt those who have the "seal of God in their foreheads" (Revelation 9:4) and these can be identified to be the same as the horses and riders of the seven seals. Given this insight, we are again reminded of the intricate yet marvelous ways our creator reveals his plan for the redemption of fallen man and of his loving desire to point his children in the way to walk. An acknowledgement that the first five trumpets terminologically and thematically pertain to those who accept the council of the last, Laodicean church in Revelation 3:18–22 and the sealed ones in Revelation 7 and who proclaim the last messages in Revelation 14 is undeniable. The believer's walk in these last days of man's probation is to understand the times and await the ultimate conclusion of this history here on earth. The following chapter expands on the link.

Chapter six also revealed that the traditionalists have avoided chronological correspondence between the sealing in Revelation 7, the final warnings in Revelation 14 and the seven trumpets by misinterpreting the sixth trumpet as the releasing of "demonic" hordes. The traditional historicist's perception violates the principle a "house divided against itself shall not stand.... if Satan cast out Satan, he is divided against himself; how shall then his kingdom stand?" (Matthew 12:25–26). Demonic hordes are not going to torment the rebels who refuse to repent and who continue to "worship devils, and idols of gold, and silver, and brass, and stone, and of wood" (Revelation 9:20). First Peter 4:17 clearly relates that judgment commences with the house of God, prior to the punishment of those who refuse to repent at the time of the sixth trumpet. The aforesaid substantiates that the opening of the trumpets conveys the consummate sorting out of the righteous from the mere professors before proceeding to plague the wicked, those who have refused to repent of their sins. There is every indication that 1 Peter 4:17 substantively conveys the antitypical Day of Atonement when "the rebelliously unrepentant will be cut off (kārat) from the congregation," which Johan Adraiaan Japp conveyed in his dissertation.

> Also, in terms of the most important event in the Levitical calendrical system, namely the Day of Atonement, repentant Israel was corporately cleansed from "all her sins" (Lev. 16:30, 34) through the atoning blood of the Lord's goat. But the same atonement ensured that the rebelliously unrepentant would be "cut off" (kārat) from the congregation of Israel (Lev. 23:29). In the same way, according to the complementary perspectives of Daniel 9:24 and 9:25–27, the Messianic Jubilee inaugurated by the atonement of the death of Messiah, would at once ensure the cleansing of repentant sinners from every aspect of sin, and the cleansing of creation from the unrepentant desecration of God's "defiled" world.[6]

The preliminary prophetic church eras convey the *Tamid* ministration of the house of God as the general intent of 1 Peter 4:17, while the trumpets convey the *Yoma* or most severe sorting of the house of God, a final corporate judgment on the antitypical Day of Atonement, an analysis which the traditional historicist's perspective ultimately cannot avoid, as in Japp's case above.

There is little debate over relating 1 Peter 4:17 to Ezekiel 9:4–5, as a professor at Wheaton College, Karen H. Jobes, affirms this in her book: *1 Peter.*

> Peter assumes that his Christian readers will be judged along with the rest of humanity. Moreover, his thought is informed by the tradition in Judaism that when God judges, he will begin with his own people, and in fact with the elders at the temple …

---

[6] Japp, "The Study of Atonement in Seventh-day Adventism," 78.

Because of the lexical affinity the prepositional phrase ἀπὸ τοῦ οἴκου τοῦ Θεοῦ (*apo tou oikou tou theou*, from the house of God) in 4:17a has with Ezek. 9:5–6 LXX, Schutter (1987) has argued that the tradition based on the Ezekiel passage is the primary background for understanding 1 Pet. 4:17a (also McKelvey 1969: 133). On the other hand, D. Johnson (1986: 292) argues that Zech. 13:9 and Mal. 3:1–3, which both refer to God's fiery presence, are more relevant for Peter's imagery than the Ezekiel passage, for they "provide the pattern for the escalation of eschatological judgment as it moves out from the house of God to those outside the covenant."[7]

Jobes conveys the suggestion that a "trial" for the elect is ongoing between the advents, which would be indicative of the general fulfillment 1 Peter 4:17 and its application to the initial prophetic church eras, conveyed *as t*he Tamid. But Jobes also maintains a consummate sense of 1 Peter 4:17 as an obvious reference to the "Great Tribulation," at the second advent, and that of "the most severe form of this testing," which corresponds with Ezekiel 9:4–6, Zechariah 13:9 and Malachi 3:1–3, and identifies it with the Day of the Lord or the antitypical Day of Atonement.

Peter is saying that eschatological judgment, understood as the sorting out of humanity, begins with God's house, defined in 2:4–5 as those who come to Christ and are built as living stones into a spiritual house. The contrast in 4:17b is between "those who reject the gospel of God" and "us," a group in which Peter probably includes himself and all whom he considers to be genuine Christians. Those who profess Christ are the first ones to

---

[7] Karen H. Jobes, *1 Peter*, (Baker Academic, 2005), 291.

be tested in God's judging action, and it occurs during their lives and throughout history. The Great Tribulation of the final days immediately preceding the return of Christ is the most severe form of this testing. The testing that persecution because of Christ presents, wherever it occurs, is of one piece with the final eschatological judgment, because persecution sorts out those who are truly Christ's from those who are not.[8]

The "trial" at the second advent, the Day of Atonement, is the consummate sorting out of "those who are truly Christ's from those who are not" according to Jobes. This is what is also symbolized in the measuring "the temple of God" in Revelation 11 (Ephesians 2:21; 1 Peter 2:5).

> And there was given me a reed like unto a rod: and the angel stood, saying, Rise, and measure the temple of God, and the altar, and them that worship therein. But the court which is without the temple leave out, and measure it not; for it is given unto the Gentiles: and the holy city shall they tread under foot forty *and* two months. (Revelation 11:1–2)

This "sorting" relates to the Day of Atonement; the Israelites who would not afflict their soul would be cut off from the house of Israel (Leviticus 23:29). The treading "under foot" of "the holy city" in Revelation 11 is merely another means of conveying the "fiery trial" upon "the house of God," that Jobes says is the most severe aspect of 1 Peter 4:17. The forty-two months the court is trodden under-foot (Revelation 11:2) parallels the thousand two hundred *and* threescore days the two witnesses prophesy, and as revealed in the sixth chapter,

---

[8] Ibid., 293.

this time period is no longer interpreted as a year-for-a-day as a result of the decree that there would be "time no longer" (Revelation 10:6).[9]

There are a number of historicists that interpret the Day of Atonement not as a corporate judgment to cast off the false believers but as a justification by works. In their view, the sins of the individual are not blotted out until their works are investigated on the antitypical Day of Atonement. The blotting of sin was first broached at the beginning of this work. The former professor of Systematic and Historical Theology at the Adventist International Institute, Woodrow W. Whidden, conveys the Wesleyan/Arminian doctrine of Ellet J. Waggoner, a past historicist, on justification.

> For Waggoner it seems that Jesus is mediating sustaining grace to keep the saints from falling into sin, but is no longer mediating justifying grace for any sort of unavoidable deficiencies. Paul Penno, Jr., expresses it this way: "The final blotting out of sins is justification by faith or forgiveness retained by the believer. This is the sanctuary message of the final atonement by Christ in the most holy." Thus the period between the close of probation, when Jesus ceases His mediation, and that of the Second Coming is the time for the initial, irrevocable gift of justification. And this permanent gift is one key explanation for their endurance during the "time of trouble," that is, the interval of crisis between the close of probation and the Second Advent... Glorification is the beginning of the eternal retention of justification.[10]

---

[9] Smith: "'Time No Longer.' What is the meaning of this most solemn declaration.... It means, rather, that no prophetic period should extend beyond the time of this message." *Daniel and Revelation*, 209.

[10] Woodrow W. Whidden, E.J. Waggoner: From the Physician of Good News to the Agent of Division (Review & Herald Publishing, 2008), 77.

The context of the citation from Whidden is the end of probation, just prior to Christ's return. Only at this time is justification a settled matter through the Wesleyan/Arminian lens that he employed to render his perception of the cleansing of the sanctuary, or the Day of Atonement. The blotting of sin occurs as a process of an investigation that commenced in 1844 A.D. in his interpretation of the prophetic time, conveyed as two-thousand and three hundred evenings and mornings in Daniel 8:14. Yet, others of Whidden's ilk remonstrate against such a notion as it defeats the propitiation of Christ that fully justified or pardoned the elect by the blotting of their sins so assuredly conveyed in Hebrews 10:10. Associate Editor of the periodical Review and Herald, Raymond F. Cottrell corrected the notion that the sins of the individual were not totally expunged by the propitiation of Christ in his article: "*That Ye May Be Clean.*"

From time to time questions arise concerning the import of Leviticus 16:30 in relation to the investigative judgment now going forward in heaven.... "For on that day [the ancient Day of Atonement] shall the priest make an atonement for you, *to cleanse you, that ye may be clean* from all your sins before the Lord." Some have construed the italicized words to mean that God expects His people on earth today to attain to absolute perfection in the flesh ... prior to the close of probation. But in addition to their relationship and responsibility to God as individuals, repentant sinners were also God's chosen people, collectively, and as such had a corporate relationship and responsibility to Him. Day by day throughout the year they had discharged their responsibility to God as individuals, and the sanctuary had accepted responsibility for all of their confessed sins. Then on the annual Day of Atonement the sanctuary was "cleansed" from these sins which had, so to speak, accumulated there during the past year. The special service of that day was not concerned with the individual's moral responsibility for his sins, from which he had already been released, but exclusively with the corporate responsibility of the sanctuary for sins that had already been confessed, forgiven, and transferred to it, and with Israel's corporate relationship to God. It provided a ritual, corporate removal of sins from the sanctuary and the camp, but there was no transfer of moral responsibility. The service did not release men from sin, nor did it in any degree alter their moral standing before God.[11]

Under the OC the daily sin offerings were made to atone for the individual; it pardoned them before God. But there was also the need to justify the corporate relationship of the nation, exhibited by the cleansing of the sanctuary on the Day of Atonement. The antitype of the former was performed by the propitiation of our sins by the blood of Christ (Romans 3:25; 1 John 4:10), while the antitype of the latter will be fulfilled by the judgment upon God's house that purges those who are truly his from those who are not, in agreement with 2 Timothy 2:20–21, the most severe form of this testing conveyed by 1 Peter 4:17.

But in a great house there are not only vessels of gold and of silver, but also of wood and of earth; and some to honour, and some to dishonour. If a man therefore purge himself from these, he shall be a vessel unto honour, sanctified, and meet for the master's use, *and* prepared unto every good work. (2 Timothy 2:20–21)

Yet, Cottrell was never able to correct the misperception of Daniel 8:14 because of his continued misapprehension that it must be

---

[11] Raymond F. Cottrell, *That Ye May Be Clean*, (Review and Herald, 1964), 13.

perceived exclusively as the Day of Atonement, which is ultimately where such misapprehension must lead and is the object of this work to correct, specifically in the following chapter. In the next chapter it will be established that Daniel 8:14 must be perceived as a bipartite phenomenon, just as the little horn in Daniel 8 was reevaluated as the bipartite phenomenon of pagan and papal Rome.

This work contends that the principal source of discord in historicism has been its failure to properly structure the four septets as John intended.[12] Certainly, Revelation 8 clues us in on the intended structuring; the first trumpet commences with the seventh seal.

> And when he had opened the seventh seal, there was silence in heaven about the space of half an hour. And I saw the seven angels which stood before God; and to them were given seven trumpets.... And the seven angels which had the seven trumpets prepared themselves to sound. (Revelation 8:1–2, 6)

True progressive revelation will correct the early historicist's attempt to severely fold the septets over themselves, which led to such untenable interpretations like the first vial or plague being fulfilled by the French Revolution.[13] It was progressive revelation that led historicists to concede that the seven vials are future, immediately preceding the return of Christ, coterminous with the period of the

---

[12] Leon Morris: "Historicist views also labour under the serious disadvantage of failing to agree." *The Book of Revelation-An Introduction and Commentary*, 19; George A. Ladd: "Obviously, such an interpretation could lead to confusion, for there are no fixed guidelines as to what historical events are meant." *A Commentary on the Revelation of John*, 11.

[13] Henry Carre Tucker: "The plague-boil, which broke out over the Papal countries on the pouring out of the first vial, appears to represent that tremendous outbreak of moral and social evil, that mixture of atheism, vice, and democratic fury, which burst forth at the French Revolution." *Brief historical explanation of the Revelation of St. John, According to the 'Horæ Apocalypticæ' of the Rev. E.B. Elliott*, 103.

seventh and last trumpet.[14] If this revelation is properly heeded, its logical conclusion establishes a pattern in the unfolding of the septets, which is: upon the period of the last era of the seventh church the phenomena of the seven seals commence, and upon the period of the seventh seal the phenomena of the seven trumpets commence. This substantiates that the book of the Revelation is structured to be folded in half; the history between the advents is conveyed in a linear narration from Revelation 1–11 and then the book folds over the first half and revisits the same frame in the succeeding chapters of Revelation 12–19, with additional details given in this second part, mainly concerning the beasts. What follows in Revelation 20–22 is the description of the eternal estate. Structuring the four septets in this manner properly renders the trumpets as covenantal judgments in harmony with Peter's epistle that judgment must commence at God's house—which establishes that the martyrdoms of the souls in the fifth seal are at the hands of their own professed brethren, in correspondence to the judgments of ancient Israel and of those conveyed in the NT (Isaiah 5:8–9, 10:2, 33:15; Jeremiah 34:8–17; Ezekiel 22:29, 45:9; Amos 2:6–8, 8:2–7; Micah 2:2; Matthew 23:4; James 5:1–6; 2 Peter 2:1–3; Revelation 18:11–13).[15] This correspondence establishes that the preliminary trumpets represent the final sorting of the house of God, a sorting out of those who are truly Christ's from those who are not. This breakthrough in structuring exposes the indefensible traditional historicist's rendition of Revelation 9:4 that the thirteenth-century

---

[14] Alberto R. Treiyer: "While the first six trumpets were partial judgments (a third), only the last and seventh trumpet was expected to be definitive in connection with the coming of the Lord (Rev 11:18: God's wrath outpoured in the seven plagues, 16:1)." *Treiyer's review of Heidi Heiks': Satin's Counterfeit Prophecy*, 5.

[15] Japp: "Because the Jews did not keep either the letter or the spirit of the sabbath year, which demanded the freeing of all Jewish slaves, without compensation, every seventh year, and the resting of the land from all agricultural activities, the principle of the sabbath year became the basis of punishment for Judah and Jerusalem(81)." *The Study of Atonement in Seventh-day Adventism*, 37.

Muslims were prohibited from harming men having "the seal of God in their foreheads." The proper structuring of the septets establishes chronological correspondence between the sealing upon the forehead, the angel's messages in Revelation 14 and the final sorting of those who are truly Christ's from those who are not, illustrated by the first five trumpets and the measuring of the temple in Revelation 11. The aforesaid structuring renders the PMI during the first and post-modern attempt at globalism as the rider on the white horse of the first seal, that "went forth conquering, and to conquer" (Revelation 6:2).

Further evidence is essential in developing the exploitation driven by markets that arose when the woman in Revelation 12 came out of the wilderness and subsequently entered the Laodicean era. In chapter six the nineteenth-century historian Arnold Toynbee was cited for his exposé of the injurious effects of the Industrial Revolution. In the posthumous publication of his lectures he expounded upon Adam Smith's now famous conception of individual liberty that led to the principle of laissez-faire. In correspondence with disestablishment, mentioned in the previous chapter, laissez-faire was touted by individualists for its positive attributes while the negative aspects were downplayed. Toynbee expounds on these judgments on laissez-faire.

> Undoubtedly related to the worship of nature—that great reaction of the eighteenth century against artificial conditions of life—and in many instances visibly confirmed by experience, this doctrine obtained an extraordinary hold upon the minds of men.... the belief in a natural or divine arrangement of human instincts lent power to it at first, so an elaborate analogy between the individual and social organism... bids fair to give fresh power to it in our own days.... But it is perfectly clear that, in the case of adulteration, of jerry-building, and of the hundred and one devices of modern trade by which a man

may grow rich at the expense of his neighbours, the
first of these assumptions breaks down. Whatever
may be the case with his higher moral interests, the
economic interest of the individual is certainly not
always identical with that of the community.[16]

Toynbee conveyed the idea that the economists of the time asserted
that laissez-faire was tantamount to a law in nature, like gravity,
and that the market could regulate itself without the church-state
restrictions, which were being denigrated in those days. What
succeeded was the ideology that free competition of equal industrial
units would lead to a wealthy society, taking little notice of the
truth that the laborer "was not a match for his employer in making a
bargain, that he was poorer, weaker, and oppressed by the law."[17] A
contemporary author, a journalist, Chris Lehmann, has joined this
controversy and has acknowledged apostate Protestantism's part in
sanctifying market determined exploitation, the PMI perception of
the rider of the white horse. Lehmann conveyed the same economic
aspect of the early controversy between the Puritan establishment
and its dissidents that Burnham, Thomas, Bailyn and Noll dealt
with as discussed in the previous chapters.

In reality, the Puritan settlement of the New World
was animated by a strong social vision of mutual
obligation and liberal charity among the parties
to the divine covenant adopted as the colonies'
founding social compact. How this vision morphed
into the sanctified capitalism of our own era is in
large part the saga of the Money Cult's ascendance.[18]

---

[16] Arnold Toynbee, *Lectures on the Industrial Revolution of the 18th Century in England*, (London Longmans, Green and Co., 1894), 20-21.
[17] Ibid., 17.
[18] Chris Lehmann, The Money Cult: Capitalism, Christianity, and the Unmaking of the American Dream (Melville House, 2016), Kindle location 410.

Lehmann also agreed with Richard Henry Tawney's observation as noted in chapter six that the dissidents persevered in their doctrine espousing prosperity as the reward for covenant fidelity and poverty as a curse for the reprobate.

> Rosenberg's plea makes perfect sense for a Protestant culture of money that has long regarded the comfortable American way of life as a self-evident sign of divine favor: Return to the true, undeviating principles of revived religion, and God shall likewise renew the material bounty he has reserved for prosperous, true-believing Americans. But in taking a more conditional view of American exceptionalism, Rosenberg also reminds us how far inward the recent course of the Money Cult has tacked. It would never have occurred to Charles Finney or other postmillennialist preachers of the Second Awakening to view God's providential designs for the American republic to be seriously in jeopardy; God's clear favor for the New World and its reformed piety was, indeed, the operating premise of the ambitious missionary activities and social reform movements undertaken under the aegis of the Benevolent Empire.[19]

(Lehmann is commenting on a book by the futurist Joel C. Rosenberg where Joel ponders the fate of America that has obviously been blessed by providence, even as he is doubtful of its inclusion in prophecy.)[20] Lehmann agrees with Mark A. Noll's observation that

---

[19] Ibid., Kindle location 6607.

[20] Joel C. Rosenberg: "At this point, nothing less than a Third Great Awakening will save us. These are not normal times. We are not facing normal problems. We cannot keep tinkering around the edges and procrastinating and living in denial. We are in mortal danger as a nation. We are on the verge of seeing God's hand of favor removed from us forever. We are on the brink of facing God's terrifying but fair judgment. Yet some deny God even exists.

the Protestants could have avoided market determined exploitation if they had heeded the principles of scripture, but Lehmann confirms that they did not and that secular influence supplanted any "moral authority to summon the idea of a higher justice."

> In the perennially fearful crouch of market consensus, it becomes imperative for some credible moral authority to summon the idea of a higher justice that transcends the impersonal, randomized verdicts delivered by the market. But it is here, much more than in the magical thinking of the prosperity-minded believers, that American religion has failed colossally to marshal any critical resources.[21]

Lehmann is correct; starting in the middle of the nineteenth-century there was no place for moral ideas "of a higher justice that transcends the impersonal, randomized verdicts delivered by the market" in our market driven society. Historicists cannot dismiss that after the twelve-hundred and sixty years of the beast system of Christendom, the "spirit of Protestantism" led capitalism and the market driven society that Lehmann wrote about; his corroboration supports the findings developed in this work regarding the detrimental influences of PMI, as well as the injustices and amorality illustrated by the apocalyptic four horsemen. Corruption and persecution did not end with the paradigm shift from papacy to Protestantism; nay, as history confirms, man's institutions always become corrupted and within

---

Others concede God exists but deny that we really need him. Some give lip service to being a 'Christian nation,' but deny Christ's power, refusing to live holy, faithful, fruitful lives...God certainly can save America. He has the power, and he has done it in the past, but he has made us no promises -and we dare not assume that because America has been such an exceptional nation in the past, she will forever remain so." *Implosion: Can America Recover from Its Economic and Spiritual Challenges in Time?* (Carol Stream, IL: Tyndale House, 2012), 290-91.

[21] Lehmann, The Money Cult: Capitalism, Christianity, and the Unmaking of the American Dream, Kindle Locations 7052-7054.

this newly formed house seeds were already being planted that would spawn an evil leading to massive scale exploitation of humanity. Theologian and author, Udo W. Middelmann also observes the consequences of a market driven Church, which lends support to the rendering of the first seal in Revelation 6 as PMI.

> In the course of a very few decades much of the church has embraced the way of mass culture in its drive to reduce everything to play and attractive entertainment. It has bowed to the demands of a consumer society and offers a message that more and often distracts for the moment than comforts for the long run.... Marketing priorities preside.... Instead the church has adapted its soul and life teaching to appeal to modern man, whose whole perception has been altered by a culture that allows him to expect entertainment, fun, and easy success. The believer-to-be expects to be confirmed in views already held, whether they are of his assumed greatness or his experienced inferiority.... To the host of other experiences he now adds also his conversion and repentance as experiences without much content or without much awareness of the conseuences.[22]

The rider of the red horse is prophesied to "take peace from the earth, and that they should kill one another" (Revelation 6:4). Historicist, Douglas S. Winnail, renders the prophecy of the rider of the red horse as being fulfilled during the last church era of Laodicea.

> Many have been told that Jesus Christ could return at any moment—perhaps even tonight! Yet the Bible reveals something *very different!* Jesus told His

---

[22] Middelmann, The Market Driven Church: The worldly Influence of Modern Culture on the Church in America, 124-125.

disciples to *watch* because His second coming would be preceded by a *recognizable series of events*. Jesus used symbols of Four Horsemen to picture major global events that would escalate out of control just before His return. Jesus said *at the end of the age* the Second Horseman—riding a fiery red horse and waving a great sword—would "take peace from the earth, and ... people should kill one another" (Revelation 6:3–4). The sobering reality of modern world news indicates that end time prophecies— of increasing violence and wars—are *coming alive* today![23]

Winnail epitomizes the thinking of the denomination of the *Church of God* that developed late in the nineteenth-century; not all historicists have followed the extensive use of recapitulation in the book of Revelation by Protestantism. Herbert W. Armstrong, this denomination's most recognized leader at one time, broke the mold of historicism, without resorting to preterism or futurism. In continuing on in the rendering of the rider of the red horse, Professor of the History of Modern Theology at the University of Oxford, Mark D. Chapman, lends support to the connection between PMI and the imperialism at the first attempt at globalism.

Three points emerge from this brief survey of sermons and addresses by Anglican churchmen and theologians during the Boer War. First is the strong sense in which the mission to civilize and Christianize shaped the way in which the indigenous population was perceived. While there was naturally little questioning the right of the Anglo-Saxon races to rule with justice and equity, equality was usually reserved only for those who were civilized

[23] Douglas S. Winnail, "Violence and War: The Second Horsemen," *Tomorrow's World magazine* vol. 6 (Issue 4, July–August 2004), 20.

or mature enough to understand its implications.... What was displayed most obviously in the Platonist ideas of the public schools, which provided the bulk of leadership for the Church of England, also structured—probably unconsciously—the rhetoric of Empire.[24]

Chapman has analyzed the connection of missionaries and colonialism throughout the period of the Laodicean era. In truth, Chapman attempts to ameliorate the missionary connection, but he could not avoid acknowledging that, through indoctrination, the missionaries consciously believed that there was an obligation to Christianize the world, while they unconsciously promoted empire at the same time, specifically Britain's in this example. Pastoral Theologian Michael Sievernich also concurs.

Christianity had spread throughout the European continent during a thousand year process that extended from Late Antiquity to the Late Middle Ages. With its variety of missionary methods (e.g. peaceful mission, mission by coercion and the conversion of tribes by first converting the ruler), Christianity had reached all European peoples. It extended from Greece to Scandinavia and Iceland; it stretched from Ireland in the far west to Eastern Europe's West Slavic and Baltic peoples. This process had brought forth European Christianity which, in turn and by stages, initiated missionary activity beyond Europe's borders. The religious missionary enterprise was generally tied to the economically

---

[24] Mark D. Chapman, Theology at War and Peace: English Theology and Germany in the First World War, (Routledge; 1 edition, 2016), 17-18.

driven power politics involved in European overseas expansion, a process of globalization.[25]

Professor of Contemporary History at the University of Marburg, Benedikt Stuchtey, also affirms the role of PMI.

> colonial rule caused complex competitions among Europeans just as much as among the indigenous population in the colonies, that it was able to simultaneously create cooperation and close webs of relationships between conquerors and the conquered, and that it was never at any time free of violence and war, despotism, arbitrariness and lawlessness.[26]

As mentioned in the previous chapter, the Protestant nations were merely following the pattern set in the ancient worship of the goddesses, which was to promote the societal acceptance that prosperity could be obtained through religion, empire, raising of the status of the merchants and the facilitating of war. The disestablishment of the church only demoted the women-church; this is illustrated by the woman riding the beast, which mirrors disestablishment, as disestablishment did not end the church-woman's usefulness in Anglo-American imperialism according to historians like Chapman. The final analysis cannot be avoided; the Protestant's part in Anglo-American imperialism is supported, even after disestablishment.

The illustrations connected with the rider of the black horse

---

[25] Michael Sievernich, "Christian Mission," *European History Online (EGO)*, Institute of European History (IEG), 2011-05-19, 3, accessed October 27, 2018, http://ieg-ego.eu/en/threads/europe-and-the-world/mission/michael-sievernich-christian-mission

[26] Benedikt Stuchtey, "Colonialism and Imperialism, 1450–1950," *European History Online* (EGO), Institute of European History (IEG), Mainz 2011-01-24, 2, accessed October 27, 2018, http://ieg-ego.eu/en/threads/backgrounds/colonialism-and-imperialism

especially lend to the interpretation of the apocalyptic four horsemen as a Laodicean era phenomenon. Black is associated with Judgment Day in Joel 2:2, 6 and this is what is exemplified in the context of the rider of the black horse. A nineteenth-century theologian, Rev. James Brown, did an excellent job of relating the illustration even though he did not apply it correctly, inasmuch as the market driven capitalism that we have today was still in its nascent form and too early for him to witness.

> The Personage here presented may be considered as the Presiding Demon, or Guardian Genius of Civil Policy, and especially of Agriculture and Commerce. And the subject set forth is clearly the introduction of Trade and Mercantile Transactions, with all their precision, exactness, and regularity; represented by the *Balance*, the *Measure*, and the *Penny*, the *price*.[27]

Brown's "Genius" demon "of Civil Policy and especially that of Agriculture and Commerce" fits the Protestant liberal spirit of capitalism perfectly in how they introduced the changes in commerce—to the entire world—beyond the monasteries and Italian city-states, during this Laodicean era. As to the interpretation of the oil and the wine, historicists have come to properly understand that they represent "His Word is available to us and none are able to hurt the oil and wine of His doctrines."[28]

The rider of the pale horse, like the previous two, is a consequence of the release of the first horsemen. The theme of Psalms 49 is about the folly of trusting in riches and the final verse provides for the

---

[27] Rev. James Brown D.D., An Attempt Towards a New Historical and Political Explanation of the Book of Revelation (London, G. Cowie & Company, 1812), 29.

[28] Bob L'Aloge, "The Four Horsemen of the Apocalypse," *Historicists.com.* accessed October 27, 2018, http://historicist.info/articles2/fourhorsemen.htm

interpretation of the beasts in the fourth seal, which substantiates the theme of this book.

> Man in his pomp yet without understanding is like the beasts that perish. (Psalms 49:20 ESV)

The beasts of the fourth seal illustrate those capitalists who are without empathy. The liberal economic policies of the first attempt at globalism succeeded in mastering at least a quarter of the earth and, as Stuchtey conveyed above, no matter how much they tried to "create cooperation and close webs of relationships between conquerors and the conquered" there was never a time "free of violence and war, despotism, arbitrariness and lawlessness."[29] Scientist John Hodges has significant testimony about the first attempt at globalism that fits perfectly into the theme of this book:

> Globally, food production per person has been increasing, but 840 million people (13%) suffer from under-nutrition, malnutrition or famine because socioeconomic systems inhibit equitable distribution (FAO, 2004).... The long-term answer to feeding the world sustainably does not lie in shipping food from the West. Any economic system which separates the poor from their land or takes away their market for selling food inevitably perpetuates poverty, increases hunger and adds to the threat of famine. Globalizing agriculture and food on the basis of free trade runs that risk.... Western governments know from their own experience over the last 200 years that food cannot be treated simply as a tradable commodity subject to unrestrained capitalism without sooner or later running into socio-economic imbalances: hunger, rationing,

---

[29] Stuchtey, "Colonialism and Imperialism, 1450–1950," Mainz 2011-01-24, 2.

famine, lost capacity to feed a nation, negative effects with hidden costs, obesity, mass movements of people off the land, unemployment etc.—all of these are Western socio-economic experiences.[30]

There is no doubt that the apocalyptic four horsemen were released in the middle of the nineteenth-century; that the church knew it not, Isaiah has something to add concerning rebellious Israel.

Therefore he hath poured upon him the fury of his anger, and the strength of battle: and it hath set him on fire round about, yet he knew not; and it burned him, yet he laid it not to heart. (Isaiah 42:25)

And the false prophets and wolves in sheep's clothing that have wreaked havoc with the flock shall be spewed out of the mouth of Christ.

So then because thou art lukewarm, and neither cold nor hot, I will spue thee out of my mouth. Because thou sayest, I am rich, and increased with goods, and have need of nothing; and knowest not that thou art wretched, and miserable, and poor, and blind, and naked: I counsel thee to buy of me gold tried in the fire, that thou mayest be rich; and white raiment, that thou mayest be clothed, and *that* the shame of thy nakedness do not appear; and anoint thine eyes with eyesalve, that thou mayest see. (Revelation 3:16–18)

---

[30] John Hodges, "Cheap Food and Feeding the World Sustainably," *Livestock Production, Science* 92 (2005), 1–16, accessed October 27, 2018, http://citeseerx. ist.psu.edu/viewdoc/download?doi=10.1.1.554.8233&rep=rep1&type=pdf

CHAPTER

TEN

The Time of the End

In continuing the Revelation narrative of the seven trumpets, Rosh Hashanah, the festival of the trumpets, is of great significance. Familiarity with Hebraic cultic symbols, along with the inspiring aid of God's spirit, is indispensable in interpreting the Revelation. In consideration of the aforementioned, two scholarly historicists, Jon Paulien and Ranko Stefanovic, maintain a linear narrative between the fifth seal and Revelation 8:3–5 based on Hebrew cultic symbolism.[1] Historicist and theological professor, R. Dean Davis, agrees; the blood of the martyrs in the fifth seal is shed by the exploits of the four horsemen of the seven seals.

> Internal evidence from the first four seals suggests that it is the righteous who suffer these negative events culminating in the martyrdom of the fifth seal.[2]

---

[1] Jon Paulien: "Thus the prayers of the saints in Rev 8:3-5 are probably cries for deliverance from the oppression visited by their enemies as depicted in the seven seals." *Interpreting the Seven Trumpets*, 6-7; Ranko Stefanovic: "Thus the plea of the slain saints under the altar 'must be seen as a legal plea in which God is asked to conduct a legal process leading to a verdict that will vindicate his martyred saints.'" *The Angel at the Altar (Revelation 8:3-5): A Case Study on Intercalations in Revelation*," 91.

[2] Davis, "The Heavenly Court Scene of Revelation 4-5," 243-244.

Again, this concedes a linear narration between the fifth seal and the Revelation 8:3–5, reckoning the sixth seal is merely a "flash-forward" of what is to come at the seventh trumpet. Even so, Dean and other progressive historicists still maintain some parts of the traditionalist historicists' structural organization of the Revelation breaking this linear narration when they place the opening of the first seal in the first-century, with the souls under the altar crying out against the persecutions by pagan Rome,[3] in the era of church of Smyrna.[4] If that is the case, then the "little season" of the fifth seal, their waiting upon the final judgment that vindicates them at the second advent, becomes inapplicable and misleading particularly since it does not account for the blood shed by the mother of Harlots, Babylon. In some traditional perceptions, the martyred souls are consoled merely by the judgment on first-century Jerusalem for its part in the persecution of the saints. Their placement of the fifth seal, besides being totally arbitrary, breaks the linear narrative established by the seven churches and dismisses the preponderance of martyrs beyond the era of the first-century. As stated in chapter six, the blood of the saints and of the martyrs shed by mystery Babylon cannot be dismissed, as it is the catastrophic offense and the catalyst to God's indignation, exasperated when the souls under the altar call out for his vengeance—which determines the interpretation of the seven trumpets as the antitype to the yearly Day of Atonement ministrations. Furthermore, the vicissitudes that the traditional historicists take with the narration of the Revelation is based on Daniel's extensive use of recapitulation. But while recapitulation should be expected, John's use of four septets introduces originality;

---

[3] Jon Paulien: "It seems best, therefore, to understand the white horse to symbolize Christ's gradual conquest of His kingdom through the preaching of the gospel by his people." *The Seven Seals in Context: A Study of Rev 4-6*, (A Paper Presented to the Daniel and Revelation Committee March, 1990), 228. https://www.scribd.com/document/7240148/The-Seven-Seals

[4] David C. Myers: "For example, the fifth seal in Revelation Six may be identified as the martyrdom under Roman Emperor Diocletian." *The Irreducible Minimum: An Examination of Basic Christian Doctrine*, (Wipf & Stock Pub, 2002), 138.

nevertheless, such extensive use of recapitulation in the Revelation cannot be taken for granted. As Frank W. Hardy, Ph.D., wrote,[5] "we should seek out facts of language that can be explained well by one model and only poorly by another."[6] The traditional historicist's model is rife with *ad hoc* explanations and has undergone corrections with the growing understanding of the seven festivals and as history has advanced. Their greatest flaw, however, has been the tendency to pay mere lip service to progressive revelation but only to support their current misapprehensions of the Revelation.

A greater adherence with Hebraic cultic guidelines is maintained in placing the sanctuary scene of the fifth seal with the Laodicean era of the church. In this way, all the martyred saints are accounted for by the fifth seal, with the exception of the last martyrs who refuse the mandates of the image to the beast in Revelation 13:16–17; thus, the "little season" the saints must wait is slight as compared to a score and more of centuries required to fulfill the traditionalist's view. Moreover, placing the fifth seal during the Laodicean era is supported forensically by copious Hebraic cultic guidelines, such as the seven new moon observances between the spring and autumnal festivals that prefigured the eras of the seven churches; these commence with Christ's ministration in Revelation 1 and never break from linear narration until the seventh trumpet. The Hebraic cultic guidelines of Rosh Hashanah through Yom Kippur outline the last church era and still maintain the *sine qua non* of historicism, the year-for-a-day precept, *and* the concession that the papacy is the sea beast. When Revelation 10:6 is taken to account the seven trumpets are short in duration—short as in a sudden collapse—following the linear narration commencing in Revelation 1. If the Revelation truly

---

[5] Hardy, "Historicism and the Judgment A Study of Revelation 4-5 and 19a," 2.

[6] Noam Chomsky: "[T]he important problem in linguistics is to discover a complex of data that differentiates between conflicting conceptions of linguistic structure in that one of these conflicting theories can describe these data only by *ad hoc* means whereas the other can explain it on the basis of some empirical assumption about the form of language." *Aspects of the Theory of Syntax* (Cambridge, MS: MIT, 1965), 26.

represents the continuous revelation of history, then adherence to the Hebrew cultic guidelines accomplishes this intent. Additionally, 1 Peter 4:17b raises the perception that judgment "upon them that obey not the gospel," is the phenomenon at the return of Christ,[7] so when we examine the prophetic events in context of the judgment prior to the return, the judgment petitioned by the saints of the fifth seal must be placed within the era of the final church, Laodicea. Then, also, judgment upon those who "obey not the gospel" must be concurrent with the time of the final church. All said, this supports that the fifth seal judgment is the judgement that obtains the saint's possession of the kingdom.

And lastly, the traditionalists have corrected their views numerous times over the centuries, as in the case where progressive revelation has discarded E. B. Elliott's perception that the first vial represented the French Revolution.[8] Historicists like Alberto R. Treiyer have accepted that Elliott was in error about the vials.[9] Care must be taken to realize that progressive revelation will correct the misrepresentations put forth by past historicists.

Maintaining this linear narration places the fifth seal sanctuary scene in the Laodicean era, pertaining to the blood shed by mystery Babylon in Revelation 17, which connects it with the sanctuary scene in Joel 2:15–17. This interpretation is completely compatible with historicism. As stated, the seven "new moon" observances between the spring and autumnal festivals prefigured the seven churches, which compels the reader to perceive the throne scene in

---

[7] Jobes: "Peter is saying that eschatological judgment, understood as the sorting out of humanity, begins with God's house…. The Great Tribulation of the final days immediately preceding the return of Christ is the most severe form of this testing." *1 Peter*, 293.

[8] Tucker, Brief historical explanation of the Revelation of St. John, According to the 'Horæ Apocalypticæ' of the Rev. E.B. Elliott, 103.

[9] Treiyer: "While the first six trumpets were partial judgments (a third), only the last and seventh trumpet was expected to be definitive in connection with the coming of the Lord (Rev 11:18: God's wrath outpoured in the seven plagues, 16:1)." *Alberto R. Treiyer's review of Heidi Heiks': Satin's Counterfeit Prophecy*, 5.

Revelation 4–5 through the outline of the seven festivals as entering the antitype of the autumnal festival of Rosh Hashanah and Yom Kippur. [10] Accordingly, the prohibitions against harming those with the seal of God in the fifth trumpet correspond with Judgment Day, as they should. And most profoundly, following said narration places the throne scene at the entrance of the Laodicean era—as opposed to forcing it into the past era of Ephesus, as the traditional historicist's have done, thus breaking the narrative repeatedly.[11] Not surprisingly, two contemporary historicists and scholars, Hardy and Davis mentioned above, view the throne scene in Revelation 4–5 as chronologically following the linear narration of the seven churches.

> The throne scene (Revelation 4–5) takes place in the timeframe to which the seven letters have brought us, i.e., the timeframe of the letter to Laodicea[12] (emphasis added)

> In Rev 5 the portrayal is that of a traditional divine council in session … an investigative-type judgment.… Contrary to the views of most modern interpreters, there is evidence for interpreting the seven-sealed scroll as the Lamb's book of life. The evidence includes: (1) the occurrences of the phrase (or equivalent) "Lamb's book of life" (13:8; 20:12), (2) the reaction of those who have a definite stake in

---

[10] Hardy: "Please notice that by comparing the letters with stairs which bring us gradually through time I am capturing the historicist idea exactly." *Historicism and the Judgment A Study of Revelation 4-5 and 19a*, 2.

[11] After citing Rev 4:1 historicist Francis Nigel Lee wrote: "And now, the trumpet-voiced Son of man went on to show His same servant John a heavenly vision of the major events which would next start occurring by and large consecutively here on this present Earth, after His administration of temporal rewards or chastisements to the Congregations of His first-century Presbytery of Western Asia Minor." *John's Revelation Unveiled*, 31.

[12] Hardy, Ph.D., Historicism and the Judgment A Study of Revelation 4-5 and 19a, 1.

the contents of the scroll, (3) the corporate solidarity between the Lamb as Redeemer and the righteous saints as the redeemed, and (4) the parallel passage of Daniel 7, which describes the same corporate solidarity between the saints of the Most High and one like a son of man who receives the saints of the Most High as his covenant inheritance.[13]

Note that the phrase "investigative-type judgment" appears in the quote from Dean, so there is no mistake that he and Hardy are referring to the same "time of the end," which is the object of this chapter. Both Dean and Hardy construe "the time of the end" as the era entering Laodicea; both link the heavenly throne scene in Revelation 4–5 with the throne scene in Daniel 7; both analyze this phenomenon occurring upon entering the Laodicean era—the era we are presently in, and have been for a while now, considering the extent to which the market-driven society has evolved.

Dean and Hardy's view is a *progressive historicist's* rendition; traditionalists will likely object. Their rendition is a move in the direction of maintaining that Revelation's seven trumpets in the Revelation represent the judgment by which the saints possess the kingdom as prophesied in Daniel 7:22. In supporting the concept that the seven trumpets represent this judgment, Daniel 7:13–22 maintains a linear narration from the time Christ appears before the throne until the time when the saints possess the kingdom, before Daniel uses recapitulation (again) in the next chapter. Hardy maintains the use of this linear narration in his argument that Christ does not enter the throne scene in Daniel 7:13–14 "after" the judgment was set and the books were opened in verse 9–10, but that "Daniel writes with a repetitious style" and "develops one aspect of the story line in vss. 8–12 and then circles back to say more about the same things in vss. 13–14."[14] In other words, Daniel does not break

---

[13] Davis, "The Heavenly Court Scene of Revelation 4-5," 244.

[14] Frank W. Hardy, Ph.D., "Revelation 4-5 and 19a," *Historicism.org*, (1995, corrected edition 2005), 23. http://www.historicism.org/Documents/

the linear narration from the time Christ comes before the Ancient of days until the saints possess the kingdom. Therefore, it becomes compelling to continue the same linear narration constantly from the time Christ appears in Revelation 5:5–6 until the time arrives to "give reward unto thy servants the prophets, and to the saints" at the seventh trumpet (Revelation 5:5–7, 11:15–19), and only then does John break the linear narrative in Revelation 12, where he revisits the time of the first church again, the woman observed in heaven. The same praxis must be applied in Revelation 6 pertaining to the sixth seal, which cannot be construed as entering upon the wrath of God because it would break the linear narration and conflict with the time of the seventh trumpet. Revelation 11:18 establishes the sixth seal as merely a "flash-forward," a practice quite acceptable in linear narrations.[15] Such is not unlike Daniel's repetition, mentioned above.

In conclusion, Hardy and Davis embrace the notion that the Revelation 4–5 throne scene occurs at the entrance of the era of Laodicea, which actually supports the thesis of this work being that the seven seals and the seven trumpets must maintain the same linear narration in Daniel, regarding Christ's entrance before the throne until the time comes for the saints to possess the kingdom. The historicist's traditional rendition interrupts the linear narrative in John's visions repeatedly. While recapitulation should be expected, John's use is clearly not as extreme. It is hard to dismiss that both throne scenes, Daniel 7 and Revelation 4–5, clearly prophecy the same, the one and only, *Final* Judgment, starting with Rosh Hashanah, the Festival of the Trumpets. Davis and Hardy merely rendered a progressive rendition of Revelation 4–5 by observing that Christ also came to the Ancient of Days for the same purpose, illustrated by Daniel 7.[16] By chronologically connecting the throne

---

Rev4-5_Book.pdf

[15] Wikipedia: "Linear narrative Flashbacks [or flashforwards] are often confused with true narratives which are not linear, but the concept is fundamentally linear." (emphasis added) s.v. "Narrative structure," last modified March 2018, https://en.wikipedia.org/wiki/Narrative_structure

[16] Christ rose to sit at the right hand of the Father at the first-advent (Revelation 3:21). The visions where Christ enter the throne before the Ancient of Days are

scenes to the era of Laodicea, Hardy and Davis move away from the traditional version of recapitulation concerning the Revelation in support of a linear narration commencing with Revelation 1 and continuing up until the time of the seventh seal and, as established in chapter six of this work, which is in agreement with Hebrew cultic calendar. Furthermore, by dismissing the traditionalist's misapplication of recapitulation and by applying the proper methodology for interpretation, we can definitively associate the apocalyptic four horsemen with the first attempt of globalism by the Anglo-Protestant empire, England, which is another significant aspect of this work.

As related above, the throne scene in Daniel 7 conveys a linear narration continuously until the next chapter, where Daniel revisits the time commencing with the second bear-like beast that is changed to illustrate a ram. Historicists also see Daniel 7 as recapitulation of the image to Nebuchadnezzar in Daniel 2. They view Daniel 7 as spanning the time from the Neo-Babylonian empire until the end of this age, the same time depicted by Nebuchadnezzar's vision. Both chapters conclude with the time of the end. If Antiochus Epiphanes is interpreted as the little horn, as many suggest, then Daniel 8 does not conclude with the time of the end and this contradicts the evidence given at the chapter's end with the little horn "broken without hand" (Daniel 8:25); Antiochus Epiphanes died ages ago, broken at the hands of the Parthians. It is undeniable that history confirms that pagan Rome "magnified" itself against Christ, the "prince of host," as well as Antiochus Epiphanes in affirmation that Daniel 8 comes to the same end as Daniel 7. Furthermore, Daniel 8 comes to the same end as Daniel 7 when it is accepted that the little horn rises from the first antecedent, one of "the four winds of heaven," as opposed to one of the four notable horns in Daniel 8:8. Dismissing both elements destroys the possibility of ending

---

connected to judgment-salvation (Daniel 7; Revelation 5). The conclusion that is draw by this work is that the autumnal festivals are depicted by the setting of the court for Judgment in Daniel 7 and the opening of the seven seals in Revelation 5, which occurs upon entering the Laodicean church era.

Daniel 7 and 8 correspondingly; it definitely opposes the vision being consummated at the time of the end, in agreement with the judgment being set and the opening of the books in Daniel 7.

> Understand, O son of man: for at the time of the end *shall be* the vision. (Daniel 8:17)

> A fiery stream issued and came forth from before him: thousand thousands ministered unto him, and ten thousand times ten thousand stood before him: the judgment was set, and the books were opened. (Daniel 7:10)

The end of Antiochus Epiphanes is hardly "the time of the end." It would seem the twenty-three hundred evenings-mornings is the time of the end, which should come down to the Laodicean era. It is hard to dismiss this recapitulation in Daniel when the antecedent, amongst other issues, points to Rome, pagan *and* papal Rome, which is a bipartite interpretation. Before the Seleucid potentate could vanquish the Jewish revolt that he instigated, he was forced to defend his kingdom from the Parthians and died in that attempt. Furthermore, the twenty-three hundred "evenings-mornings" do not *accurately* represent the time that the Jewish temple was desecrated nor the time that Judea was victimized by the potentate without *ad hoc* explanations, because he is clearly not the object of the prophecy. The Seleucid potentate simply fails in fulfilling the prophecy that he would wax exceedingly greater than Cyrus (the second beast in Daniel 7), or Alexander, the "great horn that was broken," in fulfillment of Daniel 8:3–8.

In truth, history records that the Roman empire entered the events in Daniel 8 from the west, one of the Four Winds, and warred with Macedonia when in 217 BC Philip V attempted to take Illryia from Rome. The "great horn that was broken" upon the goat in Daniel 8:8 is indisputably Alexander the Great and the "four notable ones" are none other than the four, Greek dominated kingdoms that emerged after Alexander's demise (Daniel 8:8). The idea that the little horn represents the Seleucid potentate must dismiss the first antecedent of the Four Winds in such a rendition. Even so, pagan Rome conquered Macedonia and waxed exceeding greater than Alexander "towards the south, and towards the east, and towards the pleasant land" (Daniel 8:9). Rome waxed to the south and Egypt was ultimately made a province of Rome in 30 BC. Antiochus Magnus was defeated by Rome and made to pay tribute and Syria became a Roman province in 65 BC as Rome waxed to the east. The pleasant land is Judea and Rome made it a province in 63 BC.

In Daniel 7, his narration develops a connection between the fourth beast and the little horn; the little horn grows out of the fourth beast. Historicists easily connect this little horn to the rise of the papacy, and the ten horns/kings to the fallen Roman empire, placing these developments (in a spiritual application of time) to occur through the church eras to Thyatira. In rejecting Antiochus Epiphanes as the little horn, historicists took a bipartite approach in interpreting the horn in Daniel 8. The popes arrogated power to themselves that matched Rome's, which is blasphemy in the perception of Protestantism. (This sentiment reveals why historicism is a Protestant phenomenon.) The dragon (pagan Rome in Revelation 12) gave the papacy, the sea beast "his power, and his seat, and great authority" (Revelation 13:2), insomuch as the papacy's wealth and power was built upon the pagan city. Imperial Rome magnified itself "even to the prince of the host," Christ, and took away the "daily" when it "cast down" the temple in Jerusalem in 70 A.D (Daniel 8:11). The Popes made themselves greater than *their* master by subjugating "the mighty and the holy people" (Daniel 8:24), as powerful pontiffs, in the rebellion of the principle that a "disciple is not above... his lord" (Matthew 10:24). The papacy arrogated supreme ecclesiastical power in Mediaeval times: worship. In a theological sense it usurped the "daily" worship in Daniel 8:11–12. The historicist's lens cannot dismiss the evidence that the papacy stood "against the Prince of princes," Christ, and destroyed "the mighty and the holy people" in its role as "corrector of heretics" to "root up" the tares. In rejecting

Antiochus Epiphanes as the horn broken without hands, historicists have taken a bipartite approach in interpreting it that allows both chapters to end with the era of the seventh church, the Laodicean church, which maintains the principle of recapitulation that Daniel intended.

In continuing with the debate that Antiochus Epiphanes is not the little horn and that the twenty-three hundred evenings-mornings represent a significant span of time, it must be noted that it was revealed to Daniel that a ram, representing the Persian power, would be overcome by a goat, who represented the greater power of the Greeks, and that would lead to the rise of an ultimate power that would take away the "daily" and cast down the "prince" of host's sanctuary. In greater detail, Daniel is informed that "in the latter time" of the four "notable ones" that emerge upon the goat (v. 8), a "king of fierce countenance" would rise (Daniel 8:23). In rendering that which is stated concerning the vision, the advocates in support of the "Antiochus Epiphanes" interpretation cannot surmount the historical fact that pagan Rome had defeated Antiochus Epiphanes's father, Antiochus Magnus, at the Battle of Magnesia at Sipylum in 190 B.C., where Antiochus Epiphanes became a hostage of Rome until his accession.[17] Antiochus Epiphanes was a vassal of Rome and this evidence alone settles the matter; the desecrations of the temple in Jerusalem by the Seleucid potentate was done under pagan Rome's authority. Rome was the "mighty power," the king of fierce countenance, spoken of in Daniel 8:23–25. It was Rome who sanctioned Antiochus Epiphanes's actions. The Parthians broke Antiochus's kingdom; the hands of man broke his kingdom. Yet, as prophesied, the "king of fierce countenance" was not to be broken similarly: "he shall also stand up against the prince of princes; but

---

[17] Thomas L. Thompson: "Antiochus Epiphanes, a Roman vassal who had actually been a hostage at Rome prior to his elevation to kingship in 175 BCE, had to adhere to the decree of the (Roman) senate (*SC* of 196 BCE).… As vassal, he also had to accept Caius Popillius' mandate—however arrogantly presented—to retreat from Egypt and from the war with Ptolemy." *Jerusalem in Ancient History and Tradition*, (Bloomsbury T&T Clark, 2004), 86.

he shall be broken without hand" (Daniel 8:25). The "king of fierce countenance" is "broken without hand," which connects his demise to "the time of the end" (Daniel 2:34, 8:17). The prophetic time span must be addressed; a significant aspect of the little horn power is that it is not like the previous beasts; it is diverse and spans millennia, in correspondence with the twenty-three hundred evenings-mornings. Daniel fell ill and fainted at the vision and some thirteen years later he *continued* to be troubled, demonstrated by his inquiry into Jeremiah's prophecy (Daniel 9:2). Daniel petitions God to "let thine anger and thy fury be turned away from thy city Jerusalem" (Daniel 9:16), and his supplications support the perception that the twenty-three hundred evenings-mornings are a protracted phenomenon, as Daniel's anxiety would not be as troublesome if the interval were merely a matter of days; only his impression that the phenomenon was a protracted event would elicit so much distress.

Further evidence that the twenty-three hundred evenings-mornings is a protracted phenomenon is textual. Frank W. Hardy pursued a doctorate in linguistics and found "it is grammatically inaccurate to translate he-ḥā-zō-wn hat-tā-mîḏ as 'the vision (of) the daily.'"[18] Hardy demonstrates the difference between absolute and construct nouns in the Hebrew by relating the issue to the possessive or genitive case in English. His findings maintain that the sentence fragment translated in many versions as "*shall be* the vision *concerning* the daily *sacrifice*, and the transgression of desolation" have led to misrepresentations (Daniel 8:13). In the Hebraic absolute construct the vision is not *about* the daily, but is taken separately in its determination. In essence, the *vision* must be taken as a separate phenomenon and not as belonging to the daily or the transgression. As related above, the span of the vision is considerable, it is not twenty-three hundred days, but conforms to the historicist's principle of a year-for-a-day, which is also how the 70 weeks are determined in the same context. Yet, Daniel was not given the starting point of

---

[18] Frank W. Hardy, "The Three-Part Question of Daniel 8:13," *Historicism. org*, (Posted 08/29/10), 3. http://www.historicism.org/Documents/Jrnl/Dan0813.pdf

this phenomenon until it was revealed in the succeeding chapter as the decree to restore the Jewish national existence and their ritual worship, which was well within the vision as it was accomplished by the ram (Daniel 9:25).

With the dismissal of the inaccurate interpretation of Antiochus Epiphanes and the subsequent revelations of progressive historicism in reference to the twenty-three evening-mornings, the exciting prospect of determining when Christ comes before the Ancient of Days opens up. But first, a look at earlier positions held in reference to these prophecies should be taken. In the fourth-century, the Ante-Nicene patriarch Jerome was one of the first to dispute that Antiochus Epiphanes was the little horn in Daniel 8. In the fifteenth-century Nicholas (Krebs) of Cusa applied the day-year hermeneutic (revealed to Joachim of Floris just before the close of the twelfth-century) to the twenty-three hundred evening-mornings in Daniel 8:14.[19] In the succeeding centuries this provoked the heated controversy over the departure from the principle of recapitulation in rendering the little horn in Daniel 8:9 as Antiochus Epiphanes. In 1644, Ephraim Huit, pastor at Windsor, Connecticut, published *"The Whole Prophecies of Daniel Explained,"* in which he disputed that Antiochus Epiphanes fulfilled the little horn.[20] Even though he and others, for the next few centuries, varied widely in their renditions of Daniel, their adherence to the principle of recapitulation and the day-year hermeneutic succeeded in moving Protestantism away from the interpretation that Antiochus Epiphanes fulfilled the little

---

[19] LeRoy Edwin Froom: "Then, after the great persecuting apostasy had come to full fruition, and the year A.D. 1260 was approaching, Joachim of Floris, just before the close of the twelfth century, was led to apply the year-day principle to the 1260 days (or forty-two months, or three and a half times) of both Daniel and the Apocalypse.... Among the Christians it was applied beyond the seventy weeks and 1260 years, to the 1290 and 1335 years, and finally under Nicholas (Krebs) of Cusa, in the fifteenth century, to the 2300 days dating their beginning from the time of the vision." *The Prophetic Faith of Our Fathers The Historical Development of Prophetic Interpretation*, (Review and Herald Pub. Association, vol. 3, 1946), 11-12.
[20] Ibid., 60-63

horn in Daniel 8. In 1646, Thomas Parker, in his publication, *The Visions and Prophecies of Daniel Expounded*, looked for the end of all things to be about 1859 on the basis of the prophetic periods and the rendering of the papacy as the little horn in Daniel 8.[21] Samuel Hutchinson, father of Anne Hutchinson, sent letters in 1659 to a friend (that were ultimately published) holding that the twenty-three hundred days-years had "not yet run out."[22] Cotton Mather in 1693 cited a contemporary, Thomas Beverley, who applied the day-year hermeneutic to the twenty-three hundred days.[23] In the succeeding centuries, after Nicholas (Krebs) of Cusa, numerous works were published applying the day-year hermeneutic, which maintained the principle of recapitulation in Daniel 8–9. In 1878, Henry Grattan Guinness published *The Approaching End of the Age*, that applied the day-year hermeneutic to the twenty-three hundred evenings-mornings and calculated their commencement from the "the restored national existence, and ritual worship of the Jews," which Sir Isaac Newton had calculated.[24] By this period the application of the day-year to the seventy weeks in Daniel 8:24 was indisputable, as it

---

[21] Ibid., 67-73

[22] Ibid., 98-104

[23] Ibid., 150

[24] H. Grattan Guinness: "Thus, from the time of the prophet Daniel, right on over the first and second advents of Christ, and over all the intervening events, these far-reaching and majestic prophecies throw their Divine light, showing both the close of the Jewish economy, and the end of the Christian dispensation, and fixing beforehand, in mystic terms, the chronological limits of both. They were not given for the wicked to understand, but for 'the wise' to ponder in their hearts, and at the time of the end, when knowledge should be increased, to comprehend with ever growing clearness.... The 2300 years, similarly predicted as the long extended period which would elapse before the final cleansing of the Sanctuary.... This predicted period of 2300 years, commences, therefore, at some point in the time of the restored national existence, and ritual worship of the Jews, and includes the entire period of their subsequent dispersion, and of the desolation of the sanctuary: Its earliest possible starting point is the decree of Artaxerxes to restore and build Jerusalem; and, reckoned thus, its opening portion is the "seventy weeks," and its second portion the 1810 years which follow, and end in A.D. 1844,

accurately prophesied the first advent of Christ, his crucifixion, and the desolation of the temple. Yet, unlike some of the expositors that attempted to maintain the principle of recapitulation and the day-year hermeneutic, Guinness did not interpret the termination of the twenty-three hundred years as the second advent or the end of this age, as mistakenly had a number of those mentioned above, which includes William Miller who wrote at the beginning of the nineteenth-century.[25]

Rendering the twenty-three hundred evenings-mornings as years in their calculations to determine the return of Christ led to the "Great Disappointment," a significant phenomenon in Protestant American occurring in the middle of the nineteenth-century![26] The expositors failed to account for the span between Rosh Hashanah and Yom Kippur in their perception of the cleansing of the sanctuary. According to ancient Judaic traditions, Judgment Day was perceived as a bipartite process that started with the Feast of the Trumpets or Rosh Hashanah and ended ten days later with Yom Kippur; judgment day was perceived as the consolidation of the first two rituals on the

---

the terminus of so many prophetic times." *The Approaching End of the Age*, (London: Hodder & Stoughton, Updated Edition 2017), 449.

[25] David L. Rowe: "It was in 1831 that his views first became public.... Three months later Miller wrote again to sister Anna Atwood and her husband Joseph, now a Universalist, continuing his exhortation but this time adding a dire warning. 'You man depend on it my friends, that Jesus will come within 12 years, in the year 1843 or before, in that year the prophecies will be completed the dead Saints or bodies will rise, those children of God who are alive then, will be changed, and caught up to meet the Lord in the air, where they will be married to him.'" *God's Strange Work: William Miller and the End of the World* (Eerdmans; 1 edition, 2008), 96.

[26] Wikipedia: "The Great Disappointment in the Millerite movement was the reaction that followed Baptist preacher William Miller's proclamations that Jesus Christ would return to the Earth in 1844, what he called the Advent. His study of the Daniel 8 prophecy during the Second Great Awakening led him to the conclusion that Daniel's "cleansing of the sanctuary" was cleansing of the world from sin when Christ would come, and he and many others prepared, but October 22, 1844 came and they were disappointed." s.v. Great Disappointment, https://en.wikipedia.org/wiki/Great_Disappointment

seventh month. Ten days in prophetic time are significant, when seen through the same lens as the seven festivals. Professor and historicist Samuele Bacchiocchi recognized the bipartite cultic meaning of the cleansing of the sanctuary, an important detail in understanding that the "cleansing of the sanctuary" in Daniel 8:14 is the consolidation of the antitypes of Rosh Hashanah and Yom Kippur. The cleansing of the sanctuary was not complete without the blast of trumpets and the solemnity of the ten days of awe, according to Bacchiocchi. Rosh Hashanah started the autumnal festivals with a ten-day trial before Yom Kippur. Bacchiocchi wrote,

> To interpret the restoration or cleansing of the sanctuary of Daniel 8:14 solely on the basis of the cleansing of the sanctuary accomplished on the Day of Atonement, appears to me to be somewhat restrictive. The reason being that the vision of Daniel 8:13–14 stand in parallel to the heavenly court vision of Daniel 7:9–10. The latter can hardly be linked exclusively to the typological cleansing of the sanctuary on the Day of Atonement, because such cleansing represented the outcome of a judgment process, rather than an actual ongoing judgment process. Therefore this study proposes to broaden the typological base of Daniel 8:14 by including the heavenly judgment process typified by the Feast of Trumpets. Ultimately this will contribute to place the doctrine of the pre-Advent judgment on a broader and stronger typological base.[27]

Bacchiocchi was correct; the "cleansing of the sanctuary" is the verdict of a process started on Rosh Hashanah; it invokes images of a court scene in the Hebrew cultus. Hence, Bacchiocchi's research affirms that the cleansing invoked a bipartite process commencing

---

[27] Samuele Bacchiocchi, *God's Festivals In Scripture and History. Part 2: The Fall Festivals*, Biblical Perspectives (Berrien Springs Michigan, 2001), 65.

with Rosh Hashanah and ending with Yom Kippur. There simply is no reason to deny the consolidation of the bipartite process in rendering the "cleansing of the sanctuary" when the little horn is handled with relatively the same manner by historicists. The advent movement in the middle of the nineteenth-century made the same mistake as related by Amos, concerning the presumptions of his fellow citizens.

> Woe unto you that desire the day of the LORD! to what end *is* it for you? the day of the LORD *is* darkness, and not light. (Amos 5:18)

Rosh Hashanah is the only festival that begins with a new moon, which sheds no light and represents darkness. Amos is relating to us that the ignorant invoke judgment without repentance, solemnity, or expectation of trial before being permitted to take possession of the promised kingdom (Deuteronomy 30:1–5). The cleansing of the sanctuary in Daniel 8:14 invokes this trial prefigured by Rosh Hashanah that ends on Yom Kippur. And as already stated, ten days in prophetic time are significant, when seen through the same lens as the seven festivals.

The most relevant OT books on the time span between the Rosh Hashanah and Yom Kippur are Amos and Joel. Both convey the Day of the Lord, or Judgment Day, as a bipartite process in correspondence with Rosh Hashanah and Yom Kippur. Head of the department of Bible studies at Bar Ilan University, Elie Assis, concurs; the bipartite nature of the cleansing of the sanctuary was prefigured in Joel, which this work supports, in that the four horsemen of the seals are the antitype of the locust army, with its appearance of horsemen in Joel.

> The descriptions of the Day of YHWH in the two parts of the book reveal the same internal relationship as described above, a problem and its solution. For example, cosmological changes are

included in descriptions of the Day of YHWH in the two parts of the book. However, the first part … tells of a disaster for the people in the present. The second part of the book … depicts a Day of YHWH when the nations, not Israel, will be punished, and Israel itself will be saved…. That is to say, unlike the first Day of YHWH in which God strikes Israel with locusts, the second future Day of YHWH is characterized by God's saving Israel…. This analysis shows that the two parts of the book are intrinsically connected.[28]

The judgment involving the locust army that has the appearance of horsemen in Joel, has long been recognized as representing the first part of the bipartite process of judgment, Rosh Hashanah, which Bacchiocchi's research uncovered while studying the analysis of the seven festivals by Jewish scholars.

For example, the prophet Joel called for blasts of the shofar in Zion to impress the people with the needed repentance: "Blow the trumpet [shofar] in Zion; sanctify a fast; call a solemn assembly" (Joel 2:15). Joel may be referring figuratively, if not, literally, to the Feast of the Trumpet, since he mentions its three major characteristics, shofar, fast, and solemn assembly.[29]

Joel 2.15–27 is included in the haftarah for *Shabbat Shuvah* (the Shabbat that precedes Yom Kippur) in several Jewish traditions (e.g., Ashkenazi, Conservative) because of its theme of repentance,

---

[28] Elie Assis, *The Book of Joel: A Prophet between Calamity and Hope* (Bloomsbury T&T Clark; Reprint edition, 2014), 30.

[29] Bacchiocchi, God's Festivals In Scripture and History. Part 2: The Fall Festivals, 59.

lamentation, divine forgiveness, and restoration. The theme is certainly appropriate for the *'Aseret Yemei Teshuvah* ("Ten Days of Repentance" from Rosh Ha-Shanah to Yom Kippur). Note especially the conclusion of the reading of 2.27.[30]

From the Old Testament texts, the שׁוֹפָר has at least three interrelated areas of usage: war, warning, and worship.... Last, in contexts of worship, the שׁוֹפָר sound through the country on the Day of Atonement (cf. Leviticus 29:9), at the opening of the Jubilee Year (Leviticus 25:10), and when a holy fast is proclaimed (cf. Joel 2:15).[31]

Associate Professor in OT Studies at School of Mission and Theology in Stavanger, Marta Høyland Lavik, substantiates, above, that Joel 2:15–17 represents the shift from Rosh Hashanah to Yom Kippur by the sounding of the trumpet, prefigured in Leviticus 25:9, which pertains to Yom Kippur when it falls on a jubilee. All the evidence developed thus far affirms that the sanctuary scene of the fifth seal precedes Joel 2:15–17 and places their antitype in the era of the last church, Laodicea, which maintains the linear narration from the first church until the time arrives to "give reward unto thy servants the prophets, and to the saints" at the seventh trumpet (Revelation 11:15–19). The trumpet in Joel 2:15 represents the jubilee Yom Kippur of liberty. In review, the sanctuary visions in Revelation 4–5 commences with the sound of the trumpet that represents the call to judgment, Rosh Hashanah, and the release of the apocalyptic four horsemen, also conveyed as locusts, paralleling the first part of Joel. Then, as the time of the apocalyptic four horsemen draws to its end, the fifth seal is invoked that leads to the announcement

---

[30] *The Jewish Study Bible: Second Edition* (edited by Adele Berlin, Marc Zvi Brettler, Oxford University Press; 2 edition, 2014) [Ehud Ben Zvi]
[31] Marta Høyland Lavik, *A People Tall and Smooth-Skinned: The Rhetoric of Isaiah 18, Volume 112*, (Brill; 1St Edition December 31, 2006), 114.

of the coming Day of Atonement, illustrated by the sixth seal, and followed by the sealing of the 144, 000 in Revelation 7 that opens the *Yoma* scene in Revelation 8:3–5 and the sounding of the trumpets. The antitypical Day of Atonement "sorts out those who are truly Christ's from those who are not" in concurrence with 1 Peter 4:17 and the scenes in Revelation 8–9.[32] The seven new moon observances between the spring and autumnal festivals commence with Christ's ministration of the seven churches in Revelation 1 and never breaks linear narration until the seventh trumpet. The historicist's paradigm is maintained while observing this linear narrative that conforms to the Hebrew cultic guidelines. In support, historicist LeRoy Edwin Froom, in his book *The Prophetic Faith of Our Fathers*, cites noted linguist and theologian, Frederick Nolan for interpreting the seventh seal as Yom Kippur, Judgment Day.

Nolan notes the … imagery of the seventh seal, he contends, was derived from the great Day of Atonement and the Jubilee. "The analogy between this description, and the service of the Temple, upon one of the most solemn festivals of the Mosaic ceremonial, is so obvious that it has often excited the attention of the antiquary and scholar".… Nolan stresses the frequent allusions to the "Temple of God" opened in heaven, the ark of-the tabernacle, the altar, and the-incense in Revelation 9 and 15. These scenes, he insists, represent occurrences "within the precincts of the same celestial structure." Reference is made not only to the "daily service" but to the "peculiar solemnity" of the, services on the *great day of Atonement*," performed "by the high priest, in the holiest place the Temple," and celebrated in the seventh month.[33]

---

[32] Jobes, *1 Peter*, 293.
[33] LeRoy Edwin Froom, "The Background of the Sanctuary Doctrine," (*Review and Herald Paper*, vol. 125, No. 36, Sep. 2, 1948), 9.

In their book, *James, 1–2 Peter, Jude, Revelation (Cornerstone Biblical Commentary)*, Robert Mulholland and Grant Osborne substantiate that the sanctuary scene in Revelation 8:3–5 illustrates the Day of Atonement. Under the designation *8:3–4 gold incense burner,* they write,

> The imagery is the incense offering in the Temple on the Day of Atonement (Lev 16:12–13), the day in the Jewish tradition when the covenant community was restored in perfect covenant relationship with God—a preview of the restoration of the kingdom of Israel.[34]

This fits well into the linear narrative presented. There is no other place for the fulfillment of the fifth seal but at the time of the end, inaugurating such prophetic texts such as Ezekiel 9:4–5, Zechariah 13:9 and Malachi 3:1–3. As concluded in the previous chapter, the antitypical Day of Atonement sorts those who are sealed from those who are not, in likeness with the phenomenon in Ezekiel 9 and in correlation with "judgment must begin at the house of God" (1 Peter 4:17). Leviticus 25:9 ordained the blowing of the trumpet on the jubilee Yom Kippur, which prefigured the seven trumpets, symbolizing perfection, in the Revelation given John. The vision of Daniel 8:14 is clearly for the time of the end.

> And I heard a man's voice between *the banks of* Ulai, which called, and said, Gabriel, make this *man* to understand the vision. So he came near where I stood: and when he came, I was afraid, and fell upon my face: but he said unto me, Understand, O son of man: for at the time of the end *shall be* the vision. (Daniel 8:16–17)

---

[34] Robert Mulholland and Grant Osborne, *James, 1-2 Peter, Jude, Revelation (Cornerstone Biblical Commentary)*, (Tyndale House Publishers, Inc., 2011), 483.

The time of the end referred to there was not Antiochus Epiphanes' end, but the end when Christ releases the apocalyptic four horsemen, representing the antitype of Joel's locust army on the antitypical Festival of the Trumpets, Rosh Hashanah.

The seven trumpets represent the sorting of those who are Christ's from those who are not. There is no recapping through the trumpets; only a linear narration runs on until the last trumpet, when the time arrives to "give reward unto thy servants the prophets, and to the saints" which is what the saints pray for in the fifth seal (Revelation 11:18). Christ prophesied in Matthew 7:19 that "every tree which bringeth not forth good fruit is hewn down, and cast into the fire," fulfilling in the illustration John held that "the third part of trees was burnt up" at the first trumpet (Revelation 8:7). Psalms 92:7 and Amos 7:2 relate the wicked are like grass and "and all green grass" will be burnt up according to John (Revelation 8:7). The great burning mountain in Revelation 8:8 is cast into the sea in the second trumpet, that is clearly revealed as mystery Babylon in Jeremiah 51:25. On being cast into the sea "the third part … became blood; And the third part of the creatures which were in the sea, and had life, died; and the third part of the ships were destroyed" (Revelation 8:8–9). Historicist, Jon Paulien does a fair job in interpreting the symbolism in the second trumpet as "economic and commercial chaos" but fails when he resorts to the traditionalist historicist's perception that it pertains to "ancient times."[35]

> The sea is most likely to be understood in terms of nations in opposition to God (Isa 57:20; 17:12,13; Jer 51:41,42; cf. Rev 13:1ff.; 16:12; 17:15). Sea creatures are a symbol of people (Ezekiel 29:5; Hab 1:14). The destruction of fish is symbolic of God's judgment upon evildoers (Hag 4:3; Zeph 1:3). Ships are symbolic of the sources of a nation's wealth and its pride in being able to take care of itself (Ezekiel 27:26; 2 Chr 20:37; Isa 2:16). The destruction

---

[35] Paulien, Interpreting the Seven Trumpets, 35.

of ships leads to economic chaos resulting in the humiliation of that nation (Rev 18:17–19).... Given the weight of evidence it is likely that a first century reader would understand the second trumpet as a prediction that the Roman Empire was soon to fall along with its entire social order.[36]

The economic woes of the collapsing Roman empire pale in comparison of the economic woes our Protestant Anglo-American empire is facing, as it is inundated by usury and debt, indicating a reckoning to come. Furthermore, the apocalyptic four horsemen of the seals represent the Protestant Anglo-American empire, which was built upon an economy that exploited their neighbors and the natural resources of the earth, epitomized by the admonitions against the Laodicean church. The economic woes depicted by the trumpets are contemporary history. In continuing, Paulien does a fair job in revealing the symbolism of the third trumpet.

The falling star is particularly reminiscent of the Lucifer account (Isa 14:12–15) and the activity of the little horn (Dan 8:10,11) in the Old Testament.... Rivers and fountains, when pure, are sources of life in the Old Testament (Deut 8:7,8; Psalms 1:3). Thus they became symbols of spiritual nourishment (Psalms 36:8,9; Jer 17:8,13; Proverbs 14:27; Ezek 47:1–12). Impure fountains, on the other hand, would have the opposite spiritual effect (Proverbs 25:26). Bitter water cannot sustain life and growth. Wormwood and bitterness are associated together in Lam 3:15,19. In Deuteronomy wormwood represents anyone who turns away from Yahweh into idolatry (Deut 29:17,18). In Jeremiah it symbolizes the punishment Yahweh was planning to mete out because of Judah's apostasy (Jer 9:15: 23:15).

---

[36] Ibid., 34.

The Marah experience is also a close parallel to the third trumpet (Exodus 15:23). The children of Israel were dying of thirst. With great anticipation, they approached the spring-fed oasis of Marah only to find that there was no life in the bitter water.[37]

The star would be Satan, in parallel with Revelation 12, representing he is come down unto you, having great wrath, because he knoweth that he hath but a short time (Revelation 12:12). The experience will be one in which Satan will foment even greater rebellion which will make the experience of those who are doomed bitter toward the saints. Entering the time of the fourth trumpet, Paulien, once again, does well in interpreting the symbolism.

> This passage is strongly based on the darkness of the ninth plague on Egypt (Exod 10:21–23) and the lamentation over Pharaoh in Ezek 32:2–8. Darkness is one of the curses of the covenant (Deut 28:29). The sun is a symbol of the Word of God in the Old Testament (Ps 19; 119:105). The moon represents beauty and fertility (SS 6:10; Deut 33:14). Stars represent angels and the people of God (Dan 8:10; 12:3). The choice of symbolism points to a partial obliteration of the Word of God resulting in spiritual darkness.[38]

Again, Paulien's interpretation of the symbols suffice, but he fails to follow the linear narration provided by the Hebrew cultic seven festivals, which renders the fourth trumpet as a future event.

The fifth and sixth trumpets are the most disputed in historicism, which chapter six of this work revealed. The traditional Protestant interpretation cannot account for the locust's prohibitions against

---

[37] Ibid., 37.
[38] Ibid., 40.

harming men with "the seal of God in their foreheads" (Revelation 9:4). Even so, Paulien delivers on the symbolism again.

> The fallen star of verse 1 connects this trumpet with the third where the star actually fell. While the star, in its primary sense refers to Satan (cf. v. 11 and Isa 14), it is connected with apostasy in the third trumpet. Thus, in some sense, the apostasy of the third trumpet may be related to the unlocking of the abyss ... the abyss is the abode of demons in the present.... The locusts here are not literal for they attack men, not vegetation, and they have a king over them, unlike natural locusts (Rev 9:4,11 cf. Prov 30:27).... These are often directed at those who have apostatized from following Him (Joel 1:4–18; 2:1–11; Jer 4; Gen 6–9). As such they could only be turned back through repentance at the Sanctuary (1 Kgs 8:35–40; 2 Chr 7:13,14; Joel 2:12–17).... God's people are safe from the demonic forces of Satan (Luke 10:17–20; 8:28–31) which arise out of the abyss. God has given them a mark of protection (Gen 4:15 cf. Ezek 9:4).[39]

Paulien rendered "the hour, day, month and year" of Revelation 9:15 moved by the decree "there should be time no longer" in Revelation 10:6.

> It is arguable whether the hour, day, month and year of 9:15 are to be understood as successive periods of time or as the point of time at which the angels are released. The grammar leans in favor of the latter. In either case the time of release should probably

---

[39] Ibid., 43.

be associated with the decisive moment of Rev 10:6 when *chronos* comes to an end.[40]

In this view, prophetic time comes to an end for the one-thousand years of Christ's kingdom to begin. Again, this places the fifth seal in the Laodicean era. Following the Hebrew cultic rituals, the seven new moon observances between the spring and autumnal festivals prefigured the eras of the seven churches that commenced with Christ's ministration in Revelation 1 and which never breaks narration until the seventh trumpet. And then John breaks the linear narration by revisiting the first advent again in Revelation 12. Pauline does well is explaining the symbols, but then he follows traditionalist's misapprehensions and breaks the linear narrative in Revelation at the last church. Some traditionalists do not even acknowledge the seven churches as prophetic eras.

The symbolism of the sixth trumpet parallels that of the two witnesses, which reveals thematic and character development as opposed to recapitulation. In Revelation 9 the angels who muster the horsemen of the sixth trumpet plague the wicked who refuse to repent after the pronouncement of "there should be time no longer" in Revelation 10; the two witnesses are developed further in Revelation 11. They represent the same phenomenon with alternative symbols, just as Daniel's change of the symbolism representing the bear-like and leopard-like beasts in Daniel 8. As developed previously, demonic hordes are not going to torment the rebels who refuse to repent and continue to "worship devils, and idols of gold, and silver, and brass, and stone, and of wood" (Revelation 9:20). The two witnesses are overcome for three days by the beast that rises out of the abyss, which clearly means that God has them end their torment of the wicked for three and a half days just prior to his return, when God finishes his work by his wrath. Their ascension "up to heaven in a cloud" (Revelation 11:12) is merely another way of expressing they "meet the Lord in the air" conveyed in 1 Thessalonians 4:15–17.

The first remonstrance by historicists against observing the

---

[40] Ibid., 49.

Hebrew cultic guidelines with such commitment will undoubtedly be accusations of futurism. Yet, the continuous-historical approach to interpreting the Revelation is truly represented by following the linear narration from the commencement of Christ's ministration in Revelation 1 up until the seventh trumpet. Furthermore, the papacy fits well as the fifth and eighth kings in Revelation 17 as does the rise of America as the sixth, which is definitely not futurism. And most importantly, the wounding of the papacy (sea-beast) is accomplished by America's rise at the demotion of the church by Protestantism and the liberal economics that followed. The demotion of the church leads to the apocalyptic four horsemen, which is easily reconciled as the Protestant Anglo-American empire. This work has demonstrated that the church that came out of the twelve-hundred-and sixty-years wilderness experience meretriciously cooperated with her demotion, consoled with leisure and luxury; viz., the dissident Puritans successfully changed the perception of the church from one which contributed knowledge and intelligence in running a civil society into one in which she was kept in leisure and luxury for her cooperation with their enterprises. This is depicted in Revelation 17 by the fornication of the woman with the kings of the earth and her compensation with leisure and luxury. This is hardly futurism but merely straightens what the traditionalists mistakenly made crooked.

Finally, Ephraim must be briefly dealt with at the end of this work; both tribes of Ephraim and Dan are absent in the 144,000. While futurists see no problem with the historical-grammatical hermeneutic in Revelation 7, historicism has imbibed the perception of the covenantalists that Israel was replaced, maintained by Amillennialists such as Vern S. Poythress. Poythress held that the meaning of Israel must change because of "the earthshaking, transformational character of the eschatological coming of God" in his book, *Understanding Dispensationalists*.[41] Yet, in contradiction he attempts to hold at the same time that "one must compare later Scripture to earlier Scripture to understand everything" and that comparison "should not undermine or contradict

---

[41] Poythress, Understanding Dispensationalists, 79.

grammatical-historical interpretation" even as it "goes beyond its bounds" and "takes account of information not available in the original historical and cultural context."[42] One must agree with Poythress on one account, the distance and earthshaking event of the eschatological context and NT revelation does diminish "the most prosaic biological sense" that Israel must be interpreted in the Revelation, but to maintain that the context *ends* the *principal sense* altogether unequivocally "undermines or contradicts the grammatical-historical interpretation," which is precisely what historicists attempt concerning eschatological prophecy. Historicists undermine or contradict the historical-grammatical interpretation persistently. This is further supported by the truth that the gentiles "were without Christ ... aliens from the commonwealth of Israel, and strangers from the covenants of promise, having no hope, and without God in the world" (Ephesians 2:12) and as such are not to be *restored* in the *principal sense* as the biological descendants. Here we have the support in viewing the apocalyptic four horsemen as prefigured by Ephraim's persistent merchant tendencies and the reason they are not included in the 144,000.

> *He is* a merchant, the balances of deceit *are* in his hand: he loveth to oppress. And Ephraim said, Yet I am become rich, I have found me out substance: *in* all my labours they shall find none iniquity in me that *were* sin. (Hosea 12:7–8)

> Thus saith the LORD; For three transgressions of Israel, and for four, I will not turn away *the punishment* thereof; because they sold the righteous for silver, and the poor for a pair of shoes; That pant after the dust of the earth on the head of the poor, and turn aside the way of the meek: and a man and his father will go in unto the *same* maid, to profane my holy name: And they lay *themselves* down upon

---

[42] Ibid., 107, 116

clothes laid to pledge by every altar, and they drink
the wine of the condemned in the house of their
god. (Amos 2:6–8)

The distant descendants of Ephraim fulfill their part in the last
days when God leaves them in bondage to their carnal, fallen nature
to victimize those who are chosen and illustrated in the fifth seal.
As related in the previous chapter, the "horsemen and bowmen"
illustrated by the first seal represent God's agent Babylon in judging
the church because "as a cage is full of birds, so *are* their houses full
of deceit: therefore they are become great, and waxen rich," fixed in
the precedent of Jeremiah 4:29 and 5:27. Babylon in the Revelation
is comprised of the vessels of dishonor that God allows in his house,
according to 2 Timothy 2:20, to test the elect in the time of the end.
Those vessels of dishonor represent the tribe of Ephraim at the time
of the end.

For what *is* our hope, or joy, or crown of rejoicing?
Are not even ye in the presence of our Lord Jesus
Christ at his coming? (1 Thessalonians 2:19)

Glossary

Anthropomorphism is the "representation of objects (especially a god) as having human form or traits." (WordWeb Pro 8.2)

Arminianism "is a school of theology based on the teachings of Dutch theologian Jacob Arminius, for whom it is named.... It stands in contrast to Calvinism, with which it has a long history of debate.... holds that man is the final arbiter of his election, and that God elects him on the basis of foreseen faith which is exercised by libertarian free will, thus making man ultimately decisive." (*Theopedia*, https://www.theopedia.com/arminianism)

Calvinism is the "theological system of John Calvin and his followers emphasizing omnipotence of God and salvation by grace alone." (WordWeb Pro 8.2)

Compatibilism is "sometimes called soft determinism, is a theological term that deals with the topics of free will and predestination. It seeks to show that God's exhaustive sovereignty is compatible with human freedom, or in other words, it claims that determinism and free will are compatible. Rather than limit the exercise of God's sovereignty in order to preserve man's freedom, compatibilists say that there must be a different way to define what freedom really means." (*Theopedia*, https://www.theopedia.com/compatibilism)

Covenant Theology (or Federal theology) "is a prominent feature in Protestant theology, especially in the Presbyterian and Reformed churches, and a similar form is found in Methodism and Reformed Baptist churches. This article primarily concerns Covenant Theology as held by the Presbyterian and Reformed churches, which use the covenant concept as an organizing principle for Christian theology and view the history of redemption under the framework of three overarching theological covenants: the Covenant of Redemption, the Covenant of Works, and the Covenant of Grace. These three are called "theological covenants" because although not explicitly presented as covenants, they are, according to covenant theologians, implicit in the Bible." (Theopedia, https://www.theopedia. com/covenant-theology)

Dispensationalism "is a religious interpretive system for the Bible. It considers Biblical history as divided by God into dispensations, defined periods or ages to which God has allotted distinctive administrative principles. According to dispensationalist theology, each age of God's plan is thus administered in a certain way, and humanity is held responsible as a steward during that time. Dispensationalists demonstrate the harmony of history as focusing on the glory of God and put God at its center - as opposed to a central focus on humanity and their need for salvation.... Dispensationalists profess a definite distinction between Israel and the Church. For dispensationalists, Israel is an ethnic nation[6] consisting of Hebrews (Israelites), beginning with Abraham and continuing in existence to the present. The Church, on the other hand, consists of all saved individuals in this present dispensation—i.e., from the "birth of the Church" in Acts until the time of the Rapture. [7]" (*Wikipedia*, last modified July 2018, https://en.wikipedia.

org/wiki/Dispensationalism#Distinction_between_
Israel_and_the_Church)

Free Grace theology "is a Christian soteriological view teaching that
everyone receives eternal life the moment that they believe in
Jesus Christ as their personal Savior and Lord. 'Lord' refers
to the belief that Jesus is the Son of God and therefore able
to be their "Savior".[1] The view distinguishes between (1)
the 'call to believe' in Christ as Savior and to receive the gift
of eternal life and (2) the 'call to follow' Christ and become
obedient disciples.[1]" (*Wikipedia*, last modified May 2018,
https://en.wikipedia.org/wiki/Free_grace_theology)

Futurism "is a Christian eschatological view that interprets portions
of the Book of Revelation and the Book of Daniel as
future events in a literal, physical, apocalyptic, and global
context.[1]" (*Wikipedia*, last modified May 2018, https://
en.wikipedia.org/wiki/Futurism_(Christianity))

historical-grammatical method "is a Christian hermeneutical
method that strives to discover the biblical authors' original
intended meaning in the text.[1] It is the primary method
of interpretation for many conservative Protestant exegetes
who reject the historical-critical method to various degrees
(from the complete rejection of historical criticism of some
fundamentalist Protestants to the moderated acceptance
of it in the Roman Catholic tradition since Pope Pius
XII),[2] in contrast to the overwhelming reliance on
historical-critical interpretation, often to the exclusion of
all other hermeneutics, in liberal Christianity." (*Wikipedia*,
last modified June 2018, https://en.wikipedia.org/wiki/
Historical-grammatical_method)

Historicism is "a method of interpretation of Biblical prophecies,
associates symbols with historical persons, nations or

events. It can result in a view of progressive and continuous fulfillment of prophecy covering the period from Biblical times to the Second Coming. Almost[*quantify*] all Protestant Reformers from the Reformation into the 19th century held historicist views.[1][*need quotation to verify*] The main primary texts of interest to Christian-historicists include apocalyptic literature, such as the Book of Daniel and the Book of Revelation. Commentators have also applied historicist methods to ancient Jewish history, to the Roman Empire, to Islam, to the Papacy, to the Modern era, and to the end time.… Traditional Protestant historicism interprets the four kingdoms in the Book of Daniel as Neo-Babylon, Medo-Persia (c. 550–330 BC), Greece under Alexander the Great, and the Roman Empire.[32] Additionally, historicists view the "little horn" in Daniel 7:8 and Daniel 8:9 as the Papacy." (*Wikipedia*, s.v. Historicism (Christianity), last modified August 2018, https://en.wikipedia.org/wiki/Historicism_(Christianity)#Historicist_views)

laissez-faire "is an economic system in which transactions between private parties are free from government intervention such as regulation, privileges, tariffs and subsidies. The phrase laissez-faire is part of a larger French phrase and basically translates to 'let (it/them) do', but in this context usually means to 'let go'.[1]" (*Wikipedia*, last modified July 2018, https://en.wikipedia.org/wiki/Laissez-faire)

Libertarian free will "maintains that for any choice made, one could always equally have chosen otherwise, or not chosen at all." (*Wikipedia*, Compatibilism, s.v. Basic beliefs, http://www.theopedia.com/compatibilism)

Open theism, also called *free will theism* and *openness theology*, "is the belief that God does not exercise meticulous control of the universe but leaves it 'open' for humans to make significant choices (free will) that impact their relationships with God and others." (*Theopedia* https://www.theopedia.com/open-theism)

Postmillennialism "holds that Jesus Christ establishes his kingdom on earth through his preaching and redemptive work in the first century and that he equips his church with the gospel, empowers her by the Spirit, and charges her with the Great Commission (Matt 28:19) to disciple all nations. Postmillennialism expects that eventually the vast majority of people living will be saved. Increasing gospel success will gradually produce a time in history prior to Christ's return in which faith, righteousness, peace, and prosperity will prevail in the affairs of men and of nations. After an extensive era of such conditions Jesus Christ will return visibly, bodily, and gloriously, to end history with the general resurrection and the final judgment after which the eternal order follows." (Wikipedia, last modified March 2018, https://en.wikipedia.org/wiki/Postmillennialism)

Predestination is theology "being determined in advance; especially the doctrine (usually associated with Calvin) that God has foreordained every event throughout eternity (including the final salvation of mankind)" (WordWeb Pro 8.2)

Preterism "is a Christian eschatological view that interprets some (partial preterism) or all (full preterism) prophecies of the Bible as events which have already happened. This school of thought interprets the Book of Daniel as referring to events that happened from the 7th century BC until the first century AD, while seeing the prophecies of Revelation as events that happened in the first century AD. Preterism holds that Ancient Israel finds its continuation or fulfillment in the Christian church at the destruction of Jerusalem in AD 70."

(*Wikipedia*, last modified July 2018, https://en.wikipedia.org/wiki/Preterism)

Prevenient grace "is a Christian theological concept rooted in Arminian theology,[1] though it appeared earlier in Catholic theology.[2] It is divine grace that precedes human decision. In other words, God will start showing love to that individual at a certain point in his lifetime.... Because everyone's nature is corrupted by the effects of sin, prevenient grace allows persons to engage their God-given free will to choose the salvation offered by God in Jesus Christ or to reject that salvific offer." (Wikipedia, last modified February 2018, https://en.wikipedia.org/wiki/Prevenient_grace)

Progressive revelation "is the concept in Christianity that the sections of the Bible that were written later contain a fuller revelation of God than the earlier sections." (*Wikipedia*, last modified October 2017, https://en.wikipedia.org/wiki/Progressive_revelation_(Christianity)

Premillennialism, in Christian eschatology, "is the belief that Jesus will physically return to the earth (the Second Coming) before the Millennium, a literal thousand-year golden age of peace. The doctrine is called 'premillennialism' because it holds that Jesus' physical return to earth will occur prior to the inauguration of the Millennium. Premillennialism is based upon a literal interpretation of Revelation 20:1–6 in the New Testament, which describes Jesus' reign in a period of a thousand years." (Wikipedia, last modified August 2018, https://en.wikipedia.org/wiki/Premillennialism)

Recapitulation perceives "several parts of the Apocalypse as somewhat repetitious, and each of these parts seems to lead to the final consummation. In other words, the author repeatedly leads his hearers and readers over the same ground, adding a new perspective each time." (Ekkehardt Mueller, "Recapitulation in Revelation 4-11," *Biblical Research Institute*, https://adventistbiblicalresearch.org/sites/default/files/pdf/rev4-11.pdf)

Theological determinism "is a form of predeterminism which states that all events that happen are pre-ordained, or predestined to happen, by a God, or that they are destined to occur given its omniscience." (*Wikipedia*, modified July 2018, https://en.wikipedia.org/wiki/Theological_determinism)

Theophany, "(meaning 'appearance of god') is the appearance of a deity to a human." (Wikipedia, last modified August 2018, https://en.wikipedia.org/wiki/Theophany)

Two House Theology "primarily focuses on the division of the ancient United Monarchy of Israel into two kingdoms, Israel and Judah. Two House Theology raises questions when applied to modern peoples who are thought to be descendants of the two ancient kingdoms, both Jews (of the Kingdom of Judah) and the ten lost tribes of the Kingdom of Israel. The phrase 'the two houses of Israel' is found in the Isaiah 8:14." (Wikipedia, last modified August 2018, https://en.wikipedia.org/wiki/Two_House_theology)

Printed in the United States
By Bookmasters